A SHOT STORY

A SHOT STORY
FROM JUVIE TO Ph.D.

DAVID BORKOWSKI

Empire State Editions
An imprint of Fordham University Press
New York   2015

Fordham University Press has no responsibility for the persistence or accuracy of URLs for external or third-party Internet websites referred to in this publication and does not guarantee that any content on such websites is, or will remain, accurate or appropriate.

Fordham University Press also publishes its books in a variety of electronic formats. Some content that appears in print may not be available in electronic books.

Visit us online at www.fordhampress.com.

Library of Congress Cataloging-in-Publication Data

Borkowski, David.
  A shot story : from juvie to Ph.D. / David Borkowski. — First edition.
    pages cm
  Summary: "David Borkowski was nearly shot to death during a botched robbery when he was 15. Soon before turning 40, he obtained a Ph.D. in Literature and Rhetoric from the CUNY Graduate School. He is now a Professor of English. A Shot Story describes that journey" — Provided by publisher.
  Includes bibliographical references.
  ISBN 978-0-8232-6599-2 (hardback)
  1. Borkowski, David. 2. Juvenile delinquents—Rehabilitation—United States. 3. Life change events—United States. 4. Education—Social aspects—United States. 5. College teachers—United States—Biography. I. Title.
  CT275.B58456A3 2015
  378.1'2092—dc23
  [B]
                          2015002949

Printed in the United States of America
17 16 15   5 4 3 2 1
First edition

Contents

1

A Grave Situation

The human body contains about seven liters of blood. By the time the ambulance arrived, I had lost more than six and a half. When it happened, though, I didn't think they were real bullets. It was a fortunate fallacy, really. I'm convinced my ignorance kept me alive long enough to reach the hospital to receive last rites before the all-night surgery that saved me. What you don't know can't kill you, but it's really no way to live.

In my mind, I figured he was firing rubber bullets. Or, more likely, he was shooting at me with a salt gun, the kind of weapon my friends and I believed the nighttime rent-a-cops carried while patrolling Moravian Cemetery, where we sometimes got high. It was located at the intersection of New Dorp and Oakwood Heights on Staten Island. Cornelius Vanderbilt's colossal tomb, erected on a finely groomed hilltop, was situated a quarter of a mile behind the rest of the cemetery. The largest private tomb in the United States, it was five times the size of the homes that most of us lived in. Landscaping legend Frederick Law Olmsted designed its grounds. The rest of the cemetery covered more than one hundred pristine acres. If we didn't feel like walking up to Vanderbilt's at night, we would hang out in the cemetery, leaning against the headstones or parading through the infinite rows of graves. Everything was meticulously managed; barely a single weed grew beside any burial site. Ancient elms and oaks lined winding roads that went to other, less impressive mausoleums. A decent-sized human-made lake anchored the entire place. It was truly a magnificent place to be dead.

Lots of kids went there to fish, play exhausting games of hide-and-seek, and get stoned, on weed, acid, cheap beer, sickly sweet wine, or all of the above. Some shot heroin, although I didn't realize that at the time. A few kids wandered around so stoned they resembled zombies. I suspect now that some of the living dead were having sex in the bushes, although I didn't realize that at the time either. Other kids simply went there because it was somewhere to go, something to do, a juvenile delinquent field trip of sorts.

This was especially true when one took the long uphill hike through wooded terrain that went directly to Vanderbilt's tomb. Taking the path avoided passage through the main cemetery grounds, where the chances of getting caught during the day were likely. During daylight hours hardly a soul hung out there. "The Tomb," as everyone called it, was the daytime destination. It seemed kids from all over the area knew where, on a dead-end street, to find the hole in the fence that protected the cemetery from trespassers. Past it, a rather steep path that wended its way through the woods led to a second fence that surrounded the tomb. That one had to be scaled. Once you were inside, it was pretty easy, as long as you didn't suffer from vertigo, for anyone to climb onto the tomb's roof from the back by slowly walking on all fours like an ape along the slanted surface toward the front. You could then sit safely and comfortably at its peak by straddling its extravagant cornice. From there you could see the Atlantic Ocean and much of Staten Island's South Shore, as well as look down on the countless dead buried in the valley below and those paying their respects to them.

Everyone knew not to be afraid of the cops, who came out only at night. They were fake cops carrying fake weapons loaded with fake ammunition. Reputedly, the function of their salt guns went something like this: When fired at their target, they slowly immobilized the person. At first they created a slow-mo effect on the victim if he were running, causing increasing paralysis, until he finally collapsed onto the ground, rendered completely incapacitated by the salt's effect on the bloodstream. However, the cops rarely, if ever, bothered coming up to the tomb, many of them finding it too creepy in the first place. Second, it was virtually impossible for the cops to do anything more than make us take flight into the surrounding brush when they showed up (we could see the oncoming headlights long before they arrived), only for us to resurface and reclaim the territory once they'd left. Sometimes we didn't need to hide because they frequently didn't unlock the fence to get a better look at who was around. As long as they could report that they'd gone up to the tomb, I guess they could say they had done their night's work. What they did do mostly was drive aimlessly around the cemetery grounds below, perhaps even getting high like the rest of us, a prospect that was quite scary. Stoned-out males performing thankless, boring jobs can be a volatile lot, itching to pop off their pieces, even if they are only "fake" guns.

Mind you, none of us ever saw any of these guns, let alone one discharged using Morton Salt bullets. But neither did anyone want to put the rumor to a test and get shot at. That's why whenever we were in the cemetery instead of at the tomb we scattered like rats through the rows of gravestones if we saw an approaching vehicle. If you see these half-assed Barney Fifes, we'd tell each other, duck behind a tombstone. And don't move. You know they're too terrified and too lazy to get out of the car and give chase, so they'll probably pretend that they never saw you. Whatever you do, don't run. Then it's like sport to these assholes, like they're hotshot safari hunters who shoot "Wilma beasts" or whatever the fuck it is safari hunters shoot from their jeeps. *That's* when they'll spray you with those salt guns. So be cool.

And that's the conversation that was inside my head the night a real cop with a real gun with real bullets shot me. I wasn't in the cemetery, so I guess I should have figured otherwise. But I was fifteen years old, so what did I know? And unlike in the cemetery, there were no tombstones to hide behind, so when he yelled, "Freeze, you assholes," I did at first. I didn't want to be a sacrificial Wilma beast for his amusement. Dougie and I had been hiding behind a boulder in an empty, unkept lot across the street from the house where the driver was making his delivery. We had called earlier to order a pizza to be sent to that address, just as we had done twice before at that same address (really dumb), and just as we had done the first time at another address. As soon as he stepped out of the car, we'd rob him—me holding a water pistol spray-painted black and Dougie clutching a knife he'd grabbed from his mother's kitchen drawer. But when we charged out of the lot toward him, it was evident he wasn't some pimply-faced college kid as had been the case the other times.

Instead, a man was holding the white cardboard box, and when he saw us rushing forward he dropped it. A gun that looked as big as a howitzer was aimed right at me. It had magically appeared in the very same hands that had previously been carrying the pizza box, and he was cupping it with both hands, just as the professional cops on TV and in the movies did. Still, it didn't make any sense that he'd be a real cop himself. Being faster than Dougie, and the one taking the initiative, I had run out first, so I was standing in front of Dougie when the cop ordered us to stop in our tracks, which I did. When I turned around, though, Dougie was racing along a tiny path that cut down the middle of the empty lot. When I saw him running, I decided I had better run too.

And I ran like hell. And I kept running, even after the cop unloaded his revolver, hitting me three times. Shots must have rung out, but I don't remember hearing them. Nor did I feel any pain when I was hit. One bullet ripped straight through my shoulder. The other two struck me in the back, one lodging itself permanently below my collarbone, the other slamming into my right lung and bringing me to my knees. It felt like a kidney punch. But they weren't real bullets, I thought, so I immediately stood up and continued running, breathing heavily as my lungs filled with blood. *Shit, the salt is already circulating throughout my system. So this is what it feels like. Wait 'til I tell everyone. It won't be long before I can't move.* As I ran, I saw Dougie running straight toward Guyon Avenue. He never looked back. I had watched enough westerns and cops-and-robbers stuff to know not to follow him. Divide and conquer. I turned left. As I did, the policeman's footsteps faded in the distance the farther I went. He knew he had hit me, so he chased Dougie, hoping to catch him.

After I made my turn, I ran another two blocks. My labored breathing had grown so intense, and I was gasping so much for air, I thought I was choking on all of the salt I believed was in my body. I had no idea I had nearly been shot to death right then and there. I was so deluded I planned on eventually walking home, as if nothing had ever happened, once what I thought were the toxins passed through me and dissipated. *As long as I can get to a place to rest and wait it out, then it'll all be over.* Three blocks from the shooting, I found a thick row of front-yard shrubs to crawl under. The house was owned by an elderly widow who lived alone. I knew it would be safe there at that time of night. It was after 11 o'clock, so she was probably fast asleep. *If she's anything like my grandmother she didn't even hear the shots. I'll be okay here until the coast is clear.*

I don't know how long I was there. It seemed like only a few minutes, but I must have passed out for a while. Later I learned from a friend who lived nearby and had come out of his house after hearing the uproar— from dozens of police cars, their screaming sirens filling the usually quiet night—that the cops had been searching for me for more than an hour. By then, they were mostly canvassing the area on foot looking for me, undoubtedly wondering where the heck the one who'd been shot had vanished to. Dougie was long gone, having outrun the cop who shot me and then disappearing into the night by sneaking along the train tracks until he reached another station. By the time they found me, he was already staying with a friend who lived across town, in New Dorp.

From my hideaway, I could see Guyon Avenue, the main road where most of the police cruisers had been scrambling up and down looking for us. Only a few vehicles lingered, the sirens turned off but the rooftop bubble gum machines still spinning like carousels on speed. I figured it was all right to head home. I wasn't breathing so heavily anymore, although my vision was blurry, almost to the point of blindness. I figured that would pass once I started walking.

I stood up, still holding the water pistol. I tossed it into some bushes across the street. I had taken no more than three or four steps when I heard a voice shout, "Freeze, asshole!"—almost the exact words hollered by the guy who'd shot me, except it wasn't his voice. This time I didn't think I had it in me to run. "Don't fuckin' move or you're fuckin' dead," another voice said. Sure enough, I couldn't move. I stood there as frozen as I'd been commanded, swirling in place. "Get your fuckin' ass on the ground or I'll blow your fuckin' head off," added yet another voice. *Where are they?* I couldn't see more than a cloudy few inches ahead of me. When I looked down at my feet they appeared to be at a great distance, minuscule, as if they weren't even mine. "Get the fuck down—now!—asshole," the last voice thundered. It sounded like the voice of the one who'd promised to decapitate me with a blizzard of bullets. I dropped to the ground, plopping onto the widow's front lawn. She still hadn't come out. At least I had chosen the right spot.

But I couldn't believe I'd been caught. I still didn't realize how seriously shot up I was. Why would anyone want *me* dead, especially over something as unimportant as sticking up pizza delivery guys with a water pistol and a kitchen knife? For Christ's sake, we were so unprofessional and harmless that the knife probably still had butter on it. And the water pistol wasn't even loaded. It didn't make any sense for someone to shoot me, with real bullets no less. But its unreality turned out to be a lifesaver—in more ways than one. It tricked me into believing I hadn't nearly bled to death. In the end, getting shot was the best thing that ever happened to me.

Almost dying saved the rest of my life.

Interestingly enough, precisely the moment I believed I *was* going to die was the moment that changed my life forever. If you want to learn how, dear reader, skip ahead to the last chapter, as long as you promise to read the rest.

Now, if you don't read the rest, you won't find out how I arrived at that moment in my life, being administered last rites in the ER and all that cosmic jazz related to it. You also won't find out how I got out of there too—metaphorically speaking—and became, of all things, an English professor. It seems as if everything before the shooting led up to that event and everything after the shooting led away from it, including my typing these very words. Like the surgery to repair my collapsed lung, which required doctors to cut me nearly in half, my life seems divided by that one incident. I guess that's all it takes. One event can turn things around, if you're lucky, rather than ass-backward, if you're not. I'm sure I'm not alone in believing this, or alone in having experienced these flashpoints that take over our lives, including the past. And what I mean is the *perception* of the past, not necessarily the actual past. Most of us can trace a certain point along our life-maps that can be seen as an end and as a start of who we are, of what we've become. Or what we could have become but didn't. It's a dividing line. Not quite a fork in the road—more like a knife's edge. My father's absence probably had much to do with the first half, of how I got to that point in my life, while my mother's presence probably had much to do with what I did—and didn't do—after it, along with becoming a "fake doctor." It still seems strange to me that I eventually became a college professor, one who teaches English no less. Imagine that. It was pretty stupid what I did, all right, but I was practically illiterate the night I was shot. Now I'm at the top of the literacy heap, so to speak. It's as if I've led two very different lives. But a person has to live a whole life. For me, accomplishing that felt divided too, almost as soon as I started "living" again.

That night in the ER I became internally centered and whole. Externally, I felt dislocated and incomplete, to rectify that I had planned on doing big things with my life, saving pieces of the world, or perhaps saving other lives, as mine had been saved. I wanted to remake myself, to better myself, for the betterment of humankind. I had really big plans in mind. My life didn't turn out that way. I'm not dissatisfied that I didn't become a life-saving surgeon, a famous scientist, a constitutional or literary scholar. Instead, I became a really good teacher—a "gifted" one, in fact. I think that's a pretty big thing, really, as big a thing as being a "real doctor." It's not something to be disappointed about. And I don't mean just for my sake; most of all, I mean for the sake of my students.

2
Tracks of My Fears

If you don't talk about something, maybe it will seem as if it never happened. Not thinking about it helps a lot too. Add them together and it becomes evident that it's a lot easier trying to forget than it is trying to understand.

According to members of my parents' generation, the ones who stoically overcame a Great Depression and a Great War, there was no such thing as a talking cure. The weak were talkers, especially men. For all of what males in my family went through during those "great" events, hardly a peep was uttered about any of it, while those who knew them solemnized their silence. It was more than just impolite to talk about yourself or someone else; it was in poor taste. Take my father's older brother Eddy, for instance, whom I knew for forty years. During World War II he served in the Navy. Two days after D-Day, his ship was navigating the English Channel when a torpedo from a German E-boat struck. Uncle Eddy's ship sank in less than an hour. Half of the crew died, some killed on board instantly and the rest later drowned waiting to be rescued. My Uncle Eddy was one of the survivors, and survival must have been harrowing. I found this out at the luncheon following his burial. Throw dirt on the man and it's suddenly okay to talk about him.

That's how it usually went. During funeral services someone might tap me on the shoulder, as I sat uncomfortably in a folding metal chair, or sidle up alongside me, as I gingerly leaned against a pockmarked accordion wall, and begin, "Did you know . . . ?" No, I didn't know. How could I have known that my mother's brother, Sammy, was involved in the liberation of Europe when what I most knew about him was the superior quality of his barbecued chicken? At every cookout it was always "Did you have some of Uncle Sammy's chicken? It's the best one yet" but never how his squad was among the first to enter the death camps. I might as well have been living with a family of ascetics. Uncle Sammy guarded information about himself as well as he guarded his chicken recipe. No wonder men like him were so angry when a subsequent generation returned from Vietnam and spilled their guts about what they'd done and what they'd seen. Some things were better left unsaid, passing through hell being one of them. For men like my Uncle Sammy, discretion demonstrated a resolute, steely character. Talking about war, or any traumatic incident for that matter, was dishonorable. Another upside of this practice assures the person that he actually has a firm handle on the situation; that, in turn, reassures those around him that he does. Achieving the nonexistence of disturbing experiences usually begins by one's blocking them from the mind. Silence emerges from the absence of anything to discuss. That's how my parents tried to raise me.

We certainly never talked in my family about anything that affected us, at least not the really important stuff. My parents split up in 1964 at a time when nobody—and I mean nobody, except maybe movie stars—divorced or separated, at least not in the largely Catholic neighborhood I grew up in. I didn't know a single other kid whose parents weren't together. And I knew lots of kids. My parents were trendsetters in a way: We were one of the first openly dysfunctional families within a ten-mile radius, if not on Staten Island entirely. To augment our dysfunction, my parents got back together seven years later, when I was in eighth grade. During those seven years, and subsequently thereafter, they never talked about the divorce, except on that one occasion when they called me into the kitchen to announce that my father was "going away for a while."

It was a late afternoon in late winter. I was six years old. My mother, father, and twelve-year-old sister were seated at the kitchen table. Clouds of blue-gray Pall-Mall smoke were stacked above a hanging ceiling light, while swirling ribbons hovered around the rest of the room. Both of my parents smoked back then, as did every adult who ever stepped inside our home. You could cure meat in our house after just one other couple came over for cake and coffee. My mother wasn't a heavy smoker, but my father made up for it. He was a borderline chainsmoker, firing up a fresh one every ten minutes or so. He wasn't smoking when I entered the room, and I didn't stay long enough to see him light one. I was standing in the door frame when my mother broke the news, as my father's bowed gaze remained fixed on his lap, which seemed a bit odd at the time. I simply said, "Oh" and started to back away. It didn't occur to me to sit down and join them. I had been summoned while I was watching TV in the next room. I remember thinking that maybe it wasn't such a bad idea if my father went on a little trip ... but couldn't I just get back to my program before the commercials end? My sister's eyes were red and puffy from crying, while my mother's face was compressed with annoyance and displeasure, a look I often saw whenever she was disappointed with someone, a look that crushed me shortly after I'd been shot. Despite my sister's tears and my mother's expression, I didn't understand the severity of the situation, which wouldn't be the last time. Maybe if they had told me outright—"Your father is leaving us, possibly forever"—I might have understood. I still don't understand. To this day, their separation (they never actually divorced), an event that radically altered all of our lives, has never been discussed in our family. It's as if it never occurred, which isn't altogether surprising. Much about my parents is a mystery. To ask them would be a breach of an unspoken agreement. Even our silences were sealed by silence.

My father's life is a near-total blank to me. He may as well have been sent to Earth from another planet for all I know about him. I know almost as little about my mother, although she's more like from another country. At least now and then she told a few stories about her childhood. Except she tended to repeat the same ones, as if they were the safest to discuss, such as how she and her older sister Rosie felt embarrassed and humiliated whenever they ate their sandwiches in front of the other grade-school children. Their bread had been freshly baked by my Italian grandmother, whereas the other "American" kids' sandwiches were made with store-bought bread. This was during the 1930s. The background to the story changes each time she tells it, with her lamenting they were as poor as the kids on *The Little Rascals,* or with her celebrating her father's shrewdness to keep them fairly comfortable during the worst days of the Depression. It wasn't much to hang a picture of a life on, but it was better than nothing, which was what I knew about my father's childhood: practically nothing.

That's why whenever the seal was broken the event stood out, like the time when he and I were driving over the Bayonne Bridge. I was home for winter recess from Johnson & Wales College. We were coming back from skiing at Camelback Mountain in the Poconos. As the car rounded over the bridge's central spine, out of nowhere he told me about how he and a childhood friend used to shimmy to the top of the bridge's span on snowy days and drop snowballs onto the barges and tugboats below. As he began telling me the story, I craned my neck under the visor and looked up at the bridge's arch, examining its height as best as I could without smashing my face against the windshield. It clearly was a dangerous thing to have done. The slightest slip would have caused him to fall to his death.

"One time," he said, "I let one go that fell directly into a pot of boiling water a cook was carrying across the deck. It splattered all over him and he dropped the pot. Boy was he surprised, and mad as hell. It was a one-in-a-million shot, but it was one of those slow-moving barges. He didn't know what happened at first, until he looked up and could see the two of us hanging there. He started shaking his fist at us and cursing like crazy, I think in Russian, but what could he do?"

"Did you intentionally try to hit him?" I asked.

"What do you think?"

"I think you did, but you missed and nailed the pot instead."

"As I said, it was one in a million."

He told me this story less than two years after I'd been shot. Maybe he did so on my behalf, as a cryptic lesson, to reveal to me that nobody's perfect or that young men are prone to do foolish things and perform wicked deeds. Still, the paucity of such personal discussions characterized our relationship, as it did with nearly every other man of my father's generation. They were stingy with expressing their emotions, or much of anything, while stubbornly adhering to rather narrow views of correct behavior. While my Uncle Sammy may have been a war hero, and famous for his barbecued chicken, he was intolerant of those who differed from his orthodoxy, which caused him not only to snub any man who didn't work with his hands but also to be a rabid racist and a staunch anti-Semite. Any stranger who deviated from his version of normalcy might have to deal with his unpredictable rage, while any intimates who did so might have to spend the remainder of their lives pitted against his wrathful apathy.

When my parents separated, he wrote off my mother practically right after my father stepped out the door. For the next thirty-five years of his life he treated her with sanctimonious indifference. During the entire time my father was gone, my mother's only brother (she had six sisters) never visited her, never came by to help her, and never once dropped in to spend time with me or my sister. To him, it had been my mother's responsibility to keep her man at home, whatever the circumstances, and so he blamed her for whatever fatal flaw in her character had caused my father to leave. He'd never tell her that. He didn't have to. I guess to him it was quite evident where he stood, just as he wouldn't say a word to my father about how he felt about his shortcomings as a husband and as a father, and just as he would never say a word about the mayhem, cruelty, and suffering he encountered in the war. He simply unleashed those restrained feelings by carrying a baseball bat in the trunk of his car and confronting the "niggers and spics" who dared to share the road with him. The man was clearly a raging sea of repressed emotions and scalding ruminations, but you'd never know it by looking at him. The stereotype of the passionate, easily eruptible Italian did not fit him in the least. He was Nordic cool, a man of few words who kept everyone at a distance, including his wife, my Aunt Grace. With his calculated respectability, he convinced those closest to him how rock-solid and self-assured he was because his gutters were always free of debris, his basement tool shed was arranged as fastidiously as a hardware store, and his symmetrical hedges, overflowing flower beds, and swollen vegetable garden all looked as if they could appear in magazines.

He worked as an auto mechanic in a garage for the New York City Police Department. He was the cleanest "grease monkey" I have ever seen. His garage served the same precinct my father worked in until my dad was transferred. They strained and stretched cordiality with each other, while neither would ever say a word about how they really felt. I think my Uncle Sammy utterly despised my father. He treated all of us with one part disregard and one part derision. My sister and I were guilty by association. He'd wiped his hands clean of their filthy separation, even if that meant disavowing my mother when she needed his help the most. It was part of his generation's code, part of being a "real" man, to speak softly (or not at all) and carry a big stick (or a baseball bat). This attitude about a man's real duty partially explains why my father urged me to remain tight-lipped about being shot.

"You shouldn't let it take over your life, letting it become such a big deal that it dominates who you are," he urged. We were on our way to the Oakwood Heights train station, located on Guyon Avenue, to buy a newspaper at a store across from it. As it turned out, he started talking to me about the shooting as we were walking along South Railroad Avenue, which paralleled the commuter train tracks running below street level, the very same tracks Dougie had scuttled along three weeks earlier. In fact, we were only a couple of blocks from where I'd been shot. I'm sure that was uppermost in his mind. He had chosen the setting to underscore his message.

"You know," he added, "it's probably a good idea to forget about it altogether and move on."

And so I did, for better and for worse. In hindsight, it looks more like it was worse than it was better to put it behind me, as if it had never happened. It took on a life of its own because the experience essentially saved my life. Getting shot, and the aftermath of the shooting, was too much a part of me to forget it and get away with making believe it hadn't happened. While I have traveled a great distance since then, inventing that rare "second act" by becoming a college professor, I wonder how much further I could have gone if I hadn't heeded his words so religiously. In the long run, they may have hindered me more than advanced me, because in my mind I was nearly grateful for the experience. It felt like a revelation. It felt like a rebirth. Granted, I never got the chance to explain it to my parents, or to anyone, for that matter, in that superlative way. But couldn't they see for themselves that I was a changed man because of it? In less than a year I went from being practically a high school dropout to sitting in an AP Calculus class. Shouldn't my father and my mother have understood the impact that getting nearly shot to death had had on me? Were they blind? Did they metaphorically gouge their eyes out like Oedipus because they preferred not to see what was too painful for them, to think their son was a thug, and how that fact would reflect upon them? Maybe they wanted me to forget it had ever happened because they wanted to forget it ever happened to *them*?

If that's true, then they wanted me to turn a blind eye, for their recovery, to what happened, thereby refusing to see how important it was for me to embrace the experience as part of mine. They simply didn't want to tackle it head-on, whereas I did. In many ways the experience had made me much wiser and more mature than they, but at the time I didn't know that. I couldn't see what they were refusing to see. In many respects, I spent far too many years following their blind lead and following in the footsteps of their ignorance. How dumb was it for them to pretend that nothing had happened? It was a lie, really.

After all, very physical proof existed that something *had* happened. One of those bullets went right through my shoulder, and another smashed into my lung, collapsing it. I have a long and large scar on my body. It was evident something had happened to me. Less evident was the impact that watching someone administer my last rites had: the impact on my sense of self. That struck far deeper and left an even bigger mark than any of the bullets. It went to the very core of my being. But I couldn't tell them about that because I couldn't talk about any of it. It's why I struggled so mightily with them to become a college professor, coming up against their lesser expectations of me, as well as their total lack of support in what I wanted to achieve in my life. Because I couldn't speak of "the accident" at all, I couldn't speak of what I'd learned that night in the ER. I couldn't mention the epiphany as my claim to a better future and a better "self" altogether. So when opportunities came along and my parents—especially my mother—discounted them as being unreachable or a waste of time, especially by someone like me, I agreed. I stayed silent. And I moved on, just as my father had asked me to do about being shot. Forget it and move on. In moving on I also became as protective about my personal life and as emotionally cautious as my parents. Partly, that was a good thing. After all, holding up a pizza truck isn't exactly something to boast about, nor is being nearly shot to death by a cop a good way to pad a CV. That part I get. But I think I understood that already on my own.

For me to have ignored it for so long seems perversely ignorant, but in a calculated, intentional way. It would be like writing a history of the United States and deciding to leave out the Civil War because it was a gruesome part of the nation's development. Sure, being shot was one of the worst things that ever happened to me, but it also was one of the best things that ever happened to me, sort of like those opening lines of *A Tale of Two Cities*, the best of things, the worst of things. For my parents, eliminating it entirely was the best solution to one of the worst things that happened to them . . . I mean, me. But you can't realistically shave off one side of a coin because you prefer the other. Even if it could be done it would be a piece of counterfeit currency. Was that what they were asking of me, to be a phony?

Facing death in such a dramatically unheroic way produced extraordinary insights. Its lasting impression bore great relevance: The moment is tattooed onto my brain, the bad and the good. My parents' insisting I shove the entire incident into a shadowy corner, by pretending it never happened, meant that its enlightening qualities couldn't be spoken of either. They believed nothing good could possibly have come from it, and therefore nothing good could possibly come from talking about it. So I didn't. Part of my recovery, so I believed, was to become The Best Damn Dutiful Son in the World. As a result, I had to perform a rather wacky self-induced exorcism of sorts. At the very least, I knew I could never share with others what I'd learned because that would mean I'd have to talk about being shot. It now seems egregiously dishonest—about about what I was, what I became, and who I am now as a consequence. If the experience doesn't exist, then how can I? As a teacher, to me the sham seems doubly unfortunate—wasted opportunities, really. Throughout these years I could have shared that story with my students, and maybe they could have learned a thing or two from it. In following my father's words to the letter, I had a hand in scripting my own personal paradox—an eclipsed epiphany. At the very least it was a magic trick: a disappearing act.

For them, I had to keep the experience stored like radioactive material buried under miles of concrete. If my being shot had leaked out, further pain and suffering would surely follow. Allowing others to know about it not only ran the risk of my becoming identified by it—what would someone think of such a person?—but it also increased the danger of what others would do with such knowledge. My mother felt that any kind of information about us, no matter how large or how small, and no matter how good or how bad, could be used against us. "Don't tell anyone how much you make on your paper route," she would say. "They'll be jealous." Imagine the slings and arrows fired at me if people knew I'd committed a crime and had been practically shot to death doing it! Only family could be trusted. They knew how to keep secrets and how to circumvent conversations about tangled feelings. These were the terms my father was trying to set as we walked along the railroad tracks.

Putting the incident behind me, as my father insisted, meant I would be able to get on with things. My father didn't want me to embrace it as *the* definitive event of my life and then recklessly bank on its uniqueness, on its juvenile coolness. Even now I understand why he saw it that way. He feared that the minor celebrity status he knew I was gaining with my peers and the attention I was receiving from the neighbors (all of it negative) would go to my head, as it had to Dougie's—he'd turned himself into a John Dillinger wannabe. According to my dad's reasoning, I might value being shot for all of the wrong reasons. He probably agreed with my mom as well. The more who knew, the worse off the family would be. It would bring further shame to them, to all of us. They had reared a criminal. What parent wants to be known for that? Already too many people knew. The story had been splashed across the front pages of the borough's leading newspaper, the *Staten Island Advance*. Although our names weren't used, given that I was underage, most people in our neighborhood knew the two families involved. Even the *New York Times* ran a piece on it, on how the son of a cop was nearly gunned down by another cop. I'm sure my dad must have been thinking about that too on the day he advised me to put it all behind me. What kind of cop was he to raise a son who turned to crime? "You need to put this behind you," he said. He certainly must have wanted to.

It seemed like good advice at the time. I said little, if anything, in response. I really didn't think I was entitled to. After all, if I hadn't been a minor at the time, I would have had a criminal record. While I wasn't a criminal in the strict legal sense of the term, I was still a crook nonetheless. All I had was my guilt and mortification to stand on. I knew that only a jerk would do such a thing as I had done, for little more than a cheap thrill and not much more than fifty bucks. I was a crooked jerk. Why wouldn't I think my father's words were wise? I didn't even turn to face him, let alone say a word in response. "What happened is done, done and over with. Forget it and move on." I nodded in agreement. I never brought it up again, and neither did he. Neither did any of them. Case closed. I knew that's what he wanted, what everyone wanted. Silence is golden. It would be my salvation.

But it was awful advice, now that I look back on it. Nonetheless, I acted on it then with the tenacity of a trained terrier. But rather than latch on to something and never let go, I latched onto the invention of nothing and never let it go. I succeeded beyond my own imagination in not letting the *fact* of being shot from becoming a preoccupation, while barring anyone and everyone from knowing about it, as if state secrets, instead of a scar, were etched on my torso.

But secrecy has its price. Rather than allow the experience to take over my life, I found that its concealment did. I replaced one indefinite obsession with a definite one. Suppressing it became my life's mission. In the simplest terms, I wasn't really dealing with what happened, which is precisely what my parents wanted from me. Now, of course, I realize this placed a premium on its irrelevancy, a ridiculous proposition when you think about it. How could being shot and coming that close to death *not* be considered relevant in anyone's life? To my parents, my recovery and redemption involved ignoring an event that would be momentous in anyone's life. Ultimately, it boiled down to concealing the truth, of what being shot had made out of me, because I couldn't admit to what had happened—including admitting it to myself. I certainly could never admit it to others.

In keeping attuned to my father's advice, I devoted myself to keeping the truth from everyone, even though it is visibly apparent that something horrible had happened to me. The scar runs from the middle of my stomach and wraps around to the middle of my back, the removed stitches leaving behind a railroad track pattern. For several years following the surgery that repaired my collapsed lung, the pink strip, as thick as clothing line, and small white cross-sections, as long as sewing needles, could be seen from a distance. (To me, it appeared as red as a traffic light and as wide as a fist.) I had been sawed nearly in half, across the center of my body, like a rusty tin can that can't be opened from its top. Possessed of such an obvious tell-tale sign, and the need to hide its meaning, I could never remove my shirt in front of anyone. Doing so would jeopardize my scripted undertaking of confidentiality, thereby invariably inviting unwanted questions about the scar's origin. I therefore avoided any circumstance that would require showing the disfigurement to anyone, including my college roommate. I engaged in all sorts of machinations and subterfuges as a result. It's not easy never getting undressed in front of someone you live with day after day. For the record: Hiding and lying are exhausting when they're a full-time job.

Before attending Boston University, I went to Johnson & Wales College in Providence, Rhode Island. Back then it was a two-year college, known mostly for its culinary school; it also had a business division where students could get associate degrees in accounting or management or, as in my case, court reporting—a career and college choice not of my choosing (more on that later). Not far from Providence was a rather unspoiled, picturesque state beach called Horseneck in Westport, Massachusetts. On warm fall and spring days, groups of students in the dorm often organized trips there. But I never went. For two years, I refused to accompany them, always employing the same lame explanation about my fair skin being too sun-sensitive to risk minutes, let alone hours, of exposure to direct sunlight. I told them that a history of melanoma on my father's side had practically relegated the entire Borkowski clan to Mole People–like status. "I'm sorry, I can't go," I said repeatedly. "I don't tan, I singe." Granted, I could have worn a T-shirt, but I had seen how T-shirts, when worn in rough, choppy waters, can sometimes rise up to the wearer's shoulders. That would mean I'd have to steer clear of going swimming. If I did accept their invitations and wear a T-shirt I'd have to devise yet one more ridiculous ruse about why saltwater was nearly as detrimental to my skin as the sun. I wasn't prepared to pile on one lie after another. One good one was enough anyway. "What is the point of going to the beach dressed like a goddamned mummy?" I'd say.

I couldn't anticipate every situation that might end in disrobing. Once, I was virtually trapped into it. In my last semester at J&W, several dorm mates and I were wandering around East Providence one weekend, undoubtedly too bored to stay in our rooms taking hits off of the bong during marathon sessions of backgammon. We stumbled across an open door on the Brown University campus. It happened to lead to an indoor swimming pool, which, for some inexplicable reason, was not only unguarded but also unattended. Someone suggested we go for a swim. Dressed in our street clothes, this meant we'd have to strip down to our underwear. Some dove in naked. Protesting sun sensitivity wouldn't cut it this time. For a second, in full mind-race, I thought of linking the chlorine to my "condition," but that seemed too much of a stretch. I never wore an undershirt, so unless I ran out of the place like some madman, I'd have to take off my shirt and expose myself, which I did.

"Holy shit," someone said almost as soon as I peeled off my shirt. "That's some scar you've got there. What the fuck happened?"

"Oh, it was a freak accident," I began, wishing I *had* dashed out of there, but what kind of freak accident? I was totally unprepared. It was bound to happen. I should have been ready with a ready-made story, except I had become so adept at hiding the scar that I didn't think the moment of truth would ever arrive. I had to think fast. For some reason, I remembered an incident years earlier when I was lying on the ground during football practice after having the wind knocked out of me. I was the tailback on my pee-wee football team and I was running full steam with the ball when a defensive player, seemingly out of nowhere, appeared in the line's opening. He buried his helmet right into my gut, with the impact causing some pain in my ribs. After the shooting, the surgeon, Dr. Rose, explained to me that he'd had to crack two of my ribs to repair my collapsed lung (two others had been damaged by the bullet) and that I'd feel "discomfort" there for some time. (He left out the "forever" part.) In my desperation to find a suitable answer, I conflated the football experience and the medical conversation. While I always knew it was no ordinary scar, this guy's reaction upon seeing it confirmed it. I felt I needed a plausibly violent explanation for its existence. I also may have gone with something relatively macho rather than something relatively tame and medical, like pulmonary arterial whatchamacallit.

"I was playing football," I said. "I was running full speed—I was a tailback—when out of nowhere this huge guy—bam!—slams into me head-on, but sort of from the side, like a rocket. Hits me right there," I say as I point to it. "Either his helmet or his face mask caught my rib cage, breaking a couple of them. One of them freakishly snapped and punctured my lung. So they had to operate."

So I lied, just as I used to lie about my father's disappearance. Whenever any of my Little League teammates asked, for instance, why my dad wasn't around like the other fathers when we had Sunday or late afternoon weekday games I had a prepared story: "He's a cop, you know. They have different hours than your dads'," I'd say, trying to sound more special than embarrassed. I learned that from my mom, who lied to her father about my dad's repeated absences at family functions. She always said he was working whenever my grandfather asked about his whereabouts. I think my grandmother knew. At the time, my grandfather was growing increasingly senile. He once flailed at me with his cane when I went to kiss him, not recognizing me and hollering something about who was "this damn stranger" who'd been invited to his house for Easter. For one thing, we weren't in his home; for another, I was all of six years old then so he mistook me for an adult. He was a bigger anti-Semite and racist than his son, Sammy, so maybe he mistook me for a Jew—on the day of Christ's resurrection no less! During my parents' separation his dementia fluctuated from day to day, hour to hour. One minute he'd ask about my father, but then in the next he'd think I was David Ben-Gurion. Whatever his condition, he remained in the dark about their separation. He always believed my mom's explanations for his absence and never asked any additional questions.

I doubt if my Little League teammates believed me. Their brains weren't so mushy, and the whispers and snickers that would follow each lie indicated they knew or had put two and two together. I may have had a better go at it with my college buddies standing at the poolside. They believed me, or at least so I thought. It didn't matter, really. The lie achieved its purpose. No more questions were asked. I'd soon be leaving J&W for good anyway, and I'd never see any of them ever again. My having been shot would remain as unknown to them as it would to countless others whose lives I furtively moved in and out of over the years. I had to move on, didn't I?

My parents would have been so proud. That day at the pool I proved I had it in me. And I could keep it there. Rather than tell the truth, I discovered the advantages of spinning a good yarn. I continued to avoid situations that might involve taking off my shirt. If I couldn't, at least I could tell that football story. Until I grew tired of it and it started to feel like plagiarism. Then I started making up all kinds of other stories, often off the top of my head. I welcomed the challenge to invent, and the opportunity to use the scar to have a different past, to be someone else. I was not only growing accustomed to it but enjoying it. More important, as my father had advised, I was demonstrating that I had put the shooting behind me, perhaps more creatively and convincingly than he had expected.

His remarks occurred not more than three weeks after I'd nearly bled to death on a neighbor's front yard. I had recovered quickly, discharged from the hospital after only a week, thanks to Dr. Rose's surgical skills. Some people attributed my rapid recovery and my survival to an act of

God, a near miracle. "God didn't want you to die," they'd say. "It wasn't your time." In God's hands, they told me, I had dodged a bullet—so to speak. I never put much faith in any of it. For one thing, I'm not that so-lipsistic to believe I was singled out by God. For another, Dr. Rose's skill and expertise, along with advances in medical science, saved me, not divine intervention. If my near-fatal gunshot wounds had happened thirty years earlier, I would have died, similar to the hundreds of thousands before me at Verdun or Gettysburg who had perished with far more superficial injuries, derived from far less disgraceful reasons.

So well had I been repaired that I returned to school a couple of days after being discharged, a lot sooner than I should have if the startled and alarmed expressions on my schoolmates' faces were any indication of how I looked. Although I was enervated and pale, one classmate graciously said I'd gained in appearance from the ordeal. "You look better thinner," she said. Bless her attempt to put a happy face on my gaunt one. I must have looked like a cadaver. I remember having to pull my belt buckle three additional spaces past the worn-out hole in order to keep my pants up. I looked starkly different from the way I had only a week before. I felt as different as if I were someone else.

I shouldn't have gone back to school that quickly, really. I sure as hell didn't want to be there, not yet anyway, to face classmates and teachers and have to explain things. But my mother wanted us to resume our "normal lives." Going back to school would convey that. If I didn't miss too much time, maybe my schoolmates wouldn't make too much of the absences I'd already accumulated. Maybe I'd get lucky and my teachers wouldn't ask what had happened when I handed them my medical note excusing me from school, as my chemistry teacher did. On my way out of his class the first day I returned to school, I handed him the slip of paper. As he folded it back in half and handed it to me he asked what had happened. When I told him, he was initially dumbfounded. I can still see his mouth opening and his thick salt-and-pepper beard dropping into his chest. He started mumbling a string of incoherent phrases, separated by audible "wows," "gees," and "holy cows," concluding with "That's really something." Once he regained his composure, he placed his hand on my shoulder and said, "Well, you're okay now and you're alive; that's what's important." Now it was my turn to be speechless. His generosity was touching. All I could muster in response was a choked-up "Thanks." We stood there for a few clumsy seconds staring at each other, until he broke the awkwardness by offering to help me in class. "You've obviously fallen behind," he said, "so if you need any assistance catching up, let me know. Come by my office or we can set up an appointment." An additional choked-up "Thanks" was the best I could do in response.

"You what!?" my mother shouted.

"I told him I'd been shot," I said. I was sitting at the kitchen table watching her prepare dinner. She stood by the stove stir-frying peppers and onions in one pan and repeatedly turning over sweet Italian sausages in another to brown them. She had asked how my first day back at school had gone. When I started telling her about my chemistry teacher she spun around, about as quickly as I'd ever seen her move before, holding the wooden spoon in her hand, the same one she would sometimes spank me and my sister with when we were naughty toddlers. It looked as if she might try to hit me with it once again, with a lot more force this time around, as she began challenging the wisdom of what I'd done.

"What's the big deal?" I asked. It was the wrong thing to say, too nonchalant under the circumstances for her taste. She became more visibly upset and annoyed, "the look" settling over her face, that cutting combination of disdain and annoyance, the same one she'd worn the evening I was informed that my father was "taking a little trip." The same one I'd observe many more times by the time I was a teen. I could recognize it from across a room, as I was doing then.

"For *heaven's* sake," she said, placing an angry emphasis on selected words, "are you *planning* on telling *everyone*? Is it *something* you're *proud* of?"

Of course I wasn't planning on telling everyone. I certainly wasn't proud of what I'd done—far from it. But my teacher had asked what had happened, so I'd told him. I knew she wasn't asking those questions to be answered, so I didn't answer them. She was making a point, to highlight the gravity of the situation, calling my attention to the disgrace I'd brought upon myself and the family by uniting my culpability with my accountability.

"Don't you *know*," she continued, "the *embarrassment* you have caused us; how *ashamed* we are, of the *shame* you've put on this house? I can *barely* look my friends in the face. And *you* want to *add* to it by *telling* people what you *did*? How *dare* you! How *dare* you!"

"I'm sorry," I said, as tears started sliding down my cheeks. "I'm sorry," I repeated, but I couldn't go on. I started crying uncontrollably, gasping for air. My lung wasn't completely healed and I could taste blood in my mouth. She whacked the wooden spoon a few times against the side of the pot to remove any food particles, calmly placed it in a dish on the counter by the stove, and walked over to the table. She put her arm around me and said nothing more. She'd made her point. It was up to my father to do the rest and drive it home.

A day or two later my father invited me to join him while he walked to the store to buy the *Daily News*, to instruct me on how to react to being shot. Only now, after all of these years, do I see that his invitation to walk with him for our little "heart-to-heart" was part of a twin effort to put "the accident," as my mother started calling it, completely to rest. Evidently, following the conversation I had with my chemistry teacher, my mother must have spoken to my father about the need to set me straight, to make sure I didn't shoot off my mouth ever again about it. From that moment on, what had taken place on that night was never mentioned again among any of us, just as neither of my parents ever came clean about their separation. If we didn't talk about our dysfunction, then maybe it didn't really exist.

"One last thing," my father said, as we walked along South Railroad Avenue and made a right onto Guyon Avenue, the main drag up and down which police cruisers had frantically scrambled looking for me several days before. "Is it true what the paper said and what I heard from some of the guys at the station house, that it wasn't the only time you did that?" By then we were approaching George's, the candy store and soda shop where my father bought the newspaper, as did many residents of Oakwood Heights. George's was patronized especially by locals who commuted into Manhattan every day by taking the train to the Staten Island Ferry Terminal. In the mornings, many of them would run into George's, grab a paper and a pack of cigarettes, and then dash across the street to the train station, while others would buy a paper and begin reading it while waiting for George or his wife, Jodie, to prepare a toasted bagel-to-go, with a cup of coffee. In the evenings the place would be packed with the same commuters, many of whom bought cigarettes, cigars, and the late afternoon local paper, the *Staten Island Advance*. At all other times of the day and night the majority of George's customers were kids of all ages, like me, who went from buying comic books as a boy to buying sodas as a teen.

My father bought the *Daily News* there, and nothing else. He liked its crossword puzzle; even to this day doing the puzzle is one of his favorite pastimes. He never lingered in George's for long, unlike other men who might exchange a few words with George about the Yankees or the Jets, or about money lost or won at the racetracks. It was rumored that George was a big-time bookie and his store was merely a front for a much more profitable operation. Maybe my dad knew about it and that's why he didn't stay there long. On this day, though, which I guess my father considered special, he offered to treat me to a vanilla egg cream, one of my favorite soda fountain drinks as a child.

In my adolescence I was still ordering them, frequently in batches of three or four after smoking a "J" with someone in an empty lot not far from the store. George's had a counter and five swivel stools, upholstered with the kind of gummy plastic fabric that stuck to the back of your thighs in the summer if you were wearing shorts. Getting up from the seat sounded like a fresh Band-Aid's being ripped from flesh. George's also had a couple of flimsy wooden tables with equally flimsy wooden chairs in a tight, triangular corner near the counter. The table and chairs were surrounded by an assortment of oversized plastic toys, dangling from rickety shelves—kites and Wiffle Ball and stickball bats stuffed into old, crumpled cardboard boxes and dusty beach chairs so ugly only a desperate sunbather would purchase them. There didn't seem to be enough room for George and Jodie in the place, let alone the ten or fifteen boys and young men (it was almost always crowded with males) who might be there at any given time. I had spent hours sitting at that soda fountain with my friends, but in particular with Dougie. Sometimes even on a Sunday morning after cutting out of church we could be found there. But we first needed to take care of our alibi by placing our prelabeled, named envelopes in the church kitty, or give them to a friend to drop into the wicker basket that was passed from parishioner to parishioner. Our prepackaged contribution was the way for the church, and for the school, to take attendance. If the church didn't receive the envelope they'd have the nuns at school inquire about it. If we didn't bring in the weekly 50 cents due, they tacked it onto the school's tuition. For parishioners' children who weren't attending St. Charles but the public elementary school, they sent a bill to the house. To me and Dougie, church was about as exciting as a bag of sand, as it was to most boys barreling toward puberty. We'd sit at George's counter sipping egg creams and sharing a package of Ding Dongs as we paged through the latest *Batman* installment. "Hey!" George would bark. "Are you kids planning on buying that?" How could listening to Father Gannon read a passage from Corinthians for the umpteenth time compare to egg creams and Batman battling the Riddler?

I doubt my father appreciated how fitting it was that we were at George's so soon after I'd been shot, the site of so much childhood and adolescent activity and mischief. It also happened to be the first stop after our first robbery, the place where we went to "celebrate." In addition to George's location at "The Station," which was what the area was called by kids and adults alike, there was a brightly lit pizza parlor, a shoe box–sized one-chair barbershop, and Sal's, a deli that catered to the largely Italian-American population in the neighborhood. Every kid in Oakwood Heights was familiar with each of those stores, knowing exactly where Sal shelved the mayonnaise or Comet or where George kept the jar containing the pretzel logs. Many of those same kids, at some point in their lives, spent a good deal of time milling about the parking lot adjacent to George's, sometimes in groups of ten, twenty, or thirty. So intimidating was the density of teens there on any given night, and so voluminous the child–teen combo there during the day, that only those among us who even had a car, let alone were old enough to drive, dared park their cars there. No one else would dream of invading our space. If they did, we punished them for it. As soon as anyone walked into George's or Sal's, two or three of us would sit on the car's hood as a half a dozen more would prop against the vehicle's side, which was easy enough to do back when 4-doors were the size of small boats. Most adults got the message and parked on the street or drove past Sal's to look for another deli at which to grab an order of baked ziti and meatballs. Sal didn't stay in business there long, to nobody's surprise. We scared off many of his customers. My mother said he went back to Italy, that's how far away he needed to be from us.

That corner of Oakwood Heights was ours. It was where a kid could buy wax lips filled with a colorful, sticky substance or buy an ounce of weed stuffed in a plastic sandwich bag rolled up like a cigar. In my youth, I sometimes played stickball in front of George's brick wall that faced the parking lot and watched Spalding balls, which George plentifully stored in a peach basket, sail over the railroad tracks, sometimes bouncing off the roofs and steps of the houses along South Railroad Avenue. There was plenty of fun and sometimes monotony at The Station. It could also be a pretty gruesome place. I once saw a kid I knew who was standing at the top of the train station's steps get jumped from behind by one of the neighborhood's biggest drug dealers. Apparently he had missed a payment for whatever drugs he'd taken on credit, being a minor peddler himself. The big-time dealer had his "muscle" with him. They both took turns beating my friend's face to a bloody pulp. He'd been so surprised he didn't utter a sound. After he collapsed to the ground, the dealer repeatedly kicked him. "You're fucking with the wrong person," he casually reminded him, as if such a beating were a common occurrence. Only then did my friend speak. "Stop, stop!" he begged. "I'll get you your money."

That happened soon after I'd been shot. While some guys around me were hooting and hollering like it was some kind of sporting event, I was so overcome by the raw savagery of it, along with the sight of all of the blood, I thought I would throw up. I didn't, but I felt faint. I surreptitiously sat down because I didn't want my friends to think I was too weak to stomach what we were witnessing. I can remember thinking how absurd it was for me to have to do that, to have to hide my aversion to violence after what I'd been through. I'm not 100 percent sure, but I believe that was the last time I went to The Station. When I was in the hospital I kept telling myself I wanted out of the life that I'd been living. *If I ever make it out of here alive,* I told myself, *I'll re-work and re-do my life so drastically that the people I know won't recognize me, however long it takes.* Steering clear of The Station was the first step.

Before that incident, though, The Station was where I and many others learned about life's vagaries, and its tedium. One way of dealing with both was to stage amusing distractions, many of which were destructive. Possessing an acerbic tongue produced just as much amusement as lighting stink bombs on the train platform as evening rush-hour commuters were disembarking. The barbs and razzing were common among us all, although some were better at it than others. The cooler and better-looking kids didn't need to be so witty. Their hipness and handsomeness gave them enough self-assurance. I was neither handsome nor hip. I stood out because of my size. I was, euphemistically speaking, diminutive. As a result, I developed a special brand of wittiness. I had to. Otherwise, I might get my ass kicked like my low-level drug-dealing friend, but for no reason other than that it could be done. I cultivated one of the sharpest tongues around, making me popular with almost everyone, including the thugs. Self-deprecating humor, rarer than the abusive, one-upmanship zingers most guys parleyed, was my specialty. It turned out to be highly prized, too, being unique. So while I was among a handful of neighborhood jokers, I must have perfected my craft to near stand-up-comic proportions. I was voted class clown when I graduated from St. Charles, an honor I wasn't terribly thrilled about when it occurred at our graduation party. I was out-of-my-mind high on acid at the time so I panicked when my name was announced and had to walk up to the podium to receive my "award." Also, I found it troubling that I had stood out in that way. Cracking wise, even at my own expense, was a defensive mechanism, not a plea for attention. I wasn't searching for the spotlight. If anything, there were times when I just wanted to be left alone, to be a ghost.

Playing the jester wasn't demonstrative. It was Darwinian, a survival tactic. As one of the smallest guys, if not the smallest, in any number of cliques we moved in and out of—both as a child and as a teen—I quickly realized that dickheads, bullies, and gangster wanna-bes preyed upon easy pickings. But they left you alone if they saw you as a harmless fool. For them, it wasn't worth the trouble taking down anybody whom they considered already beneath them, in a nonphysical sense. They often weren't the brightest bulbs in town so they probably figured anyone who played the self-deprecating card, anyone who'd belittle themselves, proved they'd encountered someone stupider than they. Only an idiot would make fun of himself. Some of the roughs and toughs weren't natural-born dickwads anyway. *They* did it for show, perhaps their own version of warding off the truly natural thugs by appearing to be a bad-ass and as crazy as they. Perhaps they recognized other showmen, like me, and left me alone for that reason. I guess those faux-mofo's tended to appreciate the show I'd put on for them to save my own skin. They were flattered I'd gone through all of that trouble to impress them verbally.

For some reason, macho a-holes seemed to be everywhere in Oakwood Heights, as well as in the surrounding neighborhoods, and pretty much a swarm throughout Staten Island. Maybe it had something to do with the water. If it was environmental it more likely had something to do with the landfill, the largest one on the planet, so big it was visible from outer space, like (supposedly) the Great Wall of China. But it was the great garbage pail heap. I suspect tons of trash are bound to affect people adversely, in more ways than inducing cancer, possibly poisoning the borough's testosterone levels, thereby propagating a larger pool of jag-offs.

Simple math, though, explains the rise in the number of assholes. Staten Island's population practically doubled every couple of years in the 1960s and '70s because of the influx of families who mostly emigrated out of Brooklyn when the Verrazano-Narrows Bridge was built, linking Staten Island and Brooklyn. Before its construction, Staten Island was more countrified than citified, even though it was a borough of New York City. It might as well have been located in the Catskills with its horse stables, farms, acres of marshlands and wooded areas, so inaccessible was it to the rest of the city. I actually grew up on a dirt road, and we're not talking about eighteenth-century Virginia, mind you. It's hard to believe that in the last half of the twentieth century some parts of New York City still had dirt roads and cornfields. But once the bridge was built, our street was paved and the pace of life accelerated to city speed. Those arriving by the truckload from other boroughs, especially Brooklyn, seemed fueled emotionally with high octane compared with us "country," low-octane types. Many of the boys from the city's meaner streets moved into the sprawling, tract-home developments that were built seemingly overnight. These kids were born and bred rougher, tougher, and, quite frankly, nastier than those of us who grew up on Staten Island. Even some of the girls from there turned out to be pretty damn unpleasant. Before the bridge, groups of rival kids might engage in "dirt bomb" or in snowball fights with one another. When the "city" and Brooklyn kids moved in and went at it, the boys—and sometimes the girls—threw rocks and bottles. Later, they'd exchange gunfire or beat one another with tire irons. Girls never went that far. But they often provoked a lot of violence with their petty jealousies, contrived rivalries, and ultra-foul mouths. I did see a couple of vicious "cat fights" that drew blood and hair.

Tough girls or not, Oakwood Heights was ultimately a man's world— well, more like a boy's world. Males were everywhere. And they roamed in packs, smoking cigarettes under the train trestle or behind the school- yards, riding bicycles up and down the same streets all day and all night, later mini-bikes and then later still motorcycles. There were enough boys in Oakwood Heights to fill up three separate baseball fields, with each team sometimes fielding nine players. That didn't even account for ev- eryone. At the same time the ball games were being played, there might be others playing basketball near the ball fields, with still more playing roller hockey in a playground above the basketball courts. Several more groups who didn't play sports roamed the streets or hung out in bunches on schoolyard stoops or street corners, chased from one corner to another by alarmed residents. You could go anywhere in Oakwood Heights at almost any time of the day and find a collection of guys doing something or absolutely nothing.

Then there was The Station. That's where ballplayers, bikers, smokers, druggies, and drunks would converge. The summer months called forth so many that it looked like a sprawling movie set of a teeming street corner. Kids from all directions went there to buy a soda between ball games, or they sat at George's counter and ordered two or three cheeseburgers in succession, or they went next door to the pizzeria to buy two slices and a Coke for a buck. Most stood in front eating their slices in about a minute, a skill many of us had developed by laying the two pieces on top of each other, curling them into a tight triangle, and then devouring it in three or four gulps. A bottle of Coke was usually pressed between our knees, or a 7-Up in a paper cup was delicately held in our free hands.

Generally, kids simply showed up to while away large blocks of the day, the entire evening, or both by standing by the side of George's. Some downed a six-pack of beer in less than two hours, the cans or bottles hidden among George's garbage bins. In my teens, we often snuck around the corner to smoke a couple of joints. We almost all smoked a pack of Marlboros or Kools, the two preferred brands, in full view during and between the drinking and pot smoking. It didn't seem to matter back then that someone's son or daughter was already smoking by the time they were thirteen or fourteen. Everyone's parents smoked, probably not starting at such a young age, but "learning" to smoke was as common as learning to ride a bike.

There were other places besides The Station where guys wasted their time, like the benches behind a public elementary school, where some kids were so high they were passed out on them, typically from sniffing glue. Some underage teens, who clearly didn't look old enough to pass for eighteen—the legal drinking age at the time—spent time in local bars. Many of them, I'd later learn, were already juvenile alcoholics. But the real place to be seen was The Station. All of those other places were peripheral, secondary hangouts. During the eighteen years I lived in Oakwood Heights, The Station was the primary meeting place for nearly every kid in the neighborhood.

Yet I never liked it much, which seems strange considering how often I was there, especially as a teenager. But it didn't seem as if I had many choices. As I got older, I was playing less and less sports, so I was going down to the ball fields less and less. I wasn't going to sit home like some old fart and watch TV all afternoon like some kids. I couldn't imagine myself sitting home reading, either, which is exactly what I did—voraciously—after I'd been shot. After my more jock-ish childhood years ended, I spent a lot of time simply hanging out. The Station was the Taj Mahal of hangouts. Still, always gnawing in the back of my mind was what a waste it seemed to be just standing around there trying to be cool and succeeding in being foolish, all the while my life going nowhere. Another reason I was secretly uncomfortable there was that some guys who hung around The Station scared the crap out of me.

At least that's one positive thing I can say about myself and the stupid shit I did: I never intended to hurt anyone, surely not with a water pistol. In the end—and this is probably true of most decent kids who try pulling off some boneheaded move as I did—the person I hurt the most was me. And that was another reason why I wanted out of the place. My father was right about the little celebrityhood that came my way following the shooting. What frightened me the most about it was that I was receiving a good deal of attention from the very same hoodlums I despised. If *they* were proud of me, that proved I'd been heading in the wrong direction.

It was time for a change, a massive, full-scale restructuring, the kind found in the *Bildungsromans* I'd later read, the kind of building blocks I promised myself I'd accrue when I was given last rites.

Soon after I'd been shot I realized that not going to The Station again wasn't enough. I needed to get the hell off of that damn island. Of course, I couldn't do so right away, knowing full well that I'd have to wait a couple of years to graduate from high school. Going away to college was my best chance of escape and of reinvention. However—and it still pains me after all these years to accept, let alone write—my parents did their best to block my escape, essentially discouraging me from trying to reinvent myself through any kind of formal education. As much as they advised me to move on after I'd been shot, they hadn't. Perhaps to them I wasn't worthy of bettering myself. So convinced were they of my unworthiness that my mother called in reinforcements to convert me to their way of thinking, just in case their words weren't enough. With the help of a cousin's husband, they actually talked me out of going to college. My mother especially seemed bent on dissuading me from my academic ambitions my entire life, right up until I was in my late thirties when she urged me to take the New York City Sanitation Department test, four months shy of obtaining my doctorate.

Because I lacked confidence and moral courage, I often bent their way, just as I had done about keeping being shot a secret. Maybe it all started from there, becoming the dutiful son. But for all of their talk about putting the shooting behind me, I think it was they who could never quite get past the idea that their son had once attempted a robbery, along with the interminable shame it had brought to them once he'd been caught—and shot. Throughout my life, I was constantly at odds with them about my desire to remake myself and constantly at odds with myself about the value of it, of having come so close to death to become truly alive. As a result, it took a long time for me finally to become what I knew all along I wanted to become and what I wanted to do—to be the kind of person who helps others find their way in life. I wanted to be someone whom I hadn't really encountered most of my life growing up. And I guess telling this story is a further fulfillment of that desire, along with stating that it *is* better to remember even the harshest of experiences and to try to learn from them. It's actually the only way to figure things out. It's also the best way to move on.

3

"So what's your name?"

kay, look: At the time, I didn't think being shot was the best thing that had ever happened to me. That came later, really not until I had survived it all and become fully conscious of its impact, in a sobering transcendental way, if you know what I mean. Granted, holding up a pizza delivery guy with a water pistol was a pretty idiotic thing to try, but I wasn't that dumb to think at the time, *Wow, I've been shot. How wonderful! Maybe I should do this more often.* As mentioned before, I didn't even *know* I had been shot, at least not in the official, real-gun/real-bullets sense. I assumed that the dizziness, the paralysis, and the wavering myopia and hyperopia were the results of the dissolving sodium chloride pellets I thought were coursing through my bloodstream. Admittedly, a nagging sense of fatality kept creeping into my head now and then. The body doesn't lie. Signals were likely being sent to my brain: *You're fucked!* Still, not even when I was lying on the ground and that cop was pressing his shoe into my blown-out shoulder did it occur to me I'd been hit by anything more than salt ammo.

In my foggy, bloodless vision, he looked like a giant, whereas the cops standing around and behind him looked as if I were seeing them through the wrong end of a pair of binoculars. I was simultaneously among the Brobdingnagians and the Lilliputians, an immobile Gulliver pinned to the ground by a muddy shoe. Weeks later, when the hospital returned, unwashed, most of the clothes I'd worn that night, there it was on my tan, zippered corduroy jacket: the pointed, circular stain he left as a souvenir. He was trying to squeeze some information out of me, no doubt following the playbook, behaving like the bad cop because the good cop before him, the first Brobdingnagian, had no success at it.

Even after all these years, I can still picture them in my mind's eye. I distinctly remember the first, or "good," Brobdingnagian's appearance, right down to some of the finer points. Did I soak it in as it dawned on me that his might be the last face I'd ever see? It is a round, flat face with bulging light eyes. He's not wearing a uniform. I know this because I can see his thick, shiny black hair, and in those days any cop in uniform always had to wear a cap. None of them are in uniform, as far as I can make out, and all of their hair glistens. It's almost magical. In fact, there's a sheen coating almost everything: The homes, the lawns, the shrubs, and even the air seem to shine in the darkness. It had rained earlier that night. I'm thinking it's been drizzling for a while or a fog has rolled in, but I can't be sure. I don't feel wet, but I don't even feel wet from the blood soaking my shirt, my pants, right down to filling up my shoes, as I'd later learn. I can't feel much of anything, while the world seems muted, like walking outside after a big snowstorm. I'm totally immobilized. I can't even move my head much. I can't see me. I can only see upward into the evening sky. He's hovering over me now, realizing that only in my direct vision can anyone be seen. His solid, athletic frame leans forward, a massive letter "C." I can hear some Lilliputians shuffling behind him, talking, while others poke around in the shrubs and scrape around on other people's lawns looking for the weapon, the spray-painted water pistol. It's not "on my person," if that's the correct law enforcement term. Someone must have already frisked me. Maybe it was the good Brobdingnagian. But when? Had I blanked out back there? He starts asking questions, bending forward deeper into his curve. He's enormous!

"Tell us who you were with?"

That's his first question? Not who am I? Later I understand they needed to find that out fast, to have me confess, before I croaked. Maybe I remained oblivious to the severity of the situation, but they sure knew I was on the brink. In time my corpse would give *me* up. But what if they never found the other guy, "my partner in crime," and never learned his name?

"What?" I say, pretending to sound all groggy and disoriented, as if I needed to.

"You heard me," he says sternly, devoid of emotion. "Your friend, the one you were with tonight pulling off that little stunt. Who is he?"

He'll have to try harder than that. I'm not going to cough up Dougie's name just because he asked me twice, however nicely. I'm aware of some criminal or gangster code, akin, really, to the one beholden by a band of noble brother warriors, the one about never being a rat fink or a traitor or a spineless prisoner and giving up the beans, if that phrase is even used anymore. I undoubtedly held that belief. It's running through my mind even though I'm close to death, having watched God only knows how many Cagney and Bogie movies. No way too would Butch or Sundance give up the other, nor would Depression-era Butch or Sundance from that other film, even though they made it look like one of them had, but that was just part of the scam. Too bad Dougie would fall for a similar trap when the cops told him I'd turned him in, when I hadn't, no matter how many times they showed up at the hospital asking me who was with me. I was prepared to die before I'd give up his name, which is pretty much what had almost happened. Sure, when the cop asked, a part of me wanted to tell him so they might find Dougie and he could be there with me. Also, for some strange reason, I wanted to say something true and honest, skip embracing the ol' silent-treatment code. Also, I had a real need to talk to someone, to say something that might elicit a conversation, like discussing where Dougie lived, whether he was holding the gun and why he never turned around to look back to see if I was okay. I was too exhausted to think of anything more than "What?" again when the cop asked me a second time whom I was with.

A Lilliputian steps forward, growing immediately larger, like a cartoon character that swallows a weird, indigestible object and his rubberized torso expands, then his arms and legs, and then his head pops into a gigantic form. He's muttering something about "Fuck this asshole." Only my eyes can move, so when I slid them right I can't make out much more than a big blurry presence, but I recognize the voice, certainly the temper of the expletives, as the one who promised to blow me to kingdom come if I didn't get the fuck on the ground. The good Brobdingnagian raises his arm, like a tollbooth gate, preventing him from reaching any closer. "Look," he says, still as dispassionately as before, "we know you were with someone. Just tell us who it was, who you were with."

I know that "What?" won't work a third time. "I don't remember," I say. There's no holding back the former Lilliputian, now turned Brobdingnagian. He bursts past the tollgate and stands over me, looming larger than the original Brobdingnagian, bulkier and more menacing. He's oozing hatred. I can't feel much, but this I can. He wants to kill me, to wrap up the night so he can go home or head to the bar for a couple of cold ones. He presses his foot into my shoulder, the one still containing shrapnel to this day, gone so numb there's not much pain, little sensation, except I suddenly begin to sink into a hole in the ground that wasn't there a second ago. He starts to grow smaller. "You little fucker," he hollers, digging the front of his shoe farther into me. "Tell us who you were with, right the fuck now!"

"Jesus," the other one says, "he's only a kid," as he pulls on the bad cop's shirt sleeve.

"Fuck that," he says angrily, kicking me in the ribs a couple of times, before flipping his arm into the air and brushing past the good cop.

"All right, all right," the lone Brobdingnagian says. "Forget it. Never mind. We'll find your buddy, anyway. What about you? So what's your name?"

"David," I say.

"'David' what?"

"David Borkowski," I tell him.

"Borkowski?" he repeats, alarmed.

"Yes, sir," I say politely, slipping into a degree of respectfulness I rarely used with the nuns or other authority figures.

"What's your father's name?"

I tell him.

"Oh, shit," he erupts, as he connects the bleeding punk on the ground to the cop he knows. After all, how many cops are there with my father's name? It's not exactly Smith or Jones, while his unusual first name, Zenon, makes it all the more obvious.

The same realization occurs to the others, based on the "Oh, craps," "Oh, damns," and "Holy shits," including one from the bad cop. This crowd is obviously from the 122nd Precinct, where my father recently worked before transferring to the City Hall station. Some of them may have worked under him. He'd been a sergeant for a few years by then.

Everything around me is getting smaller. As the hole beneath me grows I begin to grasp that I may be in a real mess of trouble—lots of real cops, labored breathing, and a literal sinking feeling. Maybe I'd been hit with real bullets too.

To think, all of this could have been avoided if I'd remained obstinate after telling Dougie at the start of the evening that I didn't want to do it any more. During the week, my restless nights grew longer and more intense. I was convinced that what we were doing was bad, or insane, or something terribly out of joint. I'd decided it had come to an end. Instead, I let him talk me out of it. "Just one more," he pleaded. "C'mon, it'll be the last one."

4
Child's Play

Whenever we walked to the train station as kids, we brought something to toss around—a Frisbee, a tennis ball, a pygmy football, a Nerf ball, anything. If we forgot, we'd improvise. We'd crush a soda can left on the street, pluck a pine cone from a tree, or even rifle through someone's trash looking for anything we could roll up into a ball or shape into a missile. Usually, it was the four of us—me, Dougie, Timmy, and Ritchie—who went. During the school year, we'd go a couple of times a week; during the summer, we'd go a couple of times a day. The destination was secondary. The primary purpose was for sport, of a very particular kind: to hurl the projectile toward a neighbor's shrubs, forcing the sprinting receiver to dive into the shrubs. Flying object, body, and flora would meet in perfect symmetry. At least that was the goal. Drawing blood was a bonus, as long as it didn't involve busting a lip or scarring a face.

This was before families from practically every economic class started hiring landscapers to tend their properties. The homeowners did all the work, much of it fancy and elaborate. And they did it as well as any professional. One yard sported a hedge shaped like a swan. It was perfectly understandable, then, that some became infuriated watching us destroy their handiwork. The most zealous greenthumbers went berserk. They might be watering their backyard lawns or sitting on their side porches and spot one of us leaping into their perfectly pruned forsythia trying to catch a shoe we'd discovered in the garbage. They would jump out of their chair, as if it had become electrified, or drop their watering hose, as if it had become red hot, and race to the curb screaming about our eternal damnation. Some ran after us waving metal rakes or pitchforks, as if we were Frankenstein's monster (the one from the film version), promising to stick the thing up our collective asses.

Quite frankly, we deliberately targeted easily agitated homeowners. It was more exciting. The ones who overreacted posed more of a threat. It was exhilarating to be the cause of their chasing us down the street tripping over their flip-flops or struggling to keep their baggy bathing trunks from falling to the ground. Little else is as amusing to a child as watching adults behave ridiculously. Not everyone in Oakwood Heights could be so easily pushed over the edge. Some attempted to reason with us, pleading for us to be more respectful of private property. It wasn't the most effective approach to take with a bunch of nine-year-old boys seeking to turn their boring suburban neighborhood into a sports arena. But it often worked. We generally bypassed their homes, but not because we'd been persuaded by their logic or had come to our senses. Saner people lived on less challenging terrain according to our code of (mis)conduct. If people refused to get all worked up over our displays of super-hero heroism, what was the point of going through all that trouble? There were even a few sweet elderly widows who practically encouraged us to wreck their property. What was the fun in that? If they told us there was nothing wrong with playing on their lawns—after mangling a hedgerow—as long as we avoided the shrubs the grandson had worked on, then we'd never go back again, unless it was to help them shovel their sidewalks or lug metal garbage cans to the curb. We weren't that thoughtlessly naughty. We may have even considered them special residents in Oakwood Heights. In a landscape dominated by sullen, often surly adults, they seemed angelic in comparison.

On the night I was shot I lay on the lawn of one such angel. Maybe it wasn't entirely coincidental. Maybe I'd sought hers out, among all the others, believing I'd find shelter and solace there. No matter how grim it got, I might be able to keep my head above water, even if some bad-ass cop worked me over. I was on sacred ground. I was protected. But memory can be a fickle thing. If it functions anything like a river, as Wordsworth metaphorically expressed, it's a fluid process, picking up pieces of real *and* imagined recollections along the way. Because it's constantly moving, constantly acquiring, *and* generating more and more material as it flows toward the sea, the older sediments collected at the start can shift around or collide against newer ones. Such fluidity can alter its composition or appearance, even changing the recollection into a new form altogether. That's not all. Other bits fall to the bottom and may never be seen again, especially when submerged deliberately, forgotten, like my parents' insistence about that entire night. Of course, like any artifact, some may rise up on their own or they can be retrieved, no matter how far to the bottom they go or how entangled they become in the weeds and the debris. This too may turn into a selective or artificial process. Someone may scoop up a handful of goop and look for what will most please him, choosing what serves her interests, while tossing the rest back into the water. What's kept can be scrubbed and polished, improving on the original.

Possibly that's what I'm doing right now in remembering the advantages of ending up on *her* lawn, not just any lawn. But I *have* to remember it that way. A shiny object from that cesspool needs to be retrieved. I need some aspect of that night to seem dignified, when everyone else directly involved behaved so dishonorably, starting with me, followed by the cop's unnecessarily unloading his gun into my back, continued by Dougie's unceremoniously leaving me for dead, and concluding with a man's tormenting another human being who is bleeding to death. Some reassuring image has to be located in all of that male despair, even if it involves what I never "saw." Otherwise, I believe I would slowly die of sadness every time I think about it, drip by drip. I simply must believe that if the old woman had come to the door she would have politely reprimanded the cop for being so cruel. Then she'd step back inside to get a pillow and a blanket.

However contrived or corrupted my memory currently is, or has been all along, it's evident I had come a long way from darting through front lawns as a boy to nearly bleeding to death on hers as a teen. There aren't many years separating my childhood from my adolescence. But it now seems as if I had lived a lifetime between the two. What happened to me—or what did I do to myself?—between those days of playing on lawns to almost dying on one? Can it be explained? Can I put the puzzle pieces into their right places? Can I even find enough of them, let alone assemble them correctly? And even if I can gather all the pieces and place them where they belong, then what? Will the final picture look more surreal than real? For that matter, can any life and its direction—or misdirection—be explained intelligently?

In some ways, my having been shot doesn't make any sense at all. No matter how many different ways I look at it and pick it apart, I'll never be able to satisfactorily explain it to myself and why I committed those robberies. That's why we've come up with metaphors and tales for the seemingly inexplicable, like The Book of Job, and less complicated terms, like The Book of Life, as in, "Shit happens." It's as if my mother was right to call it an "accident." It was just bad timing, like getting hit by a drunk driver who runs a red light. Granted, I was doing something wrong so something wrong occurred, or it was more bound to occur than if I hadn't been. But lots of people do bad things and they don't nearly get their heads blown off—not at fifteen years of age, anyway. Lots of people do the right thing too and do get their heads blown off, or something like it. That's Job's woeful story, the fickle (middle) finger of fate. Either way you look at it, my getting shot was as random as Job's terrible losses and physical afflictions. It wasn't his fault he lost everything. He wasn't being punished. He didn't do anything wrong. Just the opposite, in fact—he was doing everything right. He was a good soul, leading a righteous life. That's the scary part. He didn't know God, and Satan had made a bet concerning his devotion, testing his allegiance to the Almighty. Even the concept of God's pulling a prank on someone doesn't quite make sense, at least not to me. What the hell?

All of that bad karma coming Job's way didn't make any sense to him, either. So it's not just me, then, or any number of the confused, who can't quite figure it out. *Nothing* makes sense to anyone, except to the Grand High Mystic Ruler, although many years ago a rabbi wrote a book, trying to explain the story and explain it *all* as well, called *When Bad Things Happen to Good People*. For most of us, though, that can't be easily explained, not in any comforting way. Sure, we all know bad things happen to good people. How come? Life seems as senseless to us as Job initially thinks it has become when his entire life heads south. He isn't in on the joke, as we are, but he realizes that despite his being a faithful, caring, honest, and all-around damned decent guy, he still loses everything. What the hell?

Except it does figure, or work itself out, at least to him—and, wink, wink, presumably to the reader too. At the conclusion of the story it's all added up for Job. But it isn't pretty, not just for him but for the story's readers as well. Ultimately, it doesn't offset the nagging feeling that capital "L" Life is altogether way too random with its outbursts of happiness, misery, joy, and suffering. In fact, the story's didactic conclusion reinforces that infuriating impression many of us have about life's rather quotidian fickleness. Simply put, according to the story, bad shit indeed happens to good people, just as the title of that rabbi's book informs us, because—and here's the kicker—God, in His infinite wisdom, made it that way. Near the end, when Job can't endure any more suffering and starts wondering about God's Great Master Plan, God steps down from His throne and angrily informs him that He, the Divine Creator, gets to create whatever He wants, including floods, plagues, and killer whales. Every now and then He throws in a cute kitten, a startling rainbow, and a cure for polio.

Message to the reader: Every person is a potential Job. So shut up if every once in a while a really devoted, righteous person, such as Job, is afflicted with disgusting boils, or a truly harmless, devoted mother gets mauled by a ferocious lion while jogging through the foothills of the Sierras. Curse the lion's presence along existence's superhighway and we're damning the Lord, the Creator of All Life. None of us therefore has any right to bitch about the existence of nasty stuff. C'est la vie.

Actually, it gets worse and even more confounding. We read the headlines. Some rather good shit happens to some rather bad-ass people, unless they get caught. But most don't. Even when they do—like all of those Watergate conspirators who turned to the Lord in prison, wrote about the experience, and made lots of money—there might still be a nifty payoff at the end. My point is that lots of good things happen to lots of bad people all the time, in full view. Life is therefore *perversely* senseless. Of course, these are the two extremes, and most of us live in the gray zone, as I likely did when I was shot. So, some bad shit happened to me, and I wasn't altogether that good or that bad. Life's senselessness may therefore be a three-ring circus: Shit happens to good, bad, and mediocre people. Great, now we're all in on God's little joke. Wouldn't most sensible people make the next leap and argue that they might as well live it up as a bad-ass because their chances of shit's happening to them is no greater than the chances of its happening to everyone else, including a Goody Two-Shoes like Job? At least they'd get to live it up a little before the shit hits the fan and sprays them with it. Yeah, one might think, why not be sitting poolside with my AK-47, doing a few lines of Bolivian Marching Powder and sipping my Courvoisier with my ho's, before I get splashed with poop? Besides, maybe I won't anyway! My God-fearing, morally upstanding neighbor might instead. C'est la (F'ing) vie!

I was probably viewed as an "average kid," despite those who considered me sneaky and mischievous. But anyone with half a brain could see that was an outcome of my being mostly lost and confused, rudderless sans papa. Overall, I was a shy, timid child and I avoided doing anything that drew attention to myself. Even when I misbehaved I did it surreptitiously, like the time I slipped a tack onto my eighth-grade teacher's chair without anyone's noticing. But by then my father had moved back in with us and I was more mixed up than I had been previously. I don't think that throughout most of my childhood I was too rotten. As a matter of fact, by being the only child around without a father, I became so self-conscious of my deficiency that I was too broken to do much damage.

In some ways, then, my getting shot makes perfect sense. The shy, self-conscious boy on the outside was cover for the misfit lurking inside. Play back the actual videotape from then and I might come up as a Junior League a-hole by the sixth grade. Who knows, maybe a toxic mixture of an increasing Napoleon complex (I was a small, if not tiny, boy) and my being raised by two skittish females (my mother and my sister) might have created a ticking time bomb. Lots of repressed turmoil churned inside of me. I was ready to explode. Sticking up pizza delivery drivers was the inevitable result. It was the result of the lid (or is it the id?) having been blown off—with my head close behind. So maybe it wasn't such a great distance after all. Sure, shit happens, but most of the time it happens for a reason. With some cautionary, careful analysis, the dots *can* be connected.

Over the years I've tried mapping the distance separating my childhood from that "fateful" experience. I've also played armchair shrink to my own psyche, seeking to trace those seemingly connectable dots that were determined by . . . by what: my character, my lack of character, a series of events and circumstances within and/or outside my control? What about growing up in an atmosphere fixated on male bravado? How about living at a time when a bad moon was rising over the nation? Maybe it was luck of the draw, and I was dealt a bad socioeconomic or parental hand. Shouldn't *something* explain why I had been shot nearly to death? My lengthy scar is visible proof that something dramatic happened. I think I'm entitled to speculate now and then on the plot leading up to that drama. I think anyone in my shoes would.

Mind you, asking these questions is largely an intellectual exercise, my personal parlor game. I'm curious. Mentally *and* emotionally I've accepted it, to the point of embracing it as the defining moment in my life. Generally speaking, it was all for the better, including making me a better teacher (eventually), which I'll get to later. I accepted it the second I watched the priest recite my last rites—had to—since I thought I was preparing to accept the Whole Enchilada, as in accepting death. Despite accepting it, I have still looked for an explanation, even a precise one, like that passage in *War and Peace* when Napoleon's head cold explains why the French lost a crucial battle and failed to subdue Moscow. How simple and neat it would be if robbing pizza delivery drivers could be explained by a toothache or something. But nothing is that simple, especially when a generally good person does some wicked things. (For the record: Tolstoy wasn't simplifying human conduct. If you haven't read the book, I don't have time to explain it here. It is, after all, a really beefy book.) In *Les Misérables*, an even beefier book, Hugo reaches a slightly different conclusion about Napoleon's failures, agreeing with early historians that if only it hadn't rained the morning of Waterloo, the great military tactician would have won that crucial battle. It rained on the night I was shot. How utterly convenient it would be to blame it on the rain.

Sometimes I think one reason I became a professor was to search quietly for the reason professionally, under the guise of the academy. It could help me understand and answer the question "Who was I?" Or better yet: "What the hell was I thinking?" Armed with my scholarly training and powers of deduction, I've examined, reexamined, deconstructed, reconstructed, and re-deconstructed my past, pulling the pieces apart and putting them back together again, Humpty Dumpy style, in order to figure out how I ended up on that old lady's lawn perforated by three bullets.

Here's what I've come up with over the years. Was it because:

1. I was a fatherless child? Answering "yes" would be the quickest and easiest explanation. End of story. Well, at least it would be the end of locating the overarching theme to a *shot story*. Obviously, this would be a bit more complicated explanation than having acquired a head cold or having watched the Weather Channel. A father's departure is more complex than that. Still, blame a parent or parents for screwing up your life and most folks, especially baby boomers, would nod their heads in agreement. But Dougie could've been the one gunned down instead of me; it could've been *his* shot story if the cop had missed his mark or if I'd thought of running first. And Dougie had a father at home. What was his excuse?

2. I grew up during the rise of the American Empire? We're all products of our times. Socially and culturally I was raised by a big bully. I learned to "be a man" at the feet of the Great White Father. Doubling its impact, this puffed-up period in American history developed alongside a culture long obsessed with guns and violence, "The Gunfighter Nation," as the historian Richard Slotkin explains. In the early '60s I came of age in a family that celebrated America's military muscle while blindly adhering to an ideology that pumped up any boy's dreams of blazing glory. It was the impetus behind Ron Kovic's joining the Marines and nearly dying from gunshot wounds in Vietnam. He regretted enlisting once he realized he'd been brainwashed into killing commie gooks. Born around Kovic's time, I might have done and felt the same. Different bullets but the same bullshit desire to be heroically and violently adventurous, to prove my manhood. The heroism part was missing from my equation, but certainly the rugged/adventure aspect of it took up a great deal of my brain space.

It was impossible to miss the cultural cue cards directing me to thump my chest back then as a boy, just as it is now. There are photos of me sitting under a sprawling Christmas tree wearing a cowboy hat and boots.

A plastic Tommy Gun lies beside me. Take a closer look at the photo and you'll notice I'm still in my diapers! I couldn't have been any older than three. Another photo from a later Christmas past shows I've been promoted into the U.S. Army. I must have been a prodigy because I'm no older than ten. In it, I'm decked out in full Army fatigues. I'm looking through a pair of binoculars directly at whoever snapped the picture. A western six-shooter in its belted holster, à la General George Patton, hangs on my hip. No surprise, then, that I had to ditch a fake gun after being shot by a real one. I wasn't doing anything much different from what my parents wanted me to pretend to do as a child, which was play with guns. But lots of boys brandished toy guns, and the neighborhood was filled with them playing Army or cowboys and Indians in their front and back yards. How come none of them ended up where I did?

3. More violent-chimp DNA coursed through my veins than other youngsters'? Some can handle it without going off the deep end, and others can't. I was one who couldn't. I struggled to grapple with an additional splash of testosterone, like some substance abuser with extra-addictive genes. My adolescence, already wobbly and off track, was further de-railed because I had a more intoxicating brew of the chemical ingredients human males inherited from their tree-swinging ancestors, as Richard Wrangham and Dale Peterson claim in *Demonic Males*. I'd grown into one fierce motherfuckin' beast. The robberies were practically inevitable. Biological determinism could explain it. Option number 3 is starting to sound pretty good.

But in my daily life I was far from aggressive. I avoided fights and con-frontations with anyone. I didn't even like arguing with girls. I never threw my weight around, mostly because I had so little to throw around. Really, I was more of a chickenshit than an ape man. And I preferred the more athletically subtle game of baseball to the smash-mouth sport of football. My stomach would turn if I came across a mangled road-kill squirrel, as it still does. And no matter how many times I've seen it, I always get a bit weepy whenever I watch Bogie in *Casablanca* standing on the train platform reading Ilsa's "Dear John" letter, the ink streaming down the page from the rain, like the tears I shed running down my face. I don't feel that I'm any more naturally sinister or hot-headed than the next guy. It doesn't seem that my wires are overloaded with demonic electricity. If they are, it can't amount to any more than a few extra volts than normal.

If it wasn't "1," "2," or "3," can it be:

4. The United States is really terrible at turning boys into men? But this one requires a good deal of explaining, so bear with me.

For one thing, lots of males prefer to remain adolescents well into their middle years. Our consumer culture wants it that way. Spoiled children are always dissatisfied, always whining for more toys and candy. It works out nicely if they continue to spoil for fancier cars or larger plasma TVs. Few "grown-up" men could be found anywhere in Oakwood Heights back in the '60s. I bet there are even fewer today. It's unfair to label boomers as the first "Me" Generation. Their parents were already working at that. In fact, they invented it. Our perpetual state of adolescent consumer dependency is a phenomenon of the immediate postwar years, the early 1950s, when the consumer republic came into full swing. It was a hyperactive, cash-flush Madison Avenue that concocted a fuller extension of the Great American Dream, with television as the perpetual selling machine. The Elizabethans weren't watching plays seven hours a day and learning how to be patriotic "Elizabethans." But Americans were watching that much TV *and* learning how to be patriotic Americans. By 1959, 90 percent of American households owned a TV set, ten years after it was introduced.

In no time at all, what we owned was who we were. It's what Americans have been told for several decades. Running parallel to this message is being told we need to have more of everything to assure fulfillment, yet whatever we do possess isn't doing the trick because something better exists, even if it's "the new and improved" version of what we already have. We are forever incomplete according to those standards and perpetually dissatisfied as well. No wonder half the country is on antidepressants. An endless cycle of instant gratification followed by instant disappointment occurs, about as fast as it takes a TV commercial to run. It's childish dependency, a culture of consumerism that encourages adults to remain as infantile as possible. My father went through it nearly fifty years ago. It's likely why he left us, a pioneer of sorts among the now common male midlife crisis managers who deal with aging by dipping back into a Fountain of Youth of immaturity and irresponsibility. And that's the good news.

Scores of males are so unprepared to face manhood when they reach it chronologically, having failed to do so emotionally and psychologically, that they end up blowing their goddamned brains out. Suicide rates among white, middle-aged American males are off the charts. (Nonwhite males have their own violent, anxiety-ridden problems.) Apparently for some males who reach middle age and haven't attained The Dream, debilitating disappointment overcomes them. Then there are those who've attained it but are left wondering why they feel so empty, having turned into straw men. For others, after sleepwalking through life, they wake from The Dream and realize it's actually been a nightmare. Nearly 30,000 people every year are killed by firearms in the United States, which amounts to roughly 80 per day, almost all of them males. Of those 80, nearly 50 are suicides (18 veterans a day), and of those 50 about four-fifths are white males between the ages of 40 and 55. That's only the daily suicide rate from *firearms*. Add to those numbers the hangings, drug overdoses, cars left idling in garages, and bodies flung from rooftops to get the fuller picture. It's an epidemic. The stereotype of females struggling with midlife crises is that they go shopping for shoes and handbags. Males should be so lucky. Men in America are at war with one another for no reason, like blowing some stranger's head off over a parking spot. More tragically, American men are at war with themselves, blowing their own heads off if they can't *find* the right parking spot, so to speak. Can you imagine if we learned that 30,000 Lebanese or Japanese or Brazilians or Jamaicans died every year from firearms? We'd be calling them barbarians, a nation of Neanderthals. Let's be realistic about such name calling, though. When we think "barbarians" we generally mean males. We don't picture a club-wielding female baring her teeth while pumping her other hairy fist over a mangled corpse. Sure enough, the 30,000 deaths a year by firearms in the United States are a male problem, not a female one.

My educated guesstimate about when this national gender crisis started is the 1950s, not uncoincidentally with the rise of the American consumer republic. For more than fifty years our consumer culture has deemed middle-aged men uncool and useless. Not only do they have nothing to teach the young, but they're in the way. With the prospect of confronting the remainder of your life as hollow, who wouldn't become morbidly depressed or lose his mind? The novelty of the uncool middle-aged man likely went down pretty hard on my dad's generation, The Greatest One, which I suppose is fitting because they essentially were the ones who invented and launched the Great Male Immaturity campaign in the first place. Starting in the early postwar years, America's consumer culture turned members of my father's generation into stick-in-the mud bogeymen, while turning their children against them. I think it's why men of his generation had trouble relating to younger males, detached from them like never before. A cultural chasm was separating sons from fathers. The culture took on the task of "raising" the nation's children and it was doing so with a cool, aloof, youth-oriented pedagogy. It was pitting one generation against another, and it was particularly problematic for males. Their old brand of male authority—largely based on obedience and restraint—had to be killed off. Restraint doesn't serve the best interests of a culture consumed by carefree consumerism.

Sure, there have always been tensions and rifts between fathers and sons. Pick up the Bible and you'll see plenty of it, like poor old King David having to deal with Absalom, or any number of ancient Greek myths and tales, such as that one very famous son who kills his (unidentified) dad during a street brawl—and then marries his mom, putting the kooky-family icing on the cake. Such father/son conflicts clearly go way back. They've been around a long time. Cave-dwelling sons and fathers probably bickered over who got to carry home the slain prey.

But something appeared on the scene that was entirely singular, a real game changer for my father's generation. Adult males had never encountered it, both in its articles of faith and in its scope. I don't think we've ever recovered from it, or at least tried to figure out how to deal with it. It was historically unprecedented: the hyperventilated social empowerment of the young, enchantingly and rigorously mediated and radiated in Technicolor through the prodigious expansion of culture, with a capital "C." Capital "C" Culture was now mass-produced and mass-consumed with the same totalizing effect as every other commodity. But it was even bigger than all of it. Culture was responsible for handling all of those other commodities, their packaging, publicity, and distribution. Culture was commodification squared. It still shared the same task as it had in bygone days, to get inside a person's head and heart, to get them to think and to feel a certain way (now mostly about things to purchase). Language—the means to the end—has always been the primary vehicle for carrying the signals to those two places. But never was it too so totalizing: the language of film, the language of television, the language of music, the language of sports, the language of suburbia, the language of shopping malls, the language of Main Street, the language of Wall Street, the language of theme parks (children's—Disney—and adults'—Las Vegas), all the way down to the language of cereal boxes and soup cans. The principal ideology these discourses conveyed was the projection of a youth culture, initially and intensely marketed at the start of the postwar years.

Even though my dad's generation eventually bought into this concept of youthful abandon (so as to keep "purchasing" it) like everybody else, it initially blindsided them. When it came time to dealing with their own children, who started to look, walk, and talk differently from them in ways that varied enormously from how fathers and sons differed in the past, they didn't know what to do. Many, it seemed, shut down completely. Others became resentful. When this situation reached its apex during the '60s, some of these men despised the young. If he could have gotten away with it, I think my Uncle Sammy would have murdered his son-in-law after he had gained conscientious objector status after he was drafted to fight in Vietnam. When I was growing up during that politically rebellious period, only women spoke to children. I can't recall a single significant conversation I had with a man, including my father. When I hit puberty, most men could barely look me in the eye. Perhaps what they most resented, without realizing it, was that their roles as mentors had been taken away from them. They saw and heard that they'd become obsolete. When they struggled to interact with *their* children, middle-aged men felt more intensely the distance that separated them from way-cool youth.

In effect, a gargantuan mass-media ethos of hipness had kidnapped their children and taken over their development. This didn't start in the '60s either. Worshipping the young and demeaning the old started in the 1950s. Watch James Dean, Natalie Wood, and Sal Mineo in *Rebel Without a Cause* dump on their parents for misunderstanding them. The fathers in the film undergo the severest shellacking. From there it was off to the races: sex, drugs, and rock 'n' roll, what has now become a culturally built-in wave of "next generation" hipster rebelliousness. Today's rappers imitate yesterday's in-your-face, go-fuck-yourself attitudes of the past, only with coarser language and catchier phrases. What real father can compete with that?

At its inception, the mass media's cool-youth ethos transcended the kind of natural antagonisms between fathers and sons that had existed for centuries. It was unlike the kind of political rights of (young) men that Thomas Paine advocated, correctly pointing out the absurdity of the previous generation's legislating "from the grave." This was different. It was a *cultural* phenomenon. In its scope and magnitude, no other civilization in history had gone through it, and in such a short span of time. Big "C" Culture became *the* dominant, pervasive force in the daily lives of every American in less than ten years. Eventually it reached even into the remotest, most segregated outposts in the nation, Native American Indian reservations, where large satellite dishes practically topple the trailer homes they're nesting in. By the end of the 1950s, the consumer-cultural imperative had reached into every corner of private and public space.

This cultural Fun Factory (Walt Disney called his production studios exactly that, a Fun Factory) was churning out Totally Cool and Way Hip youngsters and shoving these newly minted aliens down my father's generation's throats. Just as their generation was maturing (chronologically), the Youth of America had taken over, and they would continue to do so for each succeeding generation. Young male punks and young female preeners ruled. A man like my dad was considered "the old man" before he'd reached forty—bye, bye, Daddy! That's when it became necessary for men like my father to find ways to stay forever young, like bailing out on the family and driving sports cars. It was the classic midlife crisis, trying to turn back the clock, to catch up backward with the youth behind you. Then there's that other option, deliberately not getting to fifty, ending it prematurely by blowing your brains out. Didn't Hemingway, Mr. Macho Man himself, swallow a shotgun for feeling inconsequential? It happened in 1961, a most appropriate time considering it was the same year JFK uttered those famous words in his inaugural address about passing the torch to a new, younger generation. Maybe Hemingway didn't want to stick around and get all burned out by the fiery youth movement.

For the first time in history, males (of my dad's generation) could no longer share expressions of basic, common experience with younger men because the world had changed so drastically and the culture had so dramatically pigeonholed them as over the hill. There was little they could pass down to the young to demonstrate their wisdom or learning, or instruct the young about age-old traditions that might capture their interest, compared with the ever-changing, fast-paced ways of the Super-Cool flashing across a TV or movie screen. Gone were opportunities to narrate the ways of being a man that had existed for generations—hell, for centuries—like plowing a field, retrofitting a roof, or riding a horse. Men could reveal these "secrets" of life to the young just as their fathers had revealed it to them and their fathers' fathers to them. My father's father taught him how to slaughter a chicken and maintain a coal-burning furnace.

Sure, I know, things are changing all the time and have been for the past 200-plus years, from around the French Revolution on, according to my reckoning. But nothing like this, nothing like what occurred, post-1945. I've read all seven volumes of the brilliant *Oxford History of the United States*, and every author discusses how monumentally the United States changed during whatever time period is under review. I get that. Yes, the telegraph and the steam engine were significant inventions, as was the intercontinental railroad. But in spite of these shifts, life in 1650, 1750, and 1850 America wasn't altogether that much different, give or take a few less people living on farms. But life in 1850 America and life in 1950 America were vastly different. The United States changed fundamentally in the immediate postwar years. So powerful was it that the nation mainly still looks the same now as it did then because of the significant impact those changes had, give or take a few more computer screens replacing TV screens. While the resolution is better, the computer screen is essentially the same pitchman as the TV screen, and it didn't take long for TV shows to be watched on it. It's "better" only because watching TV and shopping can now be done with the same flick of a finger.

The advent of the Electric-Histrionic age after World War II meant the spread of jazzed-up knowledge and information at increasingly larger degrees of influence, with increasingly greater speed, and with increasingly greater means for its dissemination. In the past, most American families shared a common doctrine, conveyed by a common document, the Bible, with a handful of other primary texts, such as *Pilgrim's Progress* and *Robinson Crusoe*, all of which reinforced this familial cultural consensus. Like a father showing his son how to pluck and slaughter a chicken, a "simpler" philosophy of life could be passed down just the same. Not anymore.

The new consumer culture has not only co-opted "raising" America's youth, it did so by proposing for the first time the advantages of adolescence and the disadvantages of maturity. Men of my dad's generation were instantaneously displaced, while being replaced by a new authority. The only fathers who knew best were on TV. They just so happened to be "cool" too, cool in their demeanor and cool in their moronic pithy expressions. They didn't do much except sit in chairs waiting for their wives to call them to the dinner table. If they had jobs, viewers didn't exactly know what they did, except for the guy married to the witch and Rob Petrie, both of whom worked in the very industries that sold them back to us as "real" fathers. Eventually, such married men with TV children would become cool for different reasons. They behaved like ass-clowns and were *proud* that they hadn't grown up. They demonstrated that night after night for our enjoyment. Their children were smarter than they—and more mature!—and everybody knew it, especially the viewers. That was the coolest thing of all. Viewers were in on the joke, the cynicism and humiliation. We ate it up. For the past thirty years especially, white middle-aged men were fools who didn't deserve the respect of their children. Even the cartoon kids were hip and the dads were chumps.

So convinced had we become of the veracity and validity of these fictional fathers that we eventually elected a couple of boys to be president, one a fake cowboy from Texas who dressed up like a soldier for our patriotic fervor and the other before him who got blowjobs in the Oval Office from a woman young enough to be his daughter. The nation giggled about cum-stained dresses and thick cigars, including grade school kids on their way to school. That presidency was soon followed by one touting the manly appeal of the phony fighter pilot's codpiece after his staged plane landing on an aircraft carrier. It ran on the news like one of our favorite TV shows. How childish had we become? Shouldn't we have grown up after Vietnam and Watergate? But that was the point. We didn't want to, or we weren't allowed to. We had to stay "innocent" and infantile. Childish attitudes and behavior make you want things.

Our presidents reflect our values and principles, and vice-versa. Even our nation's highest elected officials were "failed boys" (the writer John Updike's words). This shouldn't be surprising given that both came of age during the postwar era. Fittingly, a president from the Greatest Generation, who aptly embodied the era's Fantasy Land, prepared us for them. Reagan lived inside the Make-Believe Fun Factory for most of his life and even accepted it as "reality," as had the nation by the time he was elected president. When Disneyland opened with great fanfare on July 17, 1955, Reagan served as master of ceremonies. For decades, it was the most-visited place in America (later replaced by Las Vegas), more than our real national treasures like Yellowstone and Yosemite. Reagan and the nation were meant for each other. As president, he recited lines from movies during real events. We were more amused by it than outraged—that is, if we even noticed.

By then, the country had been so afflicted by cultural immaturity that it didn't want to grow up historically anyway. If anything, we could disregard realistically looking at ourselves in the mirror. The country preferred Reagan's "Morning in America" to the harsh truths of our recent dysfunctional past (the hostage crisis, Watergate, assassinations, Pinochet, Vietnam, Kent State, Jim Crow, and on and on). It was as if we were a new nation once more, starting from scratch. It was *morning* in America, after all, not even early afternoon. Reagan showed us that we needn't dig too far into our past to recapture our youth, just like my own dad who had to reach only a decade or so into the past to recapture his. We could be reborn again by summoning the Golden Age of the Fifties. If only our illusions *and* amnesia were meant to be ironic. Our sunny future could be reclaimed by returning to the place where the culturally manufactured morning-in-us-all exuberance began, where it all started, the birth of TV, fast food, highways, and malls. To celebrate it all, we inserted "God" into the Pledge of Allegiance, to confirm that our new (shopping) cathedrals were graced by the Almighty.

Reagan was truly the perfect postmodern president, a man from the Greatest Generation who had trouble dealing with his own children, like most men of his age, and who once announced when walking into a sound studio to make a political ad that "the bar of soap has arrived." He was more comfortable *playing* a role than at *being* a real person. As one biographer put it, being president was the "greatest role" of his life. Ronnie—a boy's name—made it safe for us to forget about our more recent adolescent mistakes because we were still the innocents we were in the '50s, no less desiring a state of forgetfulness than what my father advised me to do about being shot. To me, Reagan was as bad a father to the nation as was my own to me when it came to guidance. Neither one dealt with the facts of life very well. If in the past we've raised the specter of Lost Generations, I wonder if it's time to consider a Lost Gender.

Which brings me back to my question (I warned you it would take a while before we got to "4"): How did I end up on that old lady's lawn? I've spent a lot of time—much of my life, really—trying to figure it out. The best answer I can come up with, after having cross-examined the facts of my childhood like an attorney, probed the psychological reverberations of my youth like a psychiatrist, observed general human behavior like an anthropologist, while reading hundreds, if not thousands, of books like the academic that I am, is "4"—America does a really crappy job of turning boys into men. Also, I'm choosing "4" because it can legitimately subsume "1," "2," and "3." All three can be viewed and explained through 4's lens. It's the macro opposite of Napoleon's head cold, or Hugo's stormy weather, the micro explanations. Furthermore, "4" is entirely human-made. I really can't blame it on the weather, including whether that's divine planning or random occurrence. Working backward, then, there's no healthy social system in play for anyone with extra chimp chromosomes ("3"), unless playing with toy guns while still in diapers counts ("2"), and about a minute after my dad left us he started driving convertibles and dressing like James Bond ("1").

The wacky thing about trying to understand how I ended up on that widow's lawn, even if "4" offers a sliver of an explanation, is that it almost doesn't matter because I'm glad I did. I'm grateful I got shot, believe it or not, which I know sounds really strange, especially after all of that soul-searching. Ultimately, I'm thankful I screwed up enough that I got the chance to be "reborn." In addition to finding "enlightenment" at the end of the priest's rosary beads, my screw-up provided a less grandiose reward. It preempted the retardation caused by an infantile culture, or so I like to think. Again, I'm well aware that being shot doesn't sound like anyone's idea of having fun, including mine. Yet in no small part, I've avoided some of the pitfalls of growing up male in America. The shooting's happening in my adolescence catapulted me into becoming a man extra-pronto. I had no choice, really. I grew up fast by witnessing my own death, so to speak. I got wise before I got old. As a general rule, wisdom doesn't come easily to people. Sometimes it doesn't come at all, ever. But it did to me, at an incredibly young age, and super-fast. Yet at the same time I was profoundly ignorant. Unlike wisdom, knowledge doesn't come to a person in a flash. I may have become wise in one grand moment, but I didn't simultaneously become knowledgeable. That takes time and work, a lifetime of work. I'm still working on it. Despite all of the time I've spent inhaling books and studying life, there are moments when I still feel like an ignoramus. Before that night I was most definitely ignorant and most certainly foolish too. I was oblivious. And I can see now that even though my dad was in his mid-forties when it happened, he was just as clueless, like a lot of men. Number "4" had begun to affect his generation, no matter how "Great" they were, maybe even more so because of the great expectations they had placed on themselves.

Most of the men I encountered throughout my life appeared as lost as my father, while most of the boys were as lost as I was—but in different ways and for different reasons. The men were more stuck and stagnant than lost. They weren't wandering around the neighborhood, as we were, looking for things to do. They weren't even wandering around inside their own heads. They may have attained the creature-comforts associated with middle-class success, but men in Oakwood Heights seemed unsatisfied and unfulfilled. Some were apathetic and depressed, unless they were drinking. Then they became angry or maudlin, like my next-door neighbor Mr. King. From his porch almost every night we could hear him cursing the weather or Mrs. King's existence, like a befuddled Lear. A few minutes later he'd be crying over the rain's beauty or ruefully weeping over mistreating his long-suffering wife. We frequently came across such men as boys while we roamed the neighborhood on our way to The Station. We came across many things, which was the point. It explains why the ten-minute walk there might take us hours.

Our trips to The Station generally followed the same route. We avoided locations like the kindly widows' and targeted the dangerous homes. It was on such an occasion we first saw him standing completely naked in the street.

"Look how little it is," Timmy said. "Half of my pinkie is bigger." He was right. It was incredibly small. But the toddler scrabbling along Isabella Avenue in tight back-and-forth semi-circles, powered by churning parenthetical legs, was no more than three years old. Just how large was his penis supposed to be?

His family had recently moved to Oakwood Heights and he was running around like that in front of his house. Over time it became a familiar scene, to see him playing in the street or on his front yard alone, although not always in a total state of undress. More often he wore a diaper. His parents had relocated from a rough neighborhood in Brooklyn. They must have assumed that the comparatively tame, traffic-free back streets of Staten Island were safe enough to let their naked child play freely.

That's how we saw him for the first time. It was really too bad for him. From then on he was called "Little Dickey." Whatever his real name was didn't matter. He became Little Dickey to the four of us that summer afternoon in 1967, and Little Dickey he remained for as long as I lived there. Once we came up with that nickname and the "rules of engagement" went into effect, everyone else in the neighborhood called him Little Dickey. The label stuck. Even when I went back to the neighborhood to visit my parents when I was in my thirties, and he was in his twenties, I continued to address him as "Dickey." For all I know, now his wife and kids call him Little Dickey. At least his older brother Anthony had the slight advantage that his nickname was a diminutive of his real name. But it was a very slight advantage.

Anthony wasn't much older than his brother, and we weren't much older than he. An undeclared rule in Oakwood Heights granted older kids the privilege of nicknaming younger ones, or peers to nickname one another. The playbook also stipulated that outside the peer group the name established by elders trumped the peer name. Being older, we had every right to determine Anthony's nickname. If kids older than we approved of the nicknames we assigned to others or to one another, they typically were permanent. This was especially true if the names were so obviously suitable, like calling Ritchie Graham "Crackers," or so ridiculously silly, like "Little Dickey," or so well suited rhythmically, like Paul "Smelly" Capelli, or so outrageously apt for underscoring an outstanding physical or behavioral characteristic, like Anthony's rather pointed head.

It was Crackers who first noticed that Anthony's head was shaped like a woman's breast. Soon thereafter, Anthony was known as "Antonio Tit-Head." Like all studious grammarians, we frequently parsed names. "Antonio Tit-Head" was reduced first to "Tit-Head" and then further still to "Tit." On the street or in George's, it was often, "Hey, Tit, what's up?" If he was with one of his parents it was only "Hey," never "Tit." It wasn't that we didn't want to humiliate him in front of them. It was that parents and adults weren't supposed to have access to our world. Ours had more flair, and most adults would have been appalled. They wouldn't have recognized the genius in having a "Tit" among us, rather than some undistinguished Anthony. There were thousands of Anthonys on Staten

Island. At least we had gone through the trouble of singling ours out, establishing a world populated with unique individuals. That wasn't a feature of the adult world, with its cookie-cutter tract homes crowded with carbon-copy appliances and furniture. Originality and creativity didn't seem part of their world, like ours, however vulgar ours was.

We didn't depend strictly on crudeness for inspiration. Some of the less coarse nicknames we borrowed from pop culture, such as "Mouse." Actually, there were two "Mice" within blocks of each other, one of whom was "Mouse" because of his appearance. Bob McAllister looked just enough like a mouse as a child, with his pointy ears, small eyes, and nose, whereas Billy Poppino was "Mouse" because of a popular novelty song. It included the lyrics, "Oh, Poppino, oh you little mouse / why won't you go away?" For years, everybody called him Mouse because of it. That changed once he hit puberty. From when he turned eleven to about when he turned thirteen he'd grown to more than six feet tall, without adding any weight. In addition to being called Mouse, he acquired the nicknames String Bean and Bean Pole. So he started lifting weights. Within a year, the weightlifting helped him overcome all of his nicknames.

On nice days, he'd be out in his back yard for hours after school, grunting, groaning, and puffing, the noise accompanied by the sound of a large transistor radio turned up full-volume to WNEW-FM, a station that played Led Zeppelin one minute and Joni Mitchell the next. In bad weather, he'd descend into his basement; from the street could be heard the sound of the weights slamming onto its concrete floor, the noise accompanied by even louder music from WNEW blaring from his more powerful stereo system. He was one of the first kids in Oakwood Heights to own an inclined bench-press. He practically slept on it. He used it in and out of doors, lugging it up and down his basement stairs depending on the weather.

Every couple of months he'd have one of his older sisters drive him to Masters department store, part of the newly built shopping center in Oakwood, one of the first department stores built in Staten Island. They'd return from there with more weights. We'd sometimes watch him pull out a box from the trunk, the bright red and blue plastic casings that sheathed the concrete discs visible through the ruptured cardboard boxes they were in. It wasn't long before all of the 25-lb. weights he owned, the biggest size sold then, couldn't fit on the longest bar available, without excluding his hands from grasping it. After a while he started wearing extra-tight T-shirts, even in the winter, stretched to the breaking point over his bulging chest and forearms. He was announcing to everyone in the neighborhood, from the sounds emanating from his back yard to wearing Fruit-of-the-Looms pulled like taffy across his upper body, that nobody was going to mess with him anymore. Billy didn't pal around much with kids his own age in our immediate neighborhood. Maybe that's because many of them picked fights with him, being an easy target, until his weightlifting regimen. The bullying stopped simultaneously with our affixing some silly nickname to him.

"String Bean" and "Bean Pole" disappeared immediately, and he was in a position to expunge "Mouse" from usage as well, even among the older boys. He began insisting that everyone call him "Pops." If anyone dared call him Mouse he'd put an end to it. For a time, he seemed to be fighting practically everyone in the neighborhood, one at a time, some of it as payback I suspect. Plenty of other kids in Oakwood Heights lifted weights, including me, but not as ferociously as Billy. Our irregular routines meant that whatever advantages we sought to gain from them—like curtailing the use of an embarrassing nickname—were offset by others in the weightlifting congregation, all of whom were equally unfaithful in their devotion to it. There was parity among the half-hearted. Not Billy. He was a true believer and a scrupulous practitioner. When the extreme weightlifting began preventing him from flexing his arms enough to hit someone or throw a football, he bought a punching bag. From his basement we were serenaded by WNEW blasting from the speakers, weights crashing to the floor, and the staccato thumping of an old-fashioned burlap bag.

But all those muscles didn't protect Billy from experiencing a transformative "bad trip" when he was seventeen, during a Deep Purple concert. Mentally, he never came back from it. I was fifteen when it happened, the summer before I was shot. A few of us had dropped acid before attending a Deep Purple concert at Madison Square Garden. Billy was someone who never should have taken LSD. His family was known to have a history of mental illness, his mother sometimes absent for days "recovering from tiredness," as it was euphemistically described. His father, a New York City fireman and plumber, was never around. One of Billy's older sisters seemed unnaturally nervous all the time and acted strange a lot of the time. Billy himself was a bit paranoid, especially whenever we played cards or Risk in his room. He often accused us of scheming against him while playing poker or conspiring to invade his game-board possessions by forming Axis powers.

His room was located in the back of his basement, attached to the large, open space where he lifted his weights. He had to remove a section of the low-lying drop ceiling in order to do military presses. Every time he stood up abruptly in his room he'd bump his head. The room's seclusion from the rest of the house allowed us to get high there freely, along with his family's clinical obliviousness to it. Between the joints passed around intermittently and six or seven guys chain-smoking cigarettes, by the end of a weekend night the room resembled San Francisco Bay in the late afternoon when the fog rolls in. Billy didn't mind. He smoked nearly two packs of Marlboros a day. That's the beauty of weightlifting: the appearance of health without necessarily living a healthful life. A person can smoke, drink, and take drugs and still lift like mad.

We had plenty of laughs and great fun for a couple of years, until Billy "freaked out." Both Dougie and I lived around the block from Billy's, so the two of us spent a lot of time there. The other guys we were palling around with lived on the other side of Oakwood Heights, almost in the next neighborhood, New Dorp. By our early teens, Dougie and I had outgrown our childhood playmates, Pee-Pocket, Crackers, and Santa. We were with a different crowd, mostly fellow potheads, the lost and illiterate, one of whom initiated the stickups. The robberies and Billy's nineteenth nervous breakdown unfolded concurrently. If any of us had known better, we would have prevented him from taking acid with us that night. His fragile mind was often adversely affected simply by his smoking Black Afghanistan, an opium-laced hashish that was our drug of choice at the time.

During the concert, when the mescaline started kicking in, he unexpectedly jumped up every few minutes, turning his head in every direction and saying how unsafe it was to stay there. We kept pushing him back down into his seat as the people sitting behind us kept shouting, "Sit the fuck down!" When he went to the bathroom, none of us trusted to let him go alone. After the show, as we walked through Madison Square Garden and rode the subway, he was dead silent, but he looked as if he'd undergone shock therapy. He didn't remain quiet for long. As soon as we boarded the Staten Island Ferry, he ran through it screaming and yelling from one end to the other, and up and down the stairs of all three decks. Much of what he was yelling was unintelligible. Whatever it was, his behavior showed how paranoid and delusional he'd become. First it was the cops who he believed were after him; then it turned into anonymous "theys." Some of our names were mentioned. Maybe he was back in his room playing Risk with us. He was never the same after that. He was in and out of mental institutions throughout his twenties.

One night one drug fried his mind for good. That's all it took to change the course of his life. It took only one night to change mine too.

That's all it takes for anyone, I guess. It seems that young men in Oakwood Heights were particularly ripe for life changes, and rarely for the better. The boxes of weights Billy brought back from the store didn't come packed with good fortune or instructions on how to deal with adolescence mentally or emotionally.

But that was Oakwood Heights for you. You played with guns when you were a child and then inflated your biceps as a teen hoping to take on the world, except that the world often took you on, without your ever knowing it. Hardly anybody lived by brains or wits, neither the preferred mode of entry into male adulthood. Both were in relative short supply and undervalued, although I did try getting by with wisecracks, a poor man's way of faking intelligence. I wish I could say I faked or strong-armed my way out of acquiring an unwelcome nickname. It would better serve the interests of the plot's arc. But that wasn't the case. My talent for self-deprecating, self-deflecting humor had nothing to do with my never having a pejorative nickname. Love saved me.

Like "Mouse" (a.k.a. "String Bean," "Bean Pole," and "Pops"), my nickname came from popular culture. During my adolescence, I was "Corn Flake" or "Flake," thanks to Ray Miller, a rather mild-mannered, affable teen who lived down the block from us. He also happened to have a mad crush on my sister. He was convinced I was the spitting image of a boy who appeared in a Kellogg's Corn Flakes TV commercial. That meant my sometimes being greeted on the streets by kids inserting my last name into the commercial's jingle: "Hey, Bor/kow/ski—new-country corn-flake." Having been given "Flake" undoubtedly spared me from being stuck with an unfavorable nickname, perhaps scarring me for life, like being called "Shit." Bobby Barnes, who was considered such a shithead by the age of ten (most likely because he was stealing bicycles when he was eight and breaking into homes when he was nine), was being called "Shit" at the start of his adolescence. He lost his eye in a barroom shootout in his late teens and a couple of years later took a header off the Verrazano Bridge. Not that his nickname directly contributed to those unfortunate twin events, but being called "Shit" several dozen times a day couldn't have been a confidence-booster or morale-builder. By comparison, "Flake" was downright ennobling. But I didn't think I looked anything like that kid on TV. It had more to do with Ray's trying to score points with my sister.

When it came to casting nicknames we drew from many different sources, not only from popular culture, like mine, or from physical characteristics, like "Tit-Head." There were also behavioral traits that we identified and used, like calling Bruce Contess "Mess." He was named Mess because he was always messed up on drugs. He obtained that ignoble moniker at a rather young age, when he was about twelve. During my jock phase, as I headed to a pair of concrete baseball diamonds adjacent to P.S. 50, I'd often spot him passed out on the wooden benches behind the school, high from sniffing glue. Hours later, when the rest of us were packing up our bats and mitts, he'd wander from the back of the building, stumbling like a Bowery drunk into right field, with hardened glue smeared over his face. In his teens his drug habits advanced to barbiturates and Quaaludes, LSD and morphine. Whenever he was in Billy's room, he rarely played cards or Risk with the rest of us, preferring instead to pass out on Billy's bed. He'd be out cold minutes after he arrived, snoring as loudly as our fathers. Billy didn't like it much, so he sometimes drew on Mess's face with a black marker. But that never stopped Mess from doing it again. If we were at The Station, Mess might quietly slip into the back of someone's parked car and pass out there. If he wasn't such a loud snorer I'm sure a few guys would have mistakenly driven home with him. Mess cleaned himself up by the time he got into a pretty decent Pennsylvania college, by then no longer even taking a single hit from a joint being passed around. It didn't matter. He was Mess and stayed Mess. He's still Mess in my mind. Maybe that's because Mess was the one who turned Dougie and me on to the idea of sticking up pizza delivery drivers. I guess we should've known not to take instructions from some kid who used to periodically conk out into a paper lunch bag full of airplane glue.

In addition to coming up with names based on outstanding traits, physical features, and pop culture, we also created puckish rhymes. We often fell back on them whenever none of the other three came to mind. In addition to Paul "Smelly" Capelli, for instance, there was Jay "Poo-Stain" Ruane. Paul didn't smell, and Jay didn't poop in his pants. The names simply had a rhythmic sound to them. Of course, the same parsing rules applied. Soon, everyone was calling Jay just "Stain."

On occasion, an original nickname could be supplanted if a more striking trait or feature was subsequently detected, like Timmy Fosket's, the very same Timmy who regularly participated in Extreme Lawn Sports. Until he was about seven, he was Timmy Tomato Head. Timmy's head wasn't shaped like a tomato, whereas Anthony's was shaped like a tit. Timmy and "Tomato" had a nice ring to it, pure and simple. I haven't the foggiest idea why "Head" was attached, other than we seemed to favor creating multi-syllabic nicknames so we could reduce their parts for variety ("Timmy Tomato Head," "Timmy Tomato," "Tomato Head," and "Tomato"). I'm sure not a single kid in Oakwood Heights knew what the word "alliteration" meant, but that's what we often went for if there weren't any outlandish options available. Timmy's first nickname fell under that category, but a second quickly replaced it. Based on a quirky hygiene habit apparent to everyone, he became "Pee-Pocket."

Timmy was in the habit of not going to the bathroom whenever he needed to, and he needed to a lot—as far as taking a pee went. Because of his affliction, he regularly had one hand thrust deeply inside one of his pockets so he could hold onto his pecker, choking off the chances that any renegade urine might dribble out. While standing, he'd often shift from one leg to the other leg, having removed his hand from one pocket and inserted it into the other one. His whole body would tilt to whatever side he was favoring. He could have been "The Leaning Tower of Timmy" if any of us had been familiar with geography. Even when we were swimming in backyard pools, Timmy stood in the water with one hand inside the pocket of his trunks. At least he had the decency not to pee in the pool. Thank God: Most of them weren't much bigger than kiddie pools. During the winter, his long winter coats provided greater cover. But anyone could see the coat's fabric bouncing around now and then. For all practical purposes, he was essentially a kid who had the use of only one arm. When it came to playing games and sports this was a major drawback.

Whenever we played baseball, for example, Timmy was always picked last, his ailment being a tremendous handicap for the team he played on. His condition wasn't so detrimental when he came up to bat. He didn't have the nerve to hit a ball holding the bat in one hand while holding his weenie with the other, although he crouched down so low to put pressure on his diaphragm that he might as well have hit with one arm. Visually, in contrast to his actual urinary needs, he looked as if he were taking a crap. Playing in position was different. His handicap was a more serious burden. No team in its right mind permitted him to play the infield. It was too risky. He couldn't react fast enough to play an infield position with any proficiency. This wasn't because of a lack of athleticism. He was actually a pretty decent athlete when he first came out of his house, no doubt thanks to his having just gone to the bathroom. Nobody wanted him in the infield because being there involved too much bending and reaching, and if he had to pee badly enough he'd let a slow grounder flitter through his legs rather than scoop it up. As a result, he was always consigned to the outfield. But he was a liability wherever he played.

Typically, he stood in the outfield with his gloved left hand covering the fidgeting taking place in his right pocket. I'm guessing it was his favorite time of year because he conducted a really good workout. He'd be so absorbed that sometimes he wouldn't notice that a ball had been hit to where he was located. Even when he did, his habit still presented a problem. It took time for him to pull his happy hand from his pocket before chasing a fly ball. If he was at the breaking point, sometimes he didn't bother taking his hand out of his pocket at all before running after a ball. He'd hobble toward a lazy pop-up that Quasimodo could snare and let it drop anywhere but in his glove. Everyone on the opposing team knew to hit the ball to him. Therefore, none of us wanted him on our team, yet none of us had the heart to tell him why. Maybe we were too embarrassed for *him*. More likely, we considered it too amusing for *us*. His handicap was worth the laughs, but we never laughed at him to his face—we'd have had to explain what we were laughing at. It could jeopardize the fun. Among us, it was "Pee-Pocket." Around him, it remained "Timmy Tomato Head."

We weren't being overly mean-spirited about it, I don't think, making fun of some kid's unfortunate handicap. It wasn't like we were joking about someone's birth defect or uncontrollable tic. Timmy's liability was rather self-induced. If he'd called a "time-out" once in a while to pee behind a tree or something, he wouldn't have had to go through all of that handwringing and we wouldn't have had cause to joke about it behind his back. Overweight David "Santa" Santoro (physical feature + alliteration = jackpot) was a different story. Not only slow and plodding whenever he played sports or games, he was also incredibly un-athletic, a "spazz." He often vied with Timmy for being chosen last—that is, whenever he came outside to play. He generally stayed indoors reading books about animals and watching TV. None of us ever went into his house to play with him, unlike all the other kids' homes we did play in. I think we feared it was haunted and we'd end up like him, never coming out, trapped inside like David seemed to be.

He unfairly had a reputation for being a momma's boy, for no right-minded kid would spend all day in his house with his mother unless he was sickly. And David wasn't. He was undoubtedly overly self-conscious of being the fattest and least athletic kid in the neighborhood. But we didn't tease him about it. Most of us probably empathized with him, knowing we were never far from being called spazzes and sissies if we dropped an easy touchdown or struck out a bunch of times—"looking like a girl." We also knew it couldn't be much fun being a chubby kid in such a competitively male neighborhood. In contrast, Pee-Pocket didn't warrant similar compassion because we assumed there was actually some advantage to fiddling with your dick all day. Both David and Timmy were terrible players, but Timmy appeared to be having a much better time at it.

Several adults in the neighborhood were given unflattering nicknames too—deservedly so, in our judgment, usually for the most egregious sin in our book, stinginess. If the parsimony was extreme, we'd assign ourselves the role of avenging (rotten) angels. They were subjected to our pranks and hijinks. If people wanted to behave like cheap bastards, even though they owned the biggest TV or had the largest backyard pool, we felt we were within our rights to punish them for their sins.

We generally learned about their stinginess through our paper routes. The *Staten Island Advance*, an afternoon daily newspaper, was delivered on foot or by bike. As the week progressed and the size of the papers increased, delivery could be done only on foot. Sunday papers required shopping carts. Anywhere from fifty to a hundred homes might be on a single route. Tightly situated tract homes at least didn't add up to great distances to be covered. Initially, Dougie had the paper route to himself (in seventh grade); then we shared it (in eighth), and then I had it alone during my freshman and sophomore years of high school. Even separately we often helped the other so afterward we could squeeze in a little more play time before we had to go home for dinner.

Collection for delivery was bi-weekly, and it might take hours to complete, even if we were both doing it. A 50-cent tip was generous, while a quarter was adequate. Anything less than that was barely acceptable. No tip was downright intolerable. The stingiest of all opted against having the paper delivered at all to avoid tipping altogether, as was the case with my next-door neighbor Mr. Weiss. He was such a miserly coot he didn't even want to give the boy who lived next door a quarter every other week for the service. Neither did Mr. King, my other next-door neighbor, who may have had an excuse: He needed the loose change for the cheap beer he drank by the six-pack. In retrospect, these were wise decisions. In time, we would have found a way to assail them too, just like the others.

Rarely did an entire family, or both husband and wife, tip poorly or not at all. Older children who answered the door and knew us frequently threw in some spare change. The males didn't spare a little invective while they were at it, just to show that they weren't total softies. They usually answered the door playing some kind of TV teen character that didn't exist yet. "Who invited you assholes to my house?" they'd ask. After placing the money in an outstretched hand they'd grab the small accounting book tucked under an armpit. "What do we have here? I bet the *Staten Island Advance* would be very upset to find out you jerks lost this." It was best when an older daughter answered. They not only tipped well, they chatted with you as if you were a normal person. "Oh, I know what you're here for. Pay day. I saw your sister in Driver's Ed. today. Our instructor is such a creep. Does she talk about him? No? Well, why should she, right? Oh, wow, it's really nasty out there," she might say, sticking her head farther out from the screen door and peering at the sky. "Would you like to come inside?" From the distance the father would shout, "No! Don't invite them in. They'll get the floor all wet!" Invariably, The Man of the House was the meanest of the lot, and the worst tipper. We always seemed to be "disturbing" him at the most inopportune time, just as he was about to sit down to dinner or just as he was getting ready to watch the news.

Almost all of the homes on Staten Island had front porches, some no more than a few feet of stone tile, while others were large, enclosed structures. Standing on them, we were at eye-level with the bay windows that also accompanied most homes. Nearly every bay window was shrouded in thick, wide drapes, but not thick enough to conceal the ever-present pulsating blue-gray TV screen, or wide enough to prevent the throbbing beam from poking around its sides. After ringing the doorbell, we could peer through a tiny parting in the curtains to see who was coming to the door, and what to expect. If The Unpleasant Man of the House was seen rising from the couch, shaking his head disgustedly, you knew you were in for plenty of guff, and possibly no tip. Some were so visibly annoyed they seemed two tics shy of one day appearing on the rooftop with a high-powered rifle ready to pick us off before ringing the bell.

Minus the rifle, The Grinch opens the door: "Why do ya always have to come around just when we're about to sit down to dinner, huh? We were just gonna eat."

I want to say, "Well, maybe it has something to do with me getting out of school at 2:30 and by the time I change out of my school uniform and walk over to the street where the delivery truck leaves the papers it's already after three and then it takes a long time to go from house to house ringing doorbells and collecting money from crabby-ass cheapskates like you and let's not forget your house is one of the last of the fifty-four on my route and really aren't you taking up more of my time by pestering me about what time it is you miserable Scrooge so why don't you just pay me so I can go on my way and whatever it is your wife is cooking sure smells good and you're lucky to have her because if it was up to me I'd be serving you puppy chow." But of course I don't say anything even remotely like that.

"Is it dinnertime already?" I say instead.

"'Is it dinner time already?' What are you, an idiot? Here," he says, thrusting a clean envelope into my hands with the words "Paper Boy" perfectly typed on the front. When I open it, I find the exact amount owed and not a penny more.

On occasion there is a slip of paper stuffed inside the envelope itemizing our transgressions and the deductions paired with them. I read it as he watches me through the screen door. "Sunday paper missing 'Parade' section (subtract 5¢); paper wet on Tuesday (subtract 5¢)." Nice. How should I react to such a calculating turd? Am I supposed to be impressed or cowed? I'm neither. I'm more baffled at how trifling people can be. I lift up my head. He's glaring at me through the screen door, looking for clues into my reaction. He wants me to be wounded. It's written all over his face.

I wish I could say, "Am I expected to go through every Sunday paper to make sure each section is there and Tuesday it poured during the middle of the route and I carried your paper under my jacket as I walked from the curb where my soaked, now probably ruined, bicycle was but what do you care and placed the paper between the storm and main door and carefully closed it and other than that really how much control do I have over whether your paper gets wet and knowing what a stingy sourpuss you are I wouldn't be surprised if what you mean by wet is that a tiny piece of the top right corner where the weather summary is was wet and so I'm really glad that I went through all of that trouble trying to keep your paper dry now that a nickel plus another nickel for the missing section must come out of my pocket to meet my payment to the paper company." But I don't say any of that either.

"Thank you," I say instead, forcing a smile and walking down the steps. The door slams shut behind me. He wants to make it clear he's upset, perhaps all the more so because I didn't seem as bothered as he wanted me to be. I let pass how good he is at making his point. Nobody was going to pull a fast one on him, especially a child, by making him read a newspaper that was one one-hundredth wet and then expect to pay for it in full. It's hard to tell if he's upset over that or something else. He's always upset. Mr. Sarnesse—The Grinch—is a grumpy bastard and he wants everyone to know it. He's mad at the world. He wasn't alone. He could have been my Uncle Sammy or my next-door neighbor Mr. King, or any number of my other neighbors or male relatives. It was a masculine mystique thing, I suppose.

Someone like Mr. Sarnesse therefore merited multiple nicknames, the more scatological the better. He was not only "Mr. Sorry-Knees" (he was in fact gimpy), "Mr. Four-Eyes" (he was in fact near-sighted), and "Mr. Sardines" (he did in fact have a fish-face) but also "Mr. Fat-Ass" (he was in fact chubby) and any number of their rude offspring—"Ass-Face,"

"Fish-Face," "Fish-Ass Face," "Fish-Fart-Face," "Fish-Fart Four-Eyes," and anything else we could imagine. And we could imagine a lot.

When customers like Sorry-Knees pushed us too far, we felt it was imperative and within our constitutional rights to punish them. Whether Dougie and I owned the route individually or collectively, payback was always done together. (Look, I know what you're thinking: sounds like a foreshadowing to the holdups. It could have been. Dougie and I perhaps were like that old TV episode of *Superman* when he divides himself to carry out two separate missions, which causes the two of him to have almost normal human strength. Separate, Dougie and I were normal. Together, we were volatile. As children, we played Batman and Robin in his basement or mine. As we grew older, we continued to imagine ourselves as a fearless pair, but by then of the more criminal kind, like Redford and Newman robbing trains or pulling off convoluted scams. One of Dougie's favorite movies was *Bonnie and Clyde*, which he saw several times, and he was all of six or seven, mind you. Bonnie's being a female obviously complicated our desire to duplicate their escapades in our imaginations. Years later, he saw *The Sting* almost as many times when it originally came out in theaters, and it came out a few months before we started our own spree of criminal activity. I'm not blaming those films for our actions, or for glorifying criminal behavior. After all, it's a bloody finale for both Bonnie and Clyde and Butch and Sundance. But the timing of the release of those films and for hanging our own wayward dispositions onto some pop cultural reference could be seen as propitious. Rather than Hugo's rainstorm fouling up Bonaparte's plans at Waterloo, a handful of big-ticket cultural events helped solidify our already formulating attitudes and sparked our foul plans. So, yeah, *maybe* the wickedest plan of them all, to stick up pizza delivery drivers, was cultivated as we were getting back at the customers we didn't like, reflected and refracted by the culture at large.)

In time, Mr. Sorry-Knees pushed us beyond nasty nicknames. We simply couldn't take it any longer. The stinginess had reached biblical proportions. His repeated deductions, based on the most trivial grounds, had to be stopped, even if that meant losing him as a customer, and certainly getting in trouble for it. One day, after a night's worth of torrential rain, we trolled his paper through a muddy puddle of water and delicately put it in his mailbox. Placed inside the newspaper, wrapped in a plastic bag, was an envelope, with his name neatly written on it. The note inside read: "One Really Wet Paper: Free." He got the message, all right. He phoned our parents and told them about it, throwing in complaints about "bad parenting" and "the state of the country," or words to that effect. I don't recall the punishment I received because it didn't matter. As expected, Fish-Fart-Face canceled delivery. Big deal. What most mattered was we had made it clear who owned the route. Some stingy-ass wasn't going to push us around! It simply never occurred to people like him that we might sacrifice money for our own crazy code of acting on principle.

When Dougie's older brother left him the route, sixty-eight homes received the paper. By the time I stopped doing it five years later there were forty-three. In our confused minds we thought we were undermining reckless and unjust adult authority, particularly when it involved titanic chintziness, such as the kind displayed by Mr. Sorry-Knees. I know I overreacted to these abuses of power. Obviously, I didn't entirely operate on the premise that unquestionable respect had to be conferred on all grownups. To me, they had to earn it. Some of them came up way short in my opinion. I'm sure that kind of defiant attitude toward authority didn't always serve me well, especially in the classroom, where I was often accused of being obstinate and bull-headed.

While generally shy and inhibited around adults, I had a rebellious streak under the surface. To this day, I can't be sure whether such an underlying trait was innate or bred over time, perhaps even accounting for the robberies, adding another wrinkle to the earlier list of possible explanations. Clear to me now, looking back on it, is the lack of faith I placed in adults as a child. For one thing, many seemed immature and intellectually stunted, especially the males (a condition that has seemingly become worse over time, in my opinion). Also, adults in those days—both males and females—were short on generating much passion for anything other than spoils and treasure. People had made a virtue out of material self-interest. Even as a boy I could see that. Acquiring things was life's goal. The not-so-funny part about it was how unhappy they seemed. Mr. Sorry-Knees lived in one of the fanciest homes in the neighborhood and he drove new, luxury-model Buicks, unlike nearly everyone else who owned older-model Fords and Chevrolets. But what good did that do him? He was discontented and hollow. He couldn't even deal humanely with a couple of kids who delivered his newspaper. It's not as if we weren't initially respectful and courteous to him, or other customers we later ambushed. We turned on someone like Sorry-Knees only if we were provoked, if their smallness interfered with our doing our jobs with some degree of dignity.

Oakwood Heights wasn't completely overrun with miserable misers like Sorry-Knees. There were plenty of "nice" men around. But they tended to be reserved and kept to themselves, almost to the point of invisibility. In effect, they were socially awkward. Nearly everyone, though, was fixated by appearances: lawns trimmed and groomed like golf courses, automobiles washed and waxed like show cars, and wardrobes and hairstyles modeled after those on *Ozzie and Harriet*. There was an endless fascination with *stuff*, especially acquiring the *right* kind of stuff, whether the right Christmas decorations or the right backyard grill. Most families owned apartment-sized aluminum sheds not only to store the rakes, shovels, hedge clippers, lawn mowers, and bags of limestone but also to accommodate some of the newly manufactured plastic junk on sale. Plastic was taking over the neighborhoods. Some families had two sheds to house the spillover of stuff that wouldn't fit in the already-packed basement, attic, back porch, or first shed. Oakwood Heights, like many of Staten Island's neighborhoods, was a working-class community aspiring to appear middle-class. Back then, that wasn't so hard to do. A person didn't need to have a secret benefactor, like Pip in *Great Expectations*, to advance themselves toward middle-class respectability.

The early postwar years were plentiful times, before the after-effects of the Vietnam War crippled the country economically and morally, not unlike how World War I crippled England in its aftermath. Despite nearly all of the families in my neighborhood being working class, they all wanted a middle class lifestyle, and many of them could afford to do so. *Appearing* middle class was a primary objective. If reached, it signified success. But it wasn't only Oakwood Height's mission. It was the nation's *modus operandi*. If we were all in the middle materially then we were all the same, all equally enjoying the good life. Richard Nixon had crowed about it during "The Kitchen Debates." Our cars, refrigerators, and TV sets demonstrated more than prosperity. They added up to equality, Nixon told Khrushchev and other Soviet visitors to the Moscow Exhibition. Mass consumerism proved we were equal among our consumer brethren. It was a special, American form of economic equality. We were *middle class*, so much better than being "bourgeoisie," which was such a foreign, outdated European term. "Bourgeoisie" also sounded like the superficial and insensitive characters in Dickens and Balzac, not that anyone in Oakwood Heights read such authors. Nobody wanted to believe they were some superficial, avaricious Victorian in mid-twentieth-century America. "Bourgeoisie" also had a Marxist ring to it, and the United States was more fervently anticommunist and antisocialist back then than it is now. Individual initiative and effort were prized: "We're (all) number one!" People privately exhibited their goods no differently from those who displayed theirs at the Moscow Exhibition. Their doing so revealed their success, demonstrating that they too had mastered the American Way of Life, which was *the* way to live a life. It's why members of the Island's working class were enslaved by their possessions.

People judged one another according to the things they owned, and *how* they were owned. Any family whose home showed any outward sign of disarray or disrepair was considered fallen. Leaving a lawn sprinkler out after it had been used bordered on insanity. Every weekend, neighbors returned from supermarket and department store safaris, their boat-sized cars overloaded with boxes and packages. Two or three people would have to make several trips back and forth from car to home as if supplying an army rather than a family. Grocery stores turned into supermarkets, any one of which could've fed half of East Asia for a month. Candy stores like George's competed with department stores, a single aisle carrying ten times as many toys as George had packed in his cardboard boxes. Store owners like Sal were competing against not only a gang of kids scaring off his customers but also supermarkets big enough to drive a forklift through its aisles. (Let's tout the entrepreneurial spirit of the Little Guy and the decency of Main Street, while actually destroying both to serve the Big Guys and Wall Street?)

Who needs all that stuff? We all did, starting in childhood. Or so it was presumed. During my father's absence what I most remember about the men who sought to fill his shoes were the gifts they bought me for my birthdays or Christmases. My Uncle Larry was a corpulent man with an equally big heart. But if he exhibited moments of a generous spirit I didn't notice or I don't remember because it was trumped by material, tangible gifts. So what I do remember vividly is a toy battleship he bought me one Christmas, as big as an ironing board. Search lights and deck lights required half a dozen double-D batteries, which had to be replaced once a week. Rockets could be fired from its control towers and planes could be launched from its expansive deck, thanks to a rubber-band propulsion system. It was magnificent, as was an electric racecar set he gave me one birthday. Believe me, I loved it, but it wasn't what I was looking for or what I really needed. And maybe no kid does when you come right down to it. But if you believe you can buy freedom and equality I guess you'll believe you can buy anything, including a child's love and well-being.

Such a consumer-oriented lifestyle requires a lot of time and effort. The pursuit of material happiness comes at a price. No wonder grownups were always busy taking care of business. Every weekend, families in Oakwood Heights scurried around their little pieces of property—the men outside, the women inside—raking leaves, cleaning carpets, clipping hedges, scrubbing stoves, cleaning gutters, washing windows, and tinkering in the remotest corners of their homes, sanding, spackling, and then painting imperfections no bigger than a half-dollar. Families with accumulated half-dollars and those who allowed saucer-sized imperfections to surface were pariahs. Two large families living on the same block as we were best-known for their poorly maintained properties. Actually, that's all they were known for. As a rule, neighbors who lived next door to or across the street from one another might exchange "Hellos" and "Good mornings." More often than not, they ignored one other by avoiding eye contact, pretending not to see someone across the street repairing his driveway or somebody getting into her car to take a child to school. If you were on the other side of the fence, literally and figuratively, repairing your driveway or taking your daughter to school, you didn't want to be noticed anyway. This practice validated the adage of how good fences make good neighbors, like the code of silence my family lived by, except this one spread throughout the neighborhood. Everyone guarded their privacy as tightly as they guarded their possessions. No wonder we pissed off so many households when we became entangled in their shrubs as boys. They weren't concerned only about their yards. They were afraid we might see something. On the other hand, concern about the general well-being of neighbors was nonexistent. Nobody cared that those two families couldn't afford to do much more than feed and clothe themselves. Knowing that their spotty grass wasn't regularly dosed with weed killer was enough information to go by. "White trash" was a term I often overhead to describe them. We too must have merited such pejorative terms because we'd fallen on such harsh times.

When my parents split up, our property went to hell. Situated on a street corner, our house had a relatively substantial side yard as far as yards went. But there was no back yard to speak of. Our unattended property was therefore fully exposed for all to see. The first summer they separated I spotted a rat camping in the waist-high grass and weeds. Ours had become a fallen household. No neighbor offered assistance, and my Uncle Sammy wouldn't set foot anywhere near us. We might be infectious. That must have been the prevailing view because not a single uncle or friend of my parents' came to our rescue. Perhaps offers were made and my mother's pride prevented her from accepting them, although I suspect the biggest obstacle was societal norms. It wouldn't be "right" for some strange man to be seen clipping our shrubs, even if it was just my mother's brother-in-law. In time, my mother had to hire a couple of older neighborhood boys to clear away the overgrowth—a further sign of our peculiarity. The next summer I was barely strong enough to push a lawn mower around and do basic yard work, which didn't exactly overshadow our difference either. No other six-year-old boy was doing his father's work.

Most other families were better equipped to hide their dysfunction. We couldn't, obviously. As I'd later learn, Oakwood Heights was rife with alcoholism, drug addiction, spousal abuse, child abuse, and clinical depression. Fucked-up families were everywhere. I didn't know it at the time, of course. These days it's rather commonplace to know about everyone else's problems. In many cases people seem to take pride in their mental and emotional disorders and the problems their families inflict upon them, announcing them on their Facebook pages right below the snapshot of the first Caesar salad they made. The pendulum has clearly swung in the opposite direction. I don't know what's worse, today's excessive true confessions or yesterday's spurious detachment. Keeping secrets seems to require more effort, as I learned about keeping my being shot a secret. In all honesty, it was exhausting. I'm sure it must have been for my mother as well to pretend we were a normal two-parent household, when in fact we weren't.

We worked tirelessly to conceal our problems, despite their being in full view. How much easier it must have been for other families to hide theirs. Our neighbors presented themselves as archetypes of stability and normalcy. They demonstrated such by turning a basement into a family room or buying the latest gadget, like a gas-powered weed-whacker. The children were expected to follow their lead. It was a big part of growing up, learning to be like our parents. If we followed along in their footsteps, we too could some day march through life clutching our accumulations and believing we had "made it." Sometimes, though, making it was pretty darned ugly.

In the Oakwood Beach section of our neighborhood, neighbors torched a black family's house shortly after they moved in. While such incidents were atypical, rabid racism wasn't atypical in Oakwood Heights and throughout most of Staten Island. I guess you could say it was a blessing the family wasn't home at the time, except that their absence didn't exactly indicate altruism on the part of the culprits. There were enough people in the neighborhood who would have torched the house even if the family had been inside.

"Come check it out," a boy shouted breathlessly from his bicycle as he pedaled toward us, his legs pumping like pistons. Dougie and I were playing Wiffle Ball in the St. Charles parking lot. "*Their* house is on fire," he hurriedly added, as if we were supposed to know whose house "theirs" was. A classmate of ours, he lived on the other side of Hylan Boulevard, the Island's major thoroughfare. It extended the fifteen-mile length of the entire Island, from the Brooklyn side to the New Jersey side. The Boulevard also divided the larger and more populated northern half from the smaller, less populated southern "beach" half, which included bungalows built prior to the tract-home developments. The beach sections had a reputation for their rough-and-tumble neighborhoods, especially the newer developments built on drained swampland. Many of them would be ravaged decades later by Hurricane Sandy in 2012. Husbands and wives often carried their loud arguments onto the streets, and their children got into bloody fights with the children of equally combative parents. If the rare shooting or stabbing was reported, it frequently took place in one of the beach neighborhoods, like New Dorp Beach or Midland Beach.

Two years before the torching incident, a shopping plaza and several subdivisions had been built in Oakwood Beach, replacing the swamps and the dense rows of tall reeds. The open land extended about two miles from the Boulevard to the ocean. Even after the developments, bunches of reeds grew in empty lots, waiting to be hacked down to make room for additional homes. What little vegetation remained sometimes caught on fire, especially during a dry summer, usually from kids hiding in them smoking cigarettes or dope. When Dougie and I first saw the smoke rising from the direction of Oakwood Beach we ignored it, thinking it was another brush fire. A house on fire was a different matter. I'd never seen one before, and I'm sure neither had Dougie. We hid the Wiffle Ball and bat in some bushes and hopped on our Sting-Ray bikes, which were leaning against the school's brick wall.

When we arrived, the street was filled with cheering onlookers. Men and women, holding their children's hands and pushing baby strollers back and forth in tight formation, seemed to be entreating the flames to spread faster. Some were angrily shouting "nigger this" and "nigger that." Others were laughing, giddy about being part of such a powerful mob. The fire trucks took forever to arrive, it seemed, whereas they reached the tiniest brush fires in minutes. The fire had started at least a half-hour before we showed up, and even after another fifteen minutes after we got there, they still hadn't arrived. Later that month, a New York City policeman was arrested for starting the fire. On the Island few expressed outrage or even dwelt on the irony of of a law man's committing such a terrible crime. If I recall, most Staten Islanders considered him a hero. Certainly those verbally fanning the flames that day did.

Oakwood Heights was similar to other communities on Staten Island, as lily-white and as restrictive as the notorious Levittowns built on Long Island and in Pennsylvania. Our residents were as vigilant in policing its "purity" as any Levitt-towner. The house was set on fire in 1965 or 1966, but the reigning temperament was stuck in 1866. Oakwood Heights residents shared the same attitudes and opinions as the rest of the Island, and the nation generally. Intolerant parents generally breed intolerant children. Most of the kids I grew up with were becoming as rabidly racist, sexist, and homophobic as their parents.

After the house burning, little had changed on Staten Island for thirty years. The children who watched the fire with their parents grew up to take their place. The sins of the fathers are truly visited upon the sons, as I observed one afternoon in the early 1990s. Both events took place on sultry summer days. Maybe it was the heat that had gotten to everyone, like the uprisings during the mid-1970s summer of the "Son of Sam."

I was temporarily living with my parents after losing two high school teaching jobs, the first in New Hampshire, the second in New Jersey. Occasionally, I spent time with guys I grew up with, most of whom I hadn't seen much after I was shot. I fled the Island after high school, thinking I'd never come back. But there I was fifteen years later, having moved back from New England two years earlier to take a teaching job in New Jersey, which I lost when cataclysmic budget cuts ravaged the public school system. The institutional euphemism was that I'd been RIF'ed. The acronym is a euphemism in and of itself, standing for "Reduction in Forces," which sounds like a military term. Heaven forbid the powers that be should admit they were firing hundreds of us because the state had reduced property taxes for the wealthy. Property taxes funded the bulk of New Jersey public schools, as it does in many states.

Until I found another position and started graduate school, I was living in my parents' basement for a few months. (It was possibly the worst seven or eight months of my life. Given the choice, I think I would rather have been shot again. At least the anguish and humiliation would have gone more quickly.) Wherever I walked around the neighborhood, I kept running into guys I used to hang around with at The Station. A few of them were even still there, standing outside of George's, smoking and drinking as if they were still sixteen, except now they were overweight and unhealthy-looking, their eyes as colorless and dim as those of dead fish. I considered my return to Oakwood Heights a personal setback, although in many respects feeling so defeated forced me to enroll in graduate school. I had had the opportunity to do so ten years earlier, on scholarships, but I'd allowed those closest to me to talk me out of it. Until my graduate studies started and I resumed teaching as an adjunct professor, along with teaching GED classes at a drug-treatment facility across the street from Manhattan's Tompkins Square Park, I'd occasionally meet old 'hood friends at bars or hang out with them in their back yards. Unlike me, some had never left their parents' homes, even though they were in their mid-thirties.

One sticky summer day about six of us were sitting in Tommy Fitheone's side yard after having gone swimming in his enormous above-ground pool. A couple of the guys had taken the day off from work, while others were there in the middle of the week because they had gone from petty to professional crime. They had graduated into becoming "Goodfellas." We were sitting in a semi-circle on the cement patio. Most chain-smoked cigarettes and went back and forth retrieving beers from a cooler placed under a tree. It wasn't much past noon, and almost all of them were drunk. Suddenly, someone shot out of his lawn chair with such force it collapsed onto the floor. "Holy fucking shit! Look what the fuck is coming our way," he said through his clenched teeth, flinging his towel to the ground.

Tommy's house sat on a small rise along Oak Avenue, which steadily climbed for a half a mile from Hylan Boulevard to the Oakwood train station. From where we were sitting, we overlooked a long stretch of the street. Two black teens had been walking up the incline and were about to pass us. The pair had canvas satchels slung over their shoulders, containing free weekly circulars supermarkets distributed. They were delivering them to the homes along Oak, gingerly and deliberately. They made sure never to cut across anyone's lawn to get to the next house, and they went only as far as the front steps before tossing a flyer onto a stoop or a porch. They knew better not to approach any doors. They apparently didn't know how unwelcome they were at all in Oakwood Heights, at least not that day and on that street.

After they'd been spotted, everyone bolted out of their chairs—except for me—and chased after them, hollering, "You fucking niggers. Get the fuck out of here." The two teens sprinted remarkably fast up the steep incline, considering the weight they bore, but who wouldn't have under the circumstances? They raced fast enough and far enough to be out of harm's way, although I don't think anyone was interested in actually confronting them. They mostly wanted to scare them, trotting well behind, and continuing the barrage of invective. Rather than catch up to them, which they likely could have done, they gathered some roadside rocks, hurling them along with the savage words they continued to express. "The next time we see you motherfuckers we hang your black fucking asses." I looked on with horror. *The street must be cursed*, I thought. Behind Tommy's house was the empty lot where Dougie and I had hid waiting for the pizza delivery car.

I remained in my chair the entire time. Once they'd chased the two teens from the area, I could hear them laughing as they walked back to the yard. When they returned, they all glared at me. To them, I was spineless for staying behind. If they thought I was cowardly, they were right. But not for the reasons they suspected. I was a coward because I said nothing. I was ashamed to be there with them, and I hated them at that moment far more than they hated those two black kids. I also was ashamed of myself, ashamed to have felt the need to rekindle friendships with a bunch of guys who may never have been my friends in the first place, other than to have gotten high with and be a jerk with twenty-five years ago. But I didn't tell them that. Doing so would have been the brave thing to do.

Those two incidents reflected Staten Island's overall social and political views. In the 1968 presidential election, Staten Island voted overwhelmingly (3 to 1) for the segregationist candidate, George Wallace, the only congressional district north of the Mason-Dixon line to do so. Nothing had changed politically over the next twenty-five years throughout the Island, just as it hadn't changed socially in Oakwood Heights from the time of the house burning to the time of the "nigger" chasing. No sooner had David Dinkins, the city's first black mayor, been elected in 1989 than the Island threatened to secede. Calls for secession ended in 1993 when Rudy Giuliani narrowly defeated Dinkins in a rematch of their 1989 race, which Dinkins had solidly won. Giuliani's round-two victory was due entirely to Staten Island's overwhelming support of him; or, to put it differently, its overwhelming hatred of Dinkins. The majority of voters in the other four boroughs—the Bronx, Brooklyn, Manhattan, and Queens—cast their ballots for Dinkins, whereas more than 90 percent of Staten Islanders voted for Giuliani, providing Giuliani with a slim overall majority. He beat Dinkins by only 3 percent. After the election Dinkins's media advisor proclaimed that "Rudy is the mayor of Staten Island now." Staten Islanders, proudly, had singlehandedly booted Dinkins out of office. It was the political equivalent of burning him out of office or chasing him from the neighborhood.

For as long as I lived in Oakwood Heights, minorities were *persona non grata*, as they were in every neighborhood surrounding it. Blacks were relegated to a corner of the Island's North Shore, which formerly had been an Italian neighborhood. My mother had grown up there, and the way she and others talked about it, it might as well have been taken over by Martians. Sure enough, minorities were considered aliens in Oakwood Heights and communities like it. In the eight years I attended St. Charles elementary school, not a single minority student attended. Diversity wasn't part of the school's enrollment policy. Nor was it part of the curriculum. And that's exactly the way the parents wanted it. It's why they sent their children there. If the school had even *considered* enrolling a minority or had proposed straying slightly from the formulaic syllabus, they would have stormed the convent and the rectory.

Such a homogeneous, narrow view of the world—imposed from without and enforced from within—meant that in school we were taught to think the same, be the same, and act the same. It wasn't just our bright green and red plaid clothing that was so uniform. Any thought or action out of the ordinary was viewed with suspicion. If that wasn't bad enough, the teachers, especially the nuns, were serially incompetent and uninspiring. They seemed to get their kicks largely out of disciplining and punishing us. I still managed to learn a few invaluable lessons, though, just not the kind they expected. For instance, it was clear that school and "the real world" had little to do with each other. There was the classroom and "out there." Not that I was terribly popular or successful "out there" as a child, but at least it was fun sometimes. There wasn't much fun involved with my schoolwork. Academically I was a total flop. School didn't necessarily have to be all fun and games, but at least the teachers could have tried harder to make it more interesting and enriching. At least they could have been more passionate about what they were doing. That might have offset my own inadequacies and inability to concentrate on my schoolwork. Then again, maybe it wouldn't have mattered at all. I might have remained a poor student no matter what the teachers did. I was lost and heading nowhere. It didn't help that I was so "giftless" academically. There wasn't anything special about me. Heck, I was well aware that there wasn't even anything terribly mediocre about me.

5

"We made the headlines, brother!"

For several nights before the robbery, I couldn't sleep. It would be my fourth attempted robbery, Dougie's fifth. Without me, he and Mess did one, which I learned about after we were caught. For the upcoming holdup we stupidly decided for the third time to use the same location and pretend to be calling from the same street address. The first time was somewhere else. Dougie and Mess also used a different location. Still, the police didn't have to be Sherlock Holmes to determine the pattern. Plus, we always robbed pizza deliverers. You'd think we'd at least have had enough sense to rob a Chinese joint once in a while. Clearly we weren't criminal masterminds. Actually, we were downright stupid. If only I'd been smart enough to walk away from the robberies earlier, or had the strength to resist one last time. Things would have been very different, but not necessarily better. That's the odd thing about it. I often think I *needed* to get shot. It liberated me from a pointless existence, one that was thoughtless and uninspiring. I know, I know. I was only fifteen at the time. Nobody at fifteen is thinking like Gandhi. Most fifteen-year-olds are hoping their acne will clear up or they won't fail algebra. Nevertheless, getting shot turned me into a better human being, or at least into someone *trying to become* a better one. It's cornball stuff, for sure. But it's true. True to how I feel about it. True to how I felt then, and still do.

As the robberies mounted, I began to have a crisis of conscience. It started to seem all wrong. It's not as though I thought it was a sin, or even much of a crime for that matter. Nor did I picture myself being punished if we were caught, locked up in jail with hardcore convicts or burning in

Hell for eternity with unrepentant evildoers. I began wondering what my parents and others who knew me would think if I were caught. But even that wasn't uppermost in my mind. Discovery and punishment weren't exactly troubling me; I wasn't tossing and turning in bed over that prospect. Rather, I started thinking that what we were doing was rotting me from the inside. It was making me depraved. I decided to tell Dougie that it was over, without explaining why. I'd keep it simple. I'd just tell him I'd had enough, that I wasn't going to do it anymore. And that would be that. There was nothing else to say. I'd tell him on the very night we were going to stick up another driver. I'd catch him off-guard and he wouldn't have time to talk me out of it. When I was done thinking this plan through, it seemed foolproof.

Earlier that night Billy picked me up at my house. As I got into the car I continued going over how I'd tell Dougie the news, practicing it in my head. I also found an excuse to keep Billy waiting in the car so I could talk to Dougie alone. Dougie and I weren't old enough to drive, but a few of our close friends were, including Mess. And only Mess among them knew what we were doing. He knew because he'd turned us on to the idea of holding up pizza delivery drivers in the first place. He was one of them. He worked for a pizza parlor in the next neighborhood, New Dorp.

One summer night, as the three of us were huddled in a corner of the St. Charles schoolyard drinking beers and smoking a jay, he pitched the idea. The best time to do it was on a Friday, he said, when he would be working and when the owner's son would be making the last delivery of the day. He'd have a lot of cash on him.

"Right before his last run he takes all of the money from the drivers and from the cash register. After he makes his last delivery, he heads over to the bank to put it all in the night deposit box."

"Why Friday? Why not Saturday or some other night?"

"It's the only night he does it. The other nights his father brings it over directly to the bank after closing. On Fridays, the old man leaves early. Friday's a busy night, you know. And you know what that means."

"How will we know he's making his last delivery and has all of that cash?"

"That's where I come in. I'll wait around 'til right before he's closing. You'll wait for me somewhere where there's a pay phone so when you see me pull up you can make the call for the last order."

"But what if he gets another call while he's making our pie?"

"They always keep a couple of made pies, large ones, warming in the oven and whoever calls for them, that's it—they're done for the night."

"How much money will he be carrying?"

"Sometimes it could be as much as $300."

Dougie and I looked at each other. "Okay," we said simultaneously. Mess laughed and said, "I knew you two were the right ones to talk to."

After we were caught, Dougie resented Mess not only for introducing us to the idea but also for keeping his involvement unknown. According to Dougie, Mess was as guilty as we were, if not more so, because he was the brainchild—and absolutely nothing happened to him. Also, Mess was involved in the first robbery and another one with Dougie. It seemed unfair that I got shot and Dougie, who was sixteen, received a criminal record, whereas nothing happened to Mess, who was involved in carrying out two robberies and whom Dougie saw as the instigator or "mastermind" behind it all. I didn't give a damn one way or the other. It didn't matter to me how many times Mess was implicated or that he'd planted the seed, *and* that he didn't pay a price for any of it. I didn't blame Mess for what happened. It wasn't his fault I almost got killed. Nor did I blame Dougie for persuading me to do another robbery, which sure did turn out to be our last. He thought I blamed him for that night, but I didn't. Not in the least.

If Heraclitus is right, that a man's character is his fate, then there was something about our characters back then that Mess identified as ripe for plunging into crimes and misdemeanors. It's why he laughed when we so quickly agreed. He had properly read our characters. Either one of us could have said no, and it would never have happened. End of story. But both of us said yes; therefore, our destiny lay ahead of us, driven forward by our characters. And therein lies the rub, the paradox of *that* night and how it drove the transformation of my life many nights later. I had to be willing to take Mess's bait, to "fall" first, or else the night I was shot would never have happened. It's similar to the way in which some view Judas's role in Christ's most glorious moment. According to them, as Jesus's best friend Judas *had* to betray him in order to set in motion the crucifixion and set the stage for his rebirth. I needed to be my own Judas. I had to mislead myself that night in order to trigger the subsequent "death watch" and encounter my own splendid moment in the ER—for my own re-birth, of sorts.

We arranged to meet Mess at a corner deli less than a mile from where he worked. A pay phone was attached to its outside brick wall. It was an ideal location. A few blocks from the deli we found a house with a large back and side yard, shaped like an inverted "L," lined thickly with pine trees. After we made the call we could walk there and easily duck into the side yard, able to see the front of the house. Mess would wait around the block on a parallel street in the getaway car.

The first time we tried it, it didn't work. Apparently the driver had left before we called. There was no answer when we did. The second time didn't pan out either because from the time Mess left to the time we called, another order came in. "I'm sorry," the store owner's son said. "I just sold my last one."

On the third try he picked up the phone and agreed to deliver a large cheese pizza to the address we provided. "I'll be there in less than ten minutes," he said. Dougie and I walked over to the spot we'd picked in which to hide. Waiting there would be less conspicuous than having Mess drop us off in front of it. We waited behind some thick shrubs planted between the trees. We had spray-painted black a purple water pistol we'd bought from Masters, the local department store, the one that replaced our giant reed-enclosed ball field. Dougie had grabbed a steak knife from his mother's kitchen drawer. We didn't know if the driver would turn over the money or laugh in our faces. What undoubtedly made us look convincing was that I wore a full-headed ski mask with only the eyes and mouth visible, and Dougie wore a stocking over his head.

Dougie insisted on holding the gun. He also said he'd do all of the talking. He was doing a hell of a lot of talking before the robbery, sounding like his favorite criminal movie characters. As we were crouched behind the bushes I could hear him breathing heavily. "My heart's racing," he said. I didn't reply. The car pulled up. We planned on robbing the driver before he went to the door. We couldn't let him ring the bell. Otherwise, he'd find out that no one at that address had made the call, and the person answering the door, suspicious of the driver, might watch him until he drove away. He got out of the car, opened the rear door, and pulled out the pizza box from the portable aluminum oven resting on the back seat. I reached for the ski mask stuffed in my jacket pocket. It was early spring and we were both wearing light jackets. I was wearing the same tan corduroy one I'd be shot in a few months from then in the fall. Dougie grabbed my wrist, clutching it tightly.

"Should we do it?" he asked.

"What?"

"What should we do?" He was still holding on to my wrist, more firmly now. He was scared but didn't want to admit it.

"What do you mean, 'What should we do?'"

"Fuck. I mean should we do it?"

"You were all gung-ho on this. Jesus."

"I was. I am. Fuck."

By then the driver was approaching the door. It was too late. But no one answered the bell. The people living in the house were evidently out and must have left the lights on to make it look as if they were home. The driver rang the bell several more times. There was still no answer. He stood dumbfounded on the large brick stoop, bordered by a waist-high black metal fence. He checked and rechecked the address written on the order slip taped to the box. He started walking down the six steps, looking back at the door a couple of times in case someone opened it. No one did.

"Give me that," I said, as I grabbed the water pistol from Dougie's hand and replaced it with the knife. "Here." I put on the ski mask and stood up without saying anything. Peripherally, I saw him reach into his jacket and pull out the stocking. I pushed through the opening between the shrub and the tree, and as I did I could hear Dougie doing the same behind me. For one of the few times in my life, I took the initiative. I'm still baffled as to why, of all times, it was just then.

Before that moment, I was a true follower, and thereafter as well, for a while. For a time, Dougie and I were inseparable. When it came to our friendship I often deferred to him. Perhaps I thought I was being a dutiful friend by letting him be top dog, no less than I became the dutiful son or the dutiful sibling and followed the lead of my family. When Dougie and I dressed up as Batman and Robin, I always played Robin. He never let me play Batman, but in all likelihood I may never have asked. When he was transferred to the other seventh-grade class with five other boys to separate the high-profile troublemakers in our class, he met a new group of friends. I eventually stopped playing with Crackers and Timmy Tomato, just as he did, and started hanging around with his new crowd, which included Mess.

I've gone over in my head many times why I picked then to take a leadership role, and it remains a mystery. Frankly, I'm largely interested in solving that mystery as a mind game, as I mentioned in an earlier chapter. I haven't exhausted too much brain matter trying to figure it out psychologically, turning myself inside out for a "criminal profile" of sorts. Really, it doesn't matter. What's done is done. I have to live with that decision, my actions, and the consequences—doing so with whatever Freudian or behavioral motives I assign to them, back then, now or later. Granted, it probably would have done me some good to talk about all of this to someone professionally, which I never did. It might even have helped to talk to *anyone* about it. But it was a package deal, as I've tried to explain: Do something entirely idiotic, get shot and almost die, and then be advised never to talk about any of it ever again to anybody. I was on my own, not unlike all of the times I spent as a child when my parents separated and I was shuttled from one "babysitter's" house to another, often sitting in a room alone staring at the walls. Maybe that's even how I felt during the first robbery when Dougie froze: on my own. He'd talked and talked beforehand about how cool it was going to be and how he'd shove the gun in the guy's face and blah, blah, blah. When the moment came, though, he couldn't back up his braggadocio with his will. I ignored his fears and pressed on. He might as well not have been there. In many ways, he wasn't.

Before the pizza driver reached his car, we cut him off. I pointed the gun at him. It was weightless. It wasn't a "loaded" gun. There wasn't even any water in it, so I felt a bit silly. For our plan to work, something other than the props will have had to take hold.

"Holy shit!" he shouted. He was terrified. He began to shake uncontrollably. Later, we learned from Mess that he'd wet his pants. And that is what I am most ashamed about—not the robberies, not my parents' and sister's finding out about them, not any of that, but how I put the fear of God into this young man.

"Shut the fuck up," I told him in the most fearsome voice I could conjure. This was what took hold, conjuring. "Say another fucking word and you're dead."

I was playing a role, just like the two cops who would catch me months later. I can see myself doing it, without necessarily experiencing it. I won't feel this way again until the night I'm shot. I don't remember the other robberies. I can hardly recall a single detail from any of them. This one and the last one, of course, I remember vividly. A movie projector still runs through my head in Technicolor and Surround sound after having captured the events of that final robbery, and the first one. To this day, it remains crystal-clear to me, even though in writing this now I am playing the film back for the first time, from end to end, in more than thirty years.

"Hand over your money, asshole."

He pulled from the inside of his jacket a roll of bills held together with a rubber band. He sheepishly offered it to me. I practically ripped it from his hand.

"What about your wallet? You have a fucking wallet, right?"

This wasn't part of the plan. I could tell Dougie was getting tense. But I didn't see him. I didn't want to. Maybe we were taking too long. I didn't care. I pulled the cash from the driver's wallet—no more than a few dollars in it—and threw it to the ground.

"Okay, asshole," I said. "You count to a hundred before you get back in the car, or else we'll come back here and you'll regret it. Got it?"

"Yeah, yeah, sure," he hurriedly replied. He wanted this to be over as fast as possible. "No problem."

We took off and ran to where Mess was parked. He saw us coming and, reaching around from the driver's seat, opened the back door. We jumped in, crushed together low so we couldn't be seen. Mess dipped below the steering wheel. In half a minute we heard the delivery guy tearing out of there. He raced fifty yards past us along a perpendicular street. There was no time for Mess to ask what happened. Dougie started bragging about how well it went, all on account of me.

"It was un-fucking-believable, Mess. You had to be there. Ba-kowsk was great, just fucking great," he said. He was excited again talking about it and he'd received an electric charge from it. Me, I was flat. "You should have heard him. *I* was fucking scared of him." Mess chuckled nervously. "And get this: He made the guy hand over his wallet." They both started laughing. I didn't. What had prompted me to do that? I wondered. Dougie was talking about something that had just happened, but it seemed light years before, or that he was talking about someone else. "You were beautiful," Dougie said.

But I didn't feel beautiful. That wasn't why I'd gone through with it, to impress Dougie or Mess, or anyone for that matter. At least I don't think so. Still, after all of these years, and after trying to sort it out, I can never be too sure of my main motivation. Despite all of my training in deconstructing stories, both imaginative and real, and reconstructing them, and then surrounding them with seemingly illuminating analysis, I must apply some doubt to my own thesis about that night, about that portion of my story. Decoding texts is one thing; decoding personal experiences is another. I'm quite aware of how subjectivity refracts and fractures vision, causing the past to be seen through rose-colored glasses or jaundice-ridden eyes. It's simply too subjective, way beyond the postmodern idea of "scientific" objectivity masquerading as subjectivity. As a result, perhaps there's no telling why I'd done it. No simple or sophisticated explanation: Because in some respect I was dead inside.

What I do know is that I didn't go through with the robberies to appear astonishingly cool or extraordinarily dangerous. In fact, I told no one about it. I may even have been ashamed of it from the start, whereas afterward I learned that Dougie had boasted about the robberies to several hardcore punks outside of our inner circle of friends. He attended a different high school from the one I did, and the guys he told eventually did jail time, or ran away to Florida to escape it, or hid from other, higher-level criminals. Some ended up as I could have: dead. Dougie regarded the robberies as his entrée into a bona fide criminal crowd he deemed more powerful and more impressive than anything any other working-class groups of kids had to offer. The robberies also provided him with a certain mystique he craved. He actually fed it by conducting more crimes and getting into more trouble with more notorious hoodlums. Unfortunately for him, their criminal acts were carried out with even less cleverness than our robberies. He and a well-known teen gangster in Oakwood Heights attempted to stick up a toll booth attendant at the Verrazano Narrows Bridge from their car. When a vehicle pulled up immediately behind them, the collector rang a bell, jumped under the half-metal door frame, like the attendant in *The Godfather*, and in seconds a Port Authority police car blocked their front escape. And I thought *we* were idiots. What was next, I wondered after hearing about it—robbing airplane passengers in mid-flight without parachutes? The ineptitude didn't deter Dougie from taking pride in what he was doing. He wasn't in the least embarrassed by it, not by the stupidity of it or by the immorality. The same was true when we were caught. In his mind the robberies demonstrated that we had become special: A bad reputation beat none at all. If asked, I'm sure he'd agree it was better to rule in Hell than to serve in Heaven. When we were caught he seemed almost grateful, but for different reasons from mine. He was happy it had become public knowledge that we were hipster thugs, right down to the robbery's appearing in the *New York Times*.

Three days after I'd been shot I was finally stabilized and fully conscious. While certainly not for the first time, my parents came to see me, although I have no recollection of their being there before, given that I was in and out of consciousness and likely medicated to the max. I don't recall a single thing we talked about that day. Whatever it was, I'm certain it was awkward, innocuous chit-chat. I do remember, however, that as soon as they walked into the ICU, my mother handed me a sealed manila envelope. "It's from Dougie," she said sternly, none too happy to be delivering something from the boy she likely blamed for my fall from grace. I waited until they left to open it. When I did, I found it contained the main section of the previous Saturday's *Staten Island Advance*, the edition put out the day after I'd been shot, with a full account of the botched robbery on the front page. A note was attached: "Get well soon. We made the headlines, brother!" To him, we were celebrities. More important, we'd become local heroes to those he believed would truly value what we did. This was the last thing I wanted. At that point I wanted to be someone else, to hide from the shame and humiliation of being some bargain-rate hoodlum, anyone other than the kid who was shot for holding up a pizza delivery driver for pocket money. We were jerks in my opinion, not Batman and Robin. If anything, we were the bad guys, the Joker and the Riddler. That was good enough for Dougie, to be known for something. It never occurred to me then or when I was doing the robberies to capitalize on it for its "gangster" value or that it was providing me with extraordinariness. To me, it was simpler than that: We decided to rob pizza delivery drivers and that's what we did and what we kept doing, carrying out something we said we'd do.

Of all of the questions I've asked myself about that period in my life, the one I've posed the most often is "Why?" Why did I do it?—as raised in a previous chapter. Honestly, I keep coming back to the same answer over and over again, despite the complex, convoluted answers included in that earlier chapter. It's the same ridiculous, pedestrian one every time: It was something to do. Forget the complicated questions and explanations from the other chapter, the possible 1, 2, 3, and 4 causes of it. Maybe I did it for very mundane and superficial reasons: It was an extreme version of diving into someone's hedges. That may have been one of the characteristics Mess detected in me when he approached us: I would be willing to take on a dare. There was a reckless adventurer's streak in me that possibly would have served me well in different times. I would have been a good pirate, highwayman, or Crusader. Who knows, like the thieves Francis Drake and Walter Raleigh I might have been knighted, dubbed a "Sir." Instead, I felt more like Sir Shithead.

In truth, robbing the delivery drivers was the only serious trouble I was getting into. Okay, that was terrible enough on its own. I wouldn't want to make it seem otherwise, as if lots of fifteen-year-olds rob pizza delivery drivers at water-pistol point. Nevertheless, it was the only activity of mine that could be considered "bad," outside of my not doing my homework and smoking a few joints now and then. Smoking pot wasn't exactly subversive at the time anyway, not in the mid- to late '70s when I was doing it. Everyone seemed to be getting high, even the jocks. Heck, a ring of reefer smoke rose out of the football team's practice huddles. I should know—I played on the JV team, and the so-called straight-and-narrow athletes were in much worse shape than I ever was. Between the heavy binge drinking and the occasional hit or two from a bong, they were heading toward plenty of trouble themselves. I was actually seen as a bit of a nerd on the team, not because of my schooling—I was an indifferent dunce—but because I was shy and reserved compared with most of them, and booze was never my thing. Actually, measured against most of the kids in my high school, I was a "good kid." While a lousy student, I didn't cause trouble in the classroom, unlike some academic train-wrecks who made life miserable for teachers. Outside of school, I kept to myself. When Stephen Malloy, a buddy from St. Charles and high school, came to the hospital, he told my parents he couldn't believe what had happened. He was stunned to learn that I, of all people, had been involved in a robbery. "David doing that, 'No way,' I said to myself," he told them. "I couldn't even get him to cut a class with me."

Stephen was right. By the standards governing troublemakers, I wasn't one of them. Stephen, on the other hand, certainly was, having been *the* ruling nuisance at St. Charles. He was "busted" in eighth grade for selling pills—"downers" and "uppers." He continued along that path right up until the day they found him dead in Great Kills Park from a heroin overdose soon after his twenty-first birthday. He had enlisted in the Marines when he turned eighteen, two years after he'd run away from home. He ended up riding around the country with some 18-wheeler truck driver who'd picked him up while he was hitchhiking in Pennsylvania. Apparently, joining the Marines hadn't cured what ailed him. It may actually have aggravated it. My parents were aware of his reputation, so I imagine when Stephen bore witness to my moral worth they listened skeptically. But he knew what he was talking about. For the most part, I was a rather well-behaved teen. Tottenville High School was an enormous place—1,200 in my graduating class alone—so it was easy to get lost there. While generally a popular kid, I wasn't tied to any one clique. I wasn't a full-fledged jock, even though I was on the football team. In spite of my mild popularity and playing football for a year, I was still a ghost. I had deliberately made myself into one. I didn't crave the attention. I preferred standing in the shadows, occasionally latching onto other ghosts. I was too timid and fearful of rejection to ask girls on dates. In the four years I was there, I went on only one, and it didn't go very well.

I went on it soon after I was shot. I was still too young to drive, so my sister drove me to the girl's house to pick her up. Like so many Tottenville students, she'd recently moved to the Island from Brooklyn. I spent days fretting over the date and worrying about what to wear. When she answered the door she was wearing super-tight jeans, spiked heels, and a long-sleeved T-shirt that seemed spray painted onto her rather large chest, which until then I hadn't noticed. Her black leather jacket was unzipped and spread wide to display her assets. She looked sexy as all hell, but she also looked like something out of *West Side Story*. I was petrified before the date began. My sister drove us to the movie theater, where we went to see, of all things, *Death Wish*. Watching Charles Bronson gun down one hoodlum after another made me dizzy, especially when I saw that one of them bore a startling resemblance to me. I practically started hyperventilating. When we walked out of the theater into the well-lit parking lot, my date looked at me and asked what was wrong. "Didn't you like the movie?" she asked in her thick Brooklyn accent, which in time became a Staten Island accent (much lampooned in numerous movies and TV shows). "Sure," I said. I could barely say much more. She took the gum out of her mouth and threw it to the ground. She lit a cigarette and started chattering. "It was great, wasn't it," she said. "I loved it." I hated it. It was one of the most violent movies I'd ever seen. And what kind of girl likes to watch all of that bloodletting? I was as overwhelmed by her as I was by the movie. We walked up to the New Dorp train station to take the train home. My stop was before hers and I got off, without seeing her home. I didn't know I was supposed to escort her home, never having been on a date before. Or maybe I just wanted to get home and crawl into bed. Whatever the reason, my sister was appalled when I told her. "I guess she won't be going out with you again." It was worse than that. When I ran into her the following Monday at school she gave me the finger. I can't say I was terribly disappointed. But I was starting to wonder what my place in the world would be. I was rather inhibited before I got shot, but I was beginning to see that having gone through that and all it meant was making me intolerant of the things others desired and their actions. In the ER, I had swiftly accrued a worldview different from that of many others, especially my peers. I was already skeptical of so-called adult wisdom. I was thinking I could become even more withdrawn, in a sort of unconscious way. Where would that lead me—right back from where I started from, alone, in those empty rooms staring at walls?

But perhaps I would never have ended up in the ER, acquiring that different point of view (that I am so grateful for!), if I had carried out my intention to tell Dougie I wasn't going to attempt another robbery with him. In many ways, I'm glad I didn't have the courage to inform him. My verbal passivity ultimately "saved" me. While Billy drove over to Dougie's, I silently practiced what I would say to him. I made sure Billy waited in the car by telling him Dougie had said his mother didn't like more than one of us waiting in the house for him. I rang the bell. His mother answered. "Dougie, David's here," she hollered in the direction of his upstairs bedroom while letting me through the door. "Be right down," he shouted back. She closed the door behind me. We were standing at the front door where it met the landing to the upstairs staircase. The sunken living room was to our left. Dougie didn't invite me up, so I couldn't tell him privately in his room. I hoped his mother wouldn't sit in the living room. She didn't. She walked back toward the family room, where I can hear a television show playing, the laugh track coughing up fits of collective amusement every few seconds.

Dougie ambled down the staircase. He was obviously in a good mood. I knew it wouldn't be easy. When I told him, he got angry. At first, he couldn't even look me in the face. Uneasily, he turned his back to me and walked halfway up the staircase. He stopped, turned around, and sat on one of the steps. "C'mon, man, you have to. I want to do this. I can't do it without you." There was more, but I can't remember what else he said. I can recall only the beginning and the end, not the middle. Whatever it was he said, he saw that I was wavering. I was torn between walking out the door and running straight home, and seeing the logic in sticking up another driver. "It'll be the last time," he said. "I promise." I waited until he was finished before replying.

"I need to go back home," I said to Billy as I plopped onto the passenger seat. The rear door slammed shut as Dougie slipped into the back of Billy's green AMC Concord. I was glumly resigned to the robbery, while Dougie's high spirits returned. He patted me on the shoulder. Billy shot me an odd look, as if to say, "What was that all about?" I turned to him as he put the car in gear, the standard shift part of the steering column. "I forgot my wallet," I explained. He rolled his eyes. First I made him wait in the car and then he had to drive me back home for something I forgot. Expecting not to pull off another holdup, I'd left the ski mask and water pistol at home. I had to go back and get them. Billy made a "K" turn in front of Dougie's house and drove the two blocks to mine.

My parents were sitting in the living room watching TV. I told them the same thing—I was back because I'd forgotten my wallet. I said it dejectedly, which I realized might draw too much attention to it. Trying to cover my tracks, I raced upstairs to my bedroom. According to them, I was always rushing around and in a hurry. I needed to act normally. As I grabbed the ski mask and water pistol from their hiding place, I knew I was about to go through something I didn't want to do. Yet I felt trapped in my inability to do the right thing, to simply say, "No!" I was fully aware of this, aware of how my failure to act wisely would lead to a certain kind of action and outcome. My inaction would have enormous consequences. In some ways, I fully knew this as I was pulling the paraphernalia out of the heating vent, although not in its enormity and severity.

The three of us were to meet our other friends at a dirt road closed off to cars. It paralleled the train tracks, and it lay almost in the middle of the Oakwood Heights and New Dorp train stations. Some of us lived in Oakwood and others in New Dorp, so it was a perfect meeting place. It also has several boulders to prevent cars from driving through, including police cruisers. It was therefore an ideal spot to go and safely drink beers or cheap wine, like Boone's Farm Apple Wine, and smoke a little weed. Back then, getting high was cheap. From a typical nickel ($5) bag of weed a dozen joints could be rolled. If five of us kicked in a dollar apiece we had enough pot for the weekend, including a possible left-over joint or two for Sunday. No matter where we were going, we'd meet at "The Rock," which is what the location was called. We sometimes hung out there all weekend if we didn't feel like dealing with the more aggressive posers at The Station. Few of us had enough money to purchase a 75-cent movie ticket or much of anything else. Hanging out at The Rock was more entertaining than most movies anyway. We told silly stories, made fun of each other, and goofed around. I was generally known for telling the funniest stories and engaging in the sharpest and wittiest "color commentary" when others were telling theirs. The Rock was like a nightclub, and other kids would come by to hang out with us, knowing we were a harmless, amusing bunch who didn't mind sharing a joint or a beer with them. The Rock was "ours," among my close-knit friends, a group I'd grown close to starting in the seventh grade when Dougie introduced me to them. The Rock also was a more sedate place to be than The Station, which was becoming overrun with uptight goons and thugs. We must have met at The Rock hundreds of times during the four years I was palling around with that crowd.

When we arrived, most of our friends were already there, wondering what had taken us so long. We were responsible for picking up the beer, so their concerns weren't only altruistic. As the time approached to call the pizza parlor, Dougie and I agreed we'd tell them we had promised to help his parents serve drinks during a party they were throwing. His parents were always having parties. His dad elaborately re-did their basement for them, including a wrap-around bar, ceiling dimmers, and a restored fireplace. We had The Rock and the adults had their party rooms. It wasn't a stretch, then, to use "playing bartenders" as a reason to leave earlier than usual.

Before we went to The Rock we had stopped at a deli in New Dorp to buy the beer. The drinking age at the time was eighteen. I'd always looked older than my age, and I'd been buying beer since I was thirteen.

I also think the times were more relaxed, and most people selling liquor seemed indifferent to following the letter of the law. Billy was eighteen, but I didn't need him to buy the beer. I walked into the deli alone and bought it.

When I walked out of the store toward Billy's car, parked a few yards away, a cop car drove alongside of me. The driver's partner looked me up and down, and as he did our eyes met. I could read his easily enough: "Guilty!" His window was rolled halfway down so he was able to get a decent look at me. He could see that while I may have had the face of a young man I had the body of someone barely past puberty. It was evident the brown paper bag I was cradling in my arms held a couple of six-packs, which could be purchased back then for merely a dollar apiece. He turned to the driver and said something as they passed. The car abruptly stopped; it rolled slowly backward. He cranked the window fully down. I pretended I hadn't noticed anything. I walked faster along the sidewalk, past where the patrol car had come to a standstill.

"You," he said, "come over here." I walked over to the car but tried not to get too close, hoping he'd be unable to see how young I was.

"I said come over here." I moved a little closer. "How old are you?"

"Nineteen, officer. Why?"

He stared at my face. He again took full stock of me, eyeing me from head to toe. "Bullshit!" he blurted out finally. "I'm not even going to bother asking you for ID. How'd you get that beer?"

I panicked. Instead of getting the store owner, a complete stranger, in trouble for selling it to me illegally, I told the cop that my friend had bought it for me. Billy and Dougie were leaning against the driver's side of his car smoking cigarettes. "Where's your friend?" he asked. "Over there," I said, gesturing toward them and passing up another chance not to get Billy involved. I easily could have said my friend had just left, or something like that, but I was too nervous to be furtive. I couldn't help but be factual. "He's standing over there," I added. Both cops turned toward them. "Which one is he?" the driver asked. "The taller one," I said. "Hey you!" he shouted, throwing his head in Billy's direction. "Get over here." Billy pointed at himself with a questioning look. "Yeah, you," the cop said. "Get over here, now."

Billy was not afraid of the cops. If anything, he was insolent toward them. He had a sharp, sarcastic tongue whenever they confronted us and chased us out of places for "loitering" or for "trespassing." He was once arrested outside the Farrell High School gym for "insolence" during one of their routine Friday Night Dances. When a cop car pulled up to the gymnasium doors, its driver asked why we were there and not inside like the other kids. "None of your damn business," Billy replied. From there it escalated to Billy's daring the "pigs" to arrest him. They took him up on it. As he walked over to the car outside of the deli, I was hoping he would keep his cool.

"Did you buy this for him?" the cop asked. Billy looked at the bag and then at me. He was simultaneously stunned and exasperated I'd been so rash. I returned his expression with one of my own acknowledging how stupid I'd been and that I already regretted it. All of this likely had a calming effect on him. He seemed resigned to the situation.

"Yeah, sure," he said.

"Let's see some ID." The driver handed Billy's license to his partner, then warned Billy about buying beer for underage kids. Billy was lucky they didn't arrest him and haul his butt to the police station.

"I bet a night in jail would cure you," the driver said.

"No, sir."

"What?"

"I mean, no, sir, there's no need for that. I'm already cured. It'll never happen again."

"Yeah, well, it better not. Give me that," the cop said, looking at the bag filled with beer. I handed it to him through the window.

As this exchange was taking place, the other cop was taking Billy's information off his license. They took my name and address as well.

Later that night, I lay on the wet grass bleeding nearly to death. Once the cops found out my name, a little detective work revealed I'd been stopped earlier by a patrol car. Another name popped up on their radar. In the middle of the night, Billy was arrested for being my accomplice.

Like mine, Billy's dad was a cop, but they arrested him anyway. His father worked in Brooklyn and there was some tension and antagonism between interborough units, largely because cops in the other, more "active" boroughs considered Staten Island cops on "paid vacation." The Staten Island cops knew they were viewed contemptuously, so maybe they took Billy in to irritate a Brooklyn cop. At the station, Billy's dad was told the details of the robbery. His father said it was impossible for Billy to have been involved. Sure, his dopey son had bought beer for the kid who'd been shot earlier in the night, but that didn't automatically mean they'd been together during the robbery. More to the point, I'd been shot before midnight and Billy had been home for almost a half an hour before then. Billy typically stayed out late, much later than when I had to be home, but he'd gotten bored with being at The Rock and was home sometime after 11:30. His father was his alibi. He was watching Johnny Carson's monologue when Billy walked through the door. He was still arrested. Not until the next morning was he finally released from the New Dorp police precinct's cell.

It didn't occur to me that Billy would be dragged into the situation. After I told the cops my name and moments before I passed out, a uniformed officer walked back from a patrol car and said something to the good Brobdingnagian.

"Were you with Billy Drigun?" he asked.

Drigun? Where'd they come up with that? Then I remembered what had happened outside the deli. They thought he was the one. "No," I said as emphatically as I could.

I felt the presence of the bad Brobdingnagian moving closer. The guy seemed to exude anger and disgust. When I told my dad about him, he wanted to find out who it was and reprimand him, perhaps even confront the guy. I begged him not to. As much as the son of a bitch overreacted, I guess I felt as though he'd thought he was doing his job. To him, I was just some punk who'd been robbing pizza delivery drivers. And he was right. That's exactly who I was. If I hadn't been, I wouldn't have been in that situation, lying on the wet grass with three bullet wounds, giving someone like him the opportunity to play his part in it.

"C'mon, stay with us," said the good Brobdingnagian. I must have been fading, slurring the few words I spoke. "William R. Drigun. That's who you were with, right?"

"No," I repeated, but I could barely marshal enough energy to get that one word out. "No, I swear."

The bad Brobdingnagian stepped even closer. "Don't," the other said. "Look, we know you were with him, so why don't you just tell us."

"I wasn't with him," I said, with as much conviction as I could generate. I also wanted to perpetuate the fiction that I'd acted alone. "I wasn't with anyone," I added.

"This fucking kid is asking for it," the bad Brobdingnagian said, kicking me again. The good one didn't stop him. "Maybe so," he said. How hard I'm kicked and where I haven't a clue. I feel nothing, just as I felt nothing when he'd dug his shoe into my injured shoulder and kicked me once before. Suddenly, I'm shrinking, sinking into an expanding, soundless hole growing below me. I'm sucked into it, and I'm too worn out to wonder if I'll resurface or come out of the other end.

6
Learning Curve

I attended St. Charles Elementary School between 1964 and 1972. It was the institutional epitome of Staten Island. When the rest of the nation was changing so drastically, St. Charles and Staten Island were stuck in time. Years later, when reading Victorian novels, I'd encounter characters trapped in insufferable boarding schools or imprisoned in dreadful orphanages and I'd be reminded of St. Charles. Minus the morning's icy wash basins those neophytes encountered, there were remarkable similarities between the places. Of course, I may simply have been responding to the misdirection and loneliness those fictional characters were experiencing and feeling, regardless of where they were. Nevertheless, St. Charles was a cold, unfriendly place for children. For a school located in one of the most diverse cities on the planet, it was astonishingly one-dimensional.

A person would be hard-pressed to decide what was more monochromatic, the student body or the curriculum. General literacy studies, for instance, varied little, or not at all, from grade to grade. For eight years I read from color-coded, gradated material I picked out from laminated cardboard boxes distributed by the diocese. Questions answered at the end of each story marked a reader's progress. It felt as if I were reading the same dreary narratives no matter the color code or the grade level. The repetitiveness didn't help me, though. My scores were as consistently dreadful as the material was consistently boring. The student body was possibly more homogeneous. Nearly a thousand students attended it every year and not a single minority passed through its doors. St. Charles was located three blocks from my house, its student body consisting largely of the Island's two most dominant ethnicities, Italian and Irish, with an occasional Pole, Swede, or German thrown in.

Chris Pogee, a Portuguese buddy of mine, was one of the most exotic students, an impression reinforced by his parents, who read books—unlike the rest of our parents, who didn't. If they did, they certainly didn't read the kinds of books the Pogees read. Those who did read books were almost entirely women. Men read trade publications and the newspaper, and a few subscribed to *Sports Illustrated* or *National Geographic*, like my father, who only flipped through the latter's pages admiring the photography. (Once I came across a copy of *Playboy* in his bachelor pad, likely the first time I'd seen a woman naked, or anyone naked for that matter.) Men mostly spent hours in their basements or garages tinkering with machines or working on hobbies. Reading was anathema to most males in my working-class family and community. Books were for sissies. Even the "sissies" (the females) didn't read much. The only time I ever saw anyone read a book was when someone's mom read a romance novel while sunbathing in the back yard. If we unexpectedly stormed in to play she would have to hide the racy cover from us. When *The Godfather* came out in 1970 a lot of local people were reading that, but so was everyone, it being the biggest-selling work of fiction ever published in the United States—at least until 1985. The Pogees, on the other hand, were different. They read history and philosophy books and classic works of literature. I recognized the literary titles because in the seventh and eighth grades we started reading the ultra-extreme, twenty-page abridged versions of such works as *Great Expectations, Moby-Dick,* and *Jane Eyre.* Despite his being a chemical engineer, Mr. Pogee "wasn't very good with his hands," a description usually applied to Jews. He simply didn't care how his yard looked or whether he needed to install new kitchen fixtures. He preferred to spend his free time reading Dostoevsky.

As unusual as Chris and his parents were ethnically and culturally, Mark Spicolla, a richly dark-skinned Sicilian, was the most glaring exception in our school and neighborhood, as were his older brother and younger sister. While no one in his family had short, curly hair, all of them were as black as the African American athletes we wished we were as good as. (I'll skip the invasion of southern Italy, the Iberian Peninsula, and other parts of Europe by the Moors as to why Mark and his family were so dark. It seems like a familiar story by now, although it wasn't back then, that's for sure.) What probably saved Mark and his siblings from a lifetime of grief (and therapy) was that Mark and his brother were two of the strongest boys in the area. In second grade Mark was bigger and stronger and tougher than most sixth-graders; by the time he was in sixth grade he could hold his own against most high school kids. Unlike Pops, he didn't need to lift weights. He was a meaty, tough kid all on his own.

When we were in fifth grade he learned that a classmate had nick-named him Mark "Spic" Spicolla. He put an end to that right away. We were shooting hoops in his side yard when he saw the boy ride past us on his bicycle. Mark dashed after him and we quickly trailed behind. Within a few yards he was running alongside the terrified kid who was pedaling furiously, but not fast enough to avoid being caught. Mark tossed the boy and the bicycle onto the street as if they were a pillow. He did it with such force that the boy remained glued to his banana seat, a tangled web of limbs, metal, and rubber tires. With his left arm, Mark pinned the knotted mess to the ground. With his cocked right arm, he circled a threatening fist over the entire configuration. He not only forced the whimpering boy to apologize but also made him promise never to utter that word or anything like it about him or anyone in his family. "Ever," Mark said em-phatically. "I swear, I swear," the boy hastily answered, close to tears. Sure enough, no one ever again developed a nickname to highlight his most outstanding physical characteristic. Mark had prevented his skin color from becoming his calling card. I'm sure if he had been a small or sickly kid his life would have been completely different.

Mark and Chris were the closest things to "minority" students at St. Charles because there weren't any within a ten-mile radius. What were in plentiful supply at St. Charles was girls. I was a serial day-dreamer in grammar school, not only bored by the material but a brooder over my broken home, so I could stare forever at the back of a girl's head sitting in front of me wondering what it would be like to stroke her hair. It didn't matter who she was or what she looked like. By the fourth grade, if even my arm grazed that of any of my female classmates, I'd swoon. I'd have to wait more than seven years to touch a girl, almost a full year after I'd been shot. Imagine that: I might have died before experiencing that small miraculous pleasure.

Each of the two classes per grade level consisted of fifty students, with equal parts boys and girls. I spent ten months a year for eight years with about the same twenty-five girls, almost all of whom I knew hardly any-thing about, at least not anything relevant. I knew that Patty Beck had nice legs and that Carrie Fox was a great speller, but that was about the extent of it. I might have steered clear of them because I wouldn't know what to do once I got anywhere near them, other than to fantasize about what I would do if I could. I received zero guidance or instruction from my parents, the school, or the Church on how to treat them or how to relate to them, which figures. They always left out the really important stuff. The useless material they fed to us like junk food.

I rarely saw my female classmates outside of school, partly because many of them lived far away (as in three or four miles) and took the bus. After class, that was the end of them. The girls whom I did see in the neighborhood were mostly my friends' younger sisters, who were "icky," and older sisters, who were off-limits. While the older ones may have entered our fantasy world, they never entered our real world, unlike the younger ones, who tried. The older girls congregated in places we didn't inhabit. Seeing one in the neighborhood was like spotting a rare bird.

Younger girls were a different story, and not only because they were less physically developed. They were close to our equals, age-wise, but as males we felt entitled to boss them around, which typically involved shunning them. We chased them from our rickety forts or backyard sand-boxes. Three or four of us might run after one we discovered hiding in our makeshift tent, or two of us might take hold of one by the hands and feet and drag her out of someone's basement, lugging her upstairs and flinging her onto a couch, after discovering her down there tinkering with the field of battle we had set up with our tiny plastic soldiers. We wouldn't even allow them to watch us play baseball in front of their own homes. Their brothers were especially vigilant about that, deliberately hitting balls right at them and clipping their knees while rounding a base as they sat curbside.

Both younger and older kept to themselves, and they mostly stayed close to home, even when they were together. Unlike the boys, they didn't hang out in groups, more like in pairs. Boys, on the other hand, were everywhere, always traveling in packs of four or five, like our foursome. It was understood that if you were alone and found a pack to play with, joining it would not offend the primary group. Large packs, composed of multiple smaller ones, often were formed to create a couple of football or baseball teams. Finding such large packs was easy, especially in the sum-mer, which was the only time of year in my childhood when I was free. It might not take more than ten minutes to form two complete nine-player softball teams.

Anywhere you went in Oakwood Heights a bunch of boys could be found. We played in the streets, in the schoolyards, in the empty lots, and, of course, at The Station. The Station wasn't quite a play destination. While a game of stickball might develop now and then, it was more like the place where packs assembled before, during, and after games. On any late afternoon in the summer there might be as many as thirty boys wandering in and out of George's and Sal's. In my youth we'd stand or sit in the parking area drinking sodas and shoving melting logs of Yodels into our mouths. In my adolescence, beers and joints replaced the sodas and cakes. Girls rarely came around the station. Even in my teens they weren't part of the scene. While we policed them in my youth, we likely scared them off as I got older by the sheer force of our inflated numbers—along with our inflated levels of testosterone. I'd imagine even the most egotistical "tease" found us intolerable.

While there were hardly any girls around, I sure was fascinated by and interested in them—from afar, and from a very, very safe emotional distance too. Looking back on it, I think the only thing I looked forward to in the morning as I walked the three blocks to St. Charles was that I'd be in the company of girls all day. I may have been in love with them all, including the ones the other boys considered physically unappealing. If I caught even a glimpse of someone's thigh as she sat in her chair, with her red plaid skirt catching a splinter in the wooden seat, with her skirt staying in place as her legs came forward, I was stirred. They all hurriedly pulled the skirt back up to its "proper" place, the thigh-sighting lasting only a few seconds. That was enough for me. I needed only a few seconds to imagine what a few hours might be like. But there was more to them than that, and I'm pretty sure I recognized it, viscerally, way back when. To me, their appeal was universal. It transcended whatever it was that made us "boys." There was something categorically different about them, well beyond the obvious physical differences. For one thing, they seemed smarter, and not only in school. They seemed to know more about the world than we did. We were too busy stomping on one another, crashing into shit, or leaping into rows of hedges to slow down long enough to figure things out, or to even try to. If we were destructive, they were reflective. I'm guessing most of the guys I palled around with were like me, covering their feelings and emotions with their aggression. Also, girls seemed less confused, at least in a harmful way. I can't imagine any female holding up a pizza delivery driver for no apparent reason. Sure, one might do it some day to pay for drugs or food for her impoverished kids, but not for "kicks." And the last time I checked there weren't any Juliet Caesars, Adele Hitlers, Paula Pots, or Josephine Stalins around. "Demonic Female" doesn't roll off of the tongue as readily as "Demonic Male" does.

At the personal level, I found girls different because they treated me differently. No girl ever goaded me about my father's absence or told me that surviving gunshots must have been "un-fucking-believable," as a few males did. Girls clearly recognized my shame, along with the sheer lunacy of what had caused it. In my childhood, they also noticed how sullen and withdrawn my parents' separation had made me, either leaving me to sulk in peace or empathizing once in a while when they saw an opening. Until about the seventh grade, when I started getting into trouble, I was an academic enigma. I was the exception to the rule, the rare shy boy who was also academically weak, almost to the breaking point. Typically, the introverted kids were the better students, while the extroverts were the "cooler," poorer ones. I was an introverted poor student.

Clearly, my parents' separation took its toll on my ability to concentrate on my school work. I had other things on my mind. In second grade, the year they separated, I failed three subjects. *Anything* that involved concentration, I couldn't deal with. It didn't take long, for instance, for my mom to stop sending me to piano lessons. I never practiced on the plastic keyboard pad the studio loaned me. I'd place my hands on it and begin to stare into space. Even organized sports were difficult to master, despite my being an active, relatively athletic kid. After playing Little League for two years, I wanted to quit. It was the summer after my parent's separation. I sucked at it, almost as much as I sucked at school. Organized baseball was different from horsing around. I was too distracted to hit or catch a baseball properly, just as I was too distracted to study my multiplication tables. I had to stay in school, but baseball I could drop out of. Who needed the additional frustration and disgrace? There was plenty of that going around in places where I had to be. During an interborough championship game—our team was the Staten Island champs—I singlehandedly lost the game as the team's second baseman. We were ahead by two runs, until I ruined it. With two men out and two men on in the last inning of the game, I booted an easy ground ball—Bill Buckner–style—and the pair raced across home plate, tying the score. The next batter drove in the winning run, driving in the kid who'd reached second base on my error. Without me, I thought, the team could have gone on to further glory. I could tell from my teammates' expressions that they shared this view.

After that embarrassing experience, I figured it was time to retire. My older cousin Tommy had done so the year before, for similarly shameful reasons, and the last time I checked he hadn't fallen off the face of the earth. Why not do the same? My mom, fortunately, stepped in. She asked Mr. Endrum, the assistant coach of that ill-fated team, to convince me otherwise. His son Billy was the team's catcher, as well as a classmate of mine at St. Charles. The Endrums didn't live far from us, and when my parents were together they sporadically socialized. Before that unfortunate day, Mr. Endrum already had noticed that my dad's absence was obviously affecting not only my play but also my psyche. I'm sure he and my mom talked about it. While he was a stern, by-the-book coach, he also treated the players fairly. He never favored the better players, or even his son, over any other child. He was both tough and instructive for everyone alike. In short, he was a good coach, and a good man. He was the ideal person to try and talk me out of quitting.

I can't recall a word he said, though. All I remember was crying like mad on the steps of our house. I kept blubbering about how I personally destroyed the team's chances of playing Japan in the World Little League Tournament. Without me, they would have been a better team. I'd be doing any team in the future a favor if I didn't play for them. Hell, I'd be doing the sport a favor if I disappeared entirely from it, I told him. Whatever he said worked because I didn't quit. My father must have learned that some other man had intervened because after that chat he put me on a healthy diet of practice drills. I remember shagging flies and practicing my swing—sometimes in the snow! Eventually, I became quite a good player—exceptional, to be perfectly frank. A couple of years later I made the Great Kills Little League "Majors" All-Star team, amassing more number-one votes from all the managers and coaches than any other player. It seems so inconsequential now. But back then it was a major accomplishment. In many respects, it was my only one as a child. My mother was wise to have asked Mr. Endrum to talk to me, to bolster my confidence and make sure I didn't become a quitter. She didn't apply similar tactics as I grew older, just the opposite, often confounding what little confidence I had. Perhaps that's because she thought of me differently after I'd been shot. I guess most parents would view their child differently if he'd been involved in a botched stick-up and nearly got his damn-fool head blown to bits.

While I was mentally restless in school, I was becoming a sojourner out of it. If my mind drifted unintentionally in class, my body was intentionally displaced every afternoon when I left the schoolroom. During the week, I was shuttled from one home to another, to different ad hoc after-school day cares. I rarely stayed at any single place more than twice in any given month. Affording a full-time babysitter or nanny—not that there were any nannies back then on Staten Island—was out of the question. My father hadn't stopped footing the bills, like the mortgage, but he was paying rent for a one-bedroom apartment on the other side of the Island. On a cop's salary, he was barely meeting whatever financial-support arrangement my parents had worked out with each other. They weren't divorced. That would have been against church principles. He therefore wasn't legally bound to give us any money because they were only separated. I guess to them "separation" was a lesser offense in the eyes of the church, and in their own. To me, it didn't matter what they called it. I came from a broken home. My father was gone, making my family different from any other. That my mother had to work once he left further proved that difference, like my cutting the grass when I was six.

She worked as a bank teller several miles from our house. It was a 9:00-to-4:00 job and by the time she drove home or took the bus from work it was after 5:00. On those nights, she didn't have to pick me up from that day's sitter. When she did, we arrived home after 5:30. My sister attended an all-girls Catholic school nearly as far away from our home, in the opposite direction, as my mother's bank. Oakwood Heights was situated in the middle of the Island's seventeen-mile stretch. Before the separation my sister was already involved in extracurricular activities. After it, she threw herself into them as if her life depended on it. Doing so was surely an expedient and constructive distraction from the domestic re/disarrangement. I've read that siblings tend to become closer when their parents divorce, unless they are adults themselves and take sides. Children are often forced to rely on each other. Not us. Our parents' separation physically separated us, so it had its emotional toll as well. I saw my sister only briefly at night and almost never on the weekend.

Family lore likes to depict us as close and tight, which is true only if certain details are ignored. But that's true of all families. Mythology is part of the equation, no matter how much unconditional love goes around, because all families are dysfunctional. Tolstoy wrote that "All happy families are alike; each unhappy family is unhappy in its own way." I believe that all families are dysfunctional and all families are dysfunctional in their own way. But that's just me. Maybe I'm more jaded than most. What's likely true for all families is that family history is composed of fact *and* fiction. Also, many families create a Bermuda Triangle, whereby things are ignored or left unsaid and end up missing. But not entirely gone, either, just out there somewhere lost at sea.

My sister often got home from school after us. Some nights my mom and I would be in the middle of dinner before she finally arrived. With neither of them home during the day something had to be done with me. No one family member or sitter supplied that care. Multiple care-providers either stepped in or were roped in. Off I went from one day to the next, to one house and another. Monday I might be at Aunt Mary's; Tuesday, with a family friend; Wednesday was the hardest to book, it being a half-day so the Catholic kids from public schools could come to ours for religious study; Thursday might find me at cousin Angela's, while the week might conclude in someone's home I'd never been to before and would never be in again.

Leading such an itinerant existence solidified my outsider status. It was bad enough I came from the weird family with no father—even genuinely freaky TV families like the Munsters and the Addams Family had both parents at home!—but I also had to suffer further public humiliation when my Aunt Rosie or my Uncle Al waited outside the school to pick me up. While my friends raced home or jumped into school buses, I climbed into a different car every day, as if I were being abducted by a different predator. When I got to their homes I stayed indoors, day-dreaming and waiting it out, patiently biding my time, knowing that the next three hours would soon be over. With any luck, so would my childhood.

Wherever I stayed, playing outside wasn't an option. Normally, I'd rather be outdoors. But these weren't normal circumstances. Not being in any one place for any period of time put me in the awkward position of being the stranger in town, always the pseudo–new kid on the block. I'd show up one day, disappear, and then reappear three weeks later, or never again. I was not reliable play material. If the situation were reversed, I can't imagine that my friends and I would go out of our way to play with such a kid. We certainly wouldn't go looking for him or invite him to join us.

When I pulled up to someone's home, a welcoming committee wasn't exactly waiting for me. No boy stood in front of a house holding a bat and tossing a baseball into the air, surrounded by his friends pounding their gloves with their fists, all of them begging me to join them because they'd heard about my great hitting and fielding. What did occur as I sheepishly emerged from the cars were long stares from unfamiliar kids wondering what I was doing getting out of Mrs. Schapane's car, wearing a forest-green jacket, matching pants, white shirt, and red plaid tie. My school uniform alone would scare most kids away. That is, if they were around in the first place. Boys weren't exactly playing in front of the homes I was staying at. If I wanted to play with them I'd have to find them. That's unrealistic for the average six- or ten-year-old to do, let alone someone as timid as I was. And then there was always that one thing uppermost in my mind: If I did gather the courage to search for playmates, then once I found them I'd either have to explain why I was there or I'd have to lie, to a bunch of kids I might see less than five times a year or maybe just once. It just wasn't worth it. So I stayed indoors.

Inside as well, no one was around to play with. All of my cousins were older than I; some were nearly as old as my mother, both she and my father being the youngest of very large families. They either were away at college or had moved out; some had started families of their own. Then there were the single friends' homes and the childless couples' homes, along with the homes where the kids who lived in them magically vanished right before I arrived. It was like being involved in the Witness Protection Program where I had to be relocated periodically, or I was an insane criminal who had to be shipped to different cells, for my own protection and for the protection of the other inmates.

Actually, it was worse than prison. At least in prison they let you watch TV. I wasn't allowed to do that anywhere I was left, either because of the times (when adults heavily regulated how much children could watch) or because my mother urged the care-providers not to let me. There were never any toys to play with, either. I was supposed to be doing my homework. But I never did. I couldn't. I was too distracted by my situation, my homelessness, and so I must have begun living too much inside my head. My day-dreaming became my home. The simplest tasks were beyond me. I couldn't concentrate on memorizing a single multiplication table, including the easy ones like 2 and 5, let alone the complete oeuvre. I still stink at basic spelling, despite all of my schooling, as a result of those days. I gazed into space sitting in strange rooms, or stared at the pictures and posters hanging on the walls of a cousin's bedroom where I was told not to touch anything. "Your cousin Marilyn won't like it if she finds out you were playing with her things when she comes home from college this weekend."

I didn't always follow their orders. I would pick through drawers and dig around in closets in search of tangible distractions. Even I was incapable of day-dreaming for three solid hours. I might come across a stack of horror magazines buried in my cousin Andrew's closet, although the disfigured faces and twisted features of Lon Chaney Jr. and Peter Cushing upset me more than soothed me. To be honest, what I was really looking for were girlie magazines. Alas, the few searches I did conduct reaped no such rewards. On the whole, I did what I was told. I was quiet and never asked for anything.

My aunts and my mother's friends often told her that they sometimes forgot I was there. Good. That's the way I wanted it. I didn't want to seem like any trouble and run the risk of not returning to a home I'd been to before or going to a new one. Why I never returned to some of them after one stay is beyond me. I'm sure it wasn't anything I did. I was the Invisible Boy. I also vanished so I couldn't be reminded by whoever was watching me that I was there in the first place. I preferred to spend three hours lost in space alone in my cousin's room than deal with the reality of my Aunt Mary's company. No matter where I was, I'd sit in a room with the door closed, if permitted, and pretend to be studying. To bide my time I'd pick up a paperweight, a stapler, or an ashtray and turn them into rocket ships, dinosaurs, or race cars, surrounded by a cast of characters involved in adventures rivaling those of any movie or comic book. I might have had other options, but invisibility worked best for me. If I hadn't become an escapist, I think either my head or my heart would have exploded before I reached puberty.

The isolation and oddity of my week were amplified on the weekends. While my nomadic weekdays lasted until about the seventh grade (when my mom started letting me be home by myself after school), the unusual weekends lasted an additional two years. I spent every Saturday with my father and every Sunday with my mother and grandmother. My sister, who was furious at my dad, never joined me on Saturday. She also was old enough to opt out of the Sunday visits to my grandmother's from the start of my parents' separation.

On Saturdays, my father would pick me up at our (his former) house in the morning and drop me off at night, often way past my bedtime, which didn't sit too well with my mom. He always drove a convertible sports car, a different one practically every other month because they kept falling apart. March might be a yellow MG; June might be a white Austin-Healey, and October might be a sky-blue Mustang. None of the vehicles were of high quality. Their ripped canvas roofs leaked when it rained and in the winter they were so cold you could store ice cream in them, even as the noisy heaters cranked out tepid air. During any season, the engines often stalled or refused to start. A garage a few blocks from his apartment specialized in selling these doomed vehicles. Almost all of them required repeatedly pumping a choke, shaped like an old vending-machine knob, to start the engine. Almost every Saturday we'd have to stop by the garage for the mechanics to inspect a faulty knob, examine a rag-top stuck in mid-position, or tinker with an engine hemorrhaging oil.

My mother viewed them as deathtraps. At the very least, they posed as perilous "toys" that could lead to my potential disfigurement. I don't think she cared one way or another about his. She was always asking me about the cars. I could tell from her tone that they represented more than danger—they symbolized my father's irresponsibility and immaturity. To her, he'd become a cliché, the mid-life-crisis male who needs to drive a sports car. It also seemed silly to her that a man of below-modest means believed he could be a jet-setting playboy by driving clunkers, sports cars or not. I was too young to know or care what his motives were. It struck me as more comical than contemptible that he couldn't afford to be 007 or a member of the Rat Pack.

"That car is dangerous," I remember overhearing her shout at him over the phone. "What's your problem?" There was a pause as my father explained his problem. "Good," she snapped, responding to his promise to get rid of the latest "Christine." Sure enough, he'd show up the following Saturday in a "new" car, just as reliable and safe as the last one. We'd pull away as the tailpipe farted black, noxious exhaust. Left behind was a saucer-sized pool of oil the engine had drooled as the car idled while he waited for me to come out of the house.

When my father first started picking me up, he'd ring the door bell and come inside. After a few weeks of that he'd ring the bell and wait on the doorsteps. Eventually, he'd honk the car horn and wait for me curbside. During the first two phases, my sister never answered the door. She couldn't bear the sight of him. My mother always answered it as I ran around the house gathering my things. I was never ready the night before or that morning, which was atypical considering how my mother encouraged me and my sister to be punctual and "always be prepared," like the good Boy and Girl Scouts we were. I think she deliberately had me get ready at the last minute just so he'd have to wait. While phases one and two lasted, I could hear them bickering from my room upstairs as I stuffed my glove, a toy or two, and a change of clothes into a brown paper shopping bag. The arguing started almost as soon as he stepped inside, or, as phase one morphed into phase two, they talked through the screen door in the summer or a crack in the storm door in the winter. By the time I ran downstairs, they were engaged in a full-blown argument, either way. Only my arrival prevented it from developing into a full-fledged shout-fest. As I pushed past both of them or individually to get outside, my brief Saturday with my mother ended and my full Saturday with my father began. He would follow me out the door or start walking behind me from where he stood on the stoop. No matter which, the front door would slam with such force the blowback caused the screen or storm door to bounce around a few times before coming to rest.

These two periods didn't last long. After a few months, my father waited for me in his car. Like my sister, I guess my mother couldn't stand the sight of him anymore either. Now the creaky automobiles belched even more exhaust as they sat there idling for increasingly lengthy periods of time, leaving behind even larger pools of oil once we pulled away. The exhaust and oil grew as my mother forced him to wait for me longer as their separation dragged on. She always had something vitally important to tell me just as I was leaving. As their separation progressed from months to years, and as they talked less and less, and whenever they did it grew more and more cantankerous, the urgency and length of my mother's "last words" swelled. As a result, these essential discourses forced my father to keep the cars running for greater amounts of time, sometimes up to twenty minutes. He couldn't turn off any of them for fear they wouldn't restart. It was one thing for that to happen if we were at the park or coming out of a movie theater. But to have my mother see him jerking the choke knob or tinkering unsuccessfully with the engine—"He's no Uncle Sammy," she liked to say—would have been too much for him to bear.

As a rule, he'd cram into a day what he believed would have been a week's worth of activities and attention. In all likelihood, it amounted to more time than most fathers spent with their sons in a month. Big and small events were planned well in advance, depending on the weather. In the winter, we'd go sleigh riding at LaTourette Golf Course, the best and most popular hill (the tenth hole) on Staten Island for the fastest and longest run. There were several bumps and ridges along the sides for the more intrepid riders to test how much vertical leap they could create by approaching them with as much pluck and speed as possible. I typically lay sprawled on top of my dad, holding onto his jacket, while he steered our long, well-made wooden and metal sleigh. Between the two of us and the heavy sleigh, we generated a ton of speed once we got going, one of the fastest sleighs every time we were there. For us, there was a double challenge—not only that of attacking the ridges fearlessly to go as high and as far off the ground as anyone else but also to see how much we could push both extremes further before I might fall off. (I rarely did.) It was buckaroo sleigh riding at its finest. We'd also go ice skating on any number of ponds still in existence before the tract homes and strip malls devoured them.

In the summer, there were Mets games, horseback riding (Staten Island still had horse stables in the late '60s and early '70s), or playing catch at any number of the Island's parks. If the weather didn't cooperate, we went to a movie. No matter what the weather or the time of year, there was always a trip to a department or toy store where he'd buy me a rather expensive toy. That drove my mother nuts. She thought he was bribing me, perhaps even establishing some kind of secular confessional. As all good Catholics know, a trip to the confessional booth on Friday or Saturday absolves the confessor's sins in order for him to receive communion on

Sunday. Post-confession he's pure enough, despite his previous indiscretions and misdeeds, to receive the holy wafer. It also means the penitent starts off each week with a clean slate, so to speak. My father's shopping ritual, according to my mom, was similarly redemptive and purifying. She was certain he bought me toys so I would newly forgive him every week for leaving us while also inducing me to look forward to seeing him the following Saturday. The toy, therefore, not his abandonment, would become uppermost in my mind. She was probably right. There was some kind of motive behind the shopping junkets, to supplant his displacement with an expensive toy.

Toys or not, there was nothing to forget and forgive. Despite its having been his decision to leave us, I didn't find fault with him. For one thing, because nobody bothered explaining it to me, there was no information on which I could base a judgment. Perhaps that's why my parents withheld it, to spare me from choosing sides. What we had there was our usual family failure to communicate. Not talking in my family had become habit, not even a conscious decision. People simply didn't talk about important things. The pattern (or pathology, if you like) lasted for decades, and it continues. But it's hard to teach old dogs new tricks, as I've learned. Only when I was told that my sister and brother-in-law were separating did I learn they'd been having marital problems for years. As a child, I imagined I would have had to torture either one of my parents before they'd talk about their separation. Today, even torture wouldn't work, so obscured is it in their memories, I suspect. Whether then, or even now, it's not a matter of assigning fault. A little useful information would've been nice. When I was a child, I didn't care very much about that either. I had other cares and concerns.

What most concerned me was that I was the kid with no father, a standout. Maybe my mother was right about my father's spending sprees, that he was trying to buy my acceptance and love. Without them, the theory went, I'd hate him for turning me into that conspicuous child. But I didn't care. I had other things on my mind. Besides, the spending sprees probably had the opposite effect anyway. The weekly toys and compressed attention actually compounded my feelings of isolation. None of the other kids I knew were receiving such special treatment. That's why I never played with the toys my father bought me when I was around them. "Wow! Where'd you get that?" I could imagine someone asking me. Like me, all of my friends were from rather humble, working-class backgrounds. If my dad plunked down twenty-five bucks—a lot of money back then— for a battery-controlled airplane, for instance, it would be noticeable. I didn't want to be noticed—at least, not for that. It was obvious enough I wasn't around most weekends to play in an empty refrigerator box or pitch two nine-inning stickball games until my arm crumbled. Sharing some exotic toy would only highlight my absence and what I was missing. I would have traded in a second all of those high-priced toys and Mets tickets for routine, "normal" playing time with my friends.

Whether my father was bribing me or whether my mother was being paranoid about the possibility made no difference to me. I was so busy simply trying to survive my childhood I didn't care who was more or less liable. Upon reflection, I probably blamed *both* of them with equal amounts of intensity for not working out their crap. They both had a hand in making me feel like an oddball, in my opinion. Today, kids from dysfunctional families have plenty of friends and confederates who come from broken homes. Not in my day. Our broken home was busted before it became commonplace. Despite my family's efforts to pretend we were normal, we clearly weren't. No other kid spent every Saturday with his dad and every Sunday with his mom. (I'll get to that in a minute.) So self-conscious was I about my father's not living with us, along with my spending Saturdays with him away from home, that I lied about it. Why not? My mother lied to her own father about it. She could fool him, easily enough, as he slipped toward dementia. It was a lot harder for me. When I said stuff to my friends like, "Yeah, I know I said I would play ball, but my family made me go with them to the Poconos for the day," I wasn't fooling anybody. They all knew, especially when I showed up to church each Sunday with blood-red lips and finger nails.

Unless we ate out for dinner, which was rare, every meal with my father was the same. He prepared all of my favorite foods, as if I were on death row. Every Saturday night it was steak, frozen french fries, string beans, and chocolate pudding or strawberry Junket for dessert. For my "appetizer" he'd break out a large bag of pistachio nuts, dyed red, the only kind available at the time. I was a nail-biter, so I was incapable of opening all of them with my fingers. Shells with hair-strand gaps had to be pried open with my mouth. Pistachio nuts were quite an expensive luxury in those days, unlike now where they can be bought inexpensively in bulk in chain drugstores, which explains why they're so damned bland. Back then, I knew what a costly, tasty treat they were. I figured he'd had to capture a lot of bad guys to be able to buy them, so I didn't waste a single one. No matter how many times I washed my hands and face, it took nearly forty-eight hours for the dye to come off. As a consequence, the next morning in church—if Dougie and I stuck around long enough to attend—my stained fingertips and lips announced to my friends and other parishioners that I'd been with my father.

"What happened to you?" I was asked. I always said I'd eaten too many pistachio nuts the night before at *home*, or in the Poconos during a family outing. Everyone knew my parents weren't together and that I'd spent Saturday with my father, but I told them otherwise, as if I hadn't been alone with him all day. As long as they kept asking, I kept lying. And they kept asking. Relentlessly. Looking back on it, I realize that some people simply liked to make me squirm, zeroing in on my vulnerabilities and watching me come undone. Eventually, most stopped asking why I showed up to church looking like a vampire. It wasn't that I didn't enjoy being with my father. I just knew that any break from "normal" family practices compounded the odds of my standing out even further. Bloody Sunday exposed it for all to see, which they did, and I knew they did. But it didn't stop me from lying. I knew that they knew I was lying. I suspect knowing that they knew furthered my unease about what I was lying about. It was fitting, though, that Sundays typically started out that way. The rest of the day was typically downright awful.

Every Sunday afternoon my mother kidnapped me to go see my grandmother for the day. It was bad enough I had to be in church in the morning, unless I skipped out with Dougie. I then had to spend most, if not all, of the afternoon at my grandmother's. If I prayed at all in church I'm sure I prayed for our car to be stolen or to learn that my grandmother had moved back to Italy during church services. If not, I'd be in for the most boring four or five hours of my life—that is, until the following Sunday.

St. Charles students were supposed to attend the 8:00 or 9:00 Mass. Several rows in the front were reserved for us. My mother insisted I follow this requirement, while she attended a later Mass. I actually preferred the early morning service. By attending such an early one, at least I'd be out playing with my friends by 10:00 or so, depending on how many papers I could deliver by 8:00 when the route was mine alone. No matter what time I started playing, the fun never lasted long. By around 12:30 it was over.

Every Sunday morning as I scampered around the house looking for whatever piece of paraphernalia I needed to play with, my mother reminded me to be home by noon so we could drive over to see my grandmother. I never was. She always had to come looking for me. She'd be furious with me for not coming home on time, even though it didn't take long to find me. I knew better than to be playing in any of the schoolyards. If she had to search for me in those more remote places, she'd have been further irritated. I usually could be found just around the corner on David "Santa's" large, hilly front lawn or in Timmy "Pee-Pocket's" side-yard sandbox. I never offered that we should play in my yard—it would have been too easy for her to find me. After driving to a couple of houses searching for me, she'd pull up to Cracker's house and see me whipping around a giant oak tree avoiding being "it" during a spirited game of tag.

"Get over here," she'd shout from the car. I'd freeze in place. I pretended to be surprised that she'd had to come for me.

"Do you know what time it is, young man?" she'd ask, as I sheepishly approached the car.

"I guess it's after twelve."

"You guessed right. Try 'many minutes after twelve.' Nearly thirty. To be exact. Now get in the car." As I did, she gave me the once-over, from top to bottom. Something was missing. Something was always missing. "Where are your things? Where's your jacket? Didn't you leave home this morning wearing a jacket?"

I'd point to the back yard or inside the house or wherever I'd dropped my things off in my mad rush to get in as much play time as possible.

"Well, you'd better go get it." I'd jump out of the car. Behind me, as the door shut, I'd hear her shout, "Hurry up about it. We're late as it is."

It was never late enough. This scenario and its accompanying charade occurred every Sunday. It was practically scripted, right down to the dialogue. I *felt* the same way every Sunday too. I didn't want to leave my friends. I didn't want to spend the second day of my weekend with my other parent. What exactly had I done wrong to deserve such a fate? I wondered. I would sit in the car silently, speculating on any number of other gloomy things: feeling singled out, how long we'd have to stay at my grandmother's—three, four, five hours?—and whether my mother was doing this to make some sort of statement, to have me to herself following the day my father did. If my father was going to spend all of Saturday with me, then she'd do the same on Sunday. It was a chess game between bitter rivals, and I was one of the pieces, the clichéd pawn. Couldn't she find a speedier, more exacting form of revenge targeted directly at *him*, like stealing his newspaper and soaking it in a muddy puddle? It's what I would have done. End of story. If she was mad at him—and she had every right to be—why did I have to get caught up or ensnared in her anger?

My grandparents lived in a one-bedroom apartment above my Uncle Sammy. My grandmother lived there alone after my grandfather died, which happened less than two years after my parents separated. Whenever we visited my grandmother, my Uncle Sammy always answered the door—sort of. Occasionally it cracked open as soon as we stepped out of the car. We would let ourselves in, and as we ascended the steps to my grandmother's we'd hear the door slam shut behind us. It was his way of demonstrating to my mom how much he disapproved of her as a "fallen woman." His mood occasionally swung so far south that it was sometimes beneath him to escort her in or to say "Hello" to her, or to me. In addition to the rudeness, it was positively spooky watching the door open slightly and inching to rest, with nobody behind it, only to close again once we were inside, with still no one visible causing it to happen. It was like something out of a horror movie, the moment when a creaky haunted castle door lures visitors into *the* room where the psychopath awaits.

Uncle Sammy may have been suffering from PTSD, but he was no Norman Bates. He was no Casper the Friendly Host either. He probably sat by the window 24/7, vigilantly keeping an eye on things, especially his precious property. I imagined him sitting there holding a shotgun, ready to blast anyone who looked suspicious or who took one step onto his beloved tiny front lawn. No golf course looked as pristine. In addition to his immaculate lawn, he had the most exquisite hedges, which, admittedly, were *Better Homes & Gardens*–perfect. He was always yelling at me to stay off the lawn and not to go anywhere near his hedges. If he'd lived in Oakwood Heights he would have been a prime candidate for our shenanigans, although he was more certifiably insane about his property than anyone in Oakwood. When the family held barbecues at his place he proudly displayed a bucket of balls and a box of toys taken from the neighbors' kids whose things had drifted into his yard. He turned absolutely giddy while describing how he confiscated their things as he ignored their pleas to return a miniature football or roll a Tonka Toy Cement Mixer back across the yard. If he could've gotten away with it I bet he would have enjoyed smashing their toys with the baseball bat he carried in the trunk of his car. As I sat at some of those family outings, I often wondered what he'd have done to *us* if he ever caught me or Crackers flinging ourselves into his hedges to catch a tennis ball. Who knows what somebody like him was capable of doing? I imagined one of our heads mounted on his wall, the other placed on a pike behind the Horror Door, a warning to any future transgressors. As it was, in all of the years I went there he never once bothered playing catch with me with one of those impounded balls. In fact, when we were visiting my grandmother he never even bothered coming upstairs. His disapproval of our "family" began as soon as we arrived, either by his avoiding meeting us at the door or his answering it as if we were strangers. When he did come to the door, he barely acknowledged our presence.

"Don't just stand there," my mother would say, nudging me. "Shake Uncle Sammy's hand." Like my mother's kidnappings, this was another routine carried out almost on a weekly basis. I stuck my hand into the open air. He barely put his out in return. I had to find it as it dangled limply by his side. When I did catch it, it was like shaking hands with a dead fish. He'd withdraw it with equal indifference. He'd stand aside and reach over one of us and push open the door behind us to my grandmother's apartment, which was accessible through the tiny hallway entrance. As we shimmied past him, he would inform my mom who was already there and who might be coming later. He was the gatekeeper and the clearing station.

"Rosie is upstairs. Muffy said she'd be here about three."

"Oh, good," my mother would say cheerfully. "Thank you. It'll be good to see Rosie." She was always so pleasant around him, possibly to show him that his surliness toward us didn't bother her. More likely, though, she was practicing a belief she extolled throughout my life: Never reveal to others how you feel, even if they are mistreating you or behaving poorly. Better to smile in their faces and never let on that you're miserable or suffering because of them. It may seem like some quasi-Zen tactic, or the manifestation of Jesus's dictum about turning the other cheek, a genuinely grand and cosmic approach to interacting with other humans. I'm all for a philosophy of life. We sometimes have to get along for the sake of getting on.

There is one large problem with this, of not expressing your opinions or feelings while behaving and acting in a contradictory manner to disguise those feelings, as I later discovered. It ties in perfectly with our family motto: Don't disclose too much information to anyone about yourself, including your emotional states. You see, it can be incredibly frustrating and unproductive not to do that. If you don't inform someone that he is making you unhappy or that he is behaving like a dick, that person will continue making you unhappy and continue behaving like a dick. Then you end up resenting him even more for not recognizing what a dick he is, or at least not recognizing that you think he's behaving like a dick, and how you're suffering as a result. Going out of your way to prove how wonderful it is to be around them, to show what little effect their behavior has on you, exacerbates the situation. Now they get the opposite impression. They may think their dickishness actually makes you happy, so why would they stop being a dick? Hell, they might even become bigger dicks. On and on it goes. And the resentment deepens. Ultimately, there's no calming effect to it. In all likelihood, the opposite is true. In the less cosmic arena of day-to-day living, and living among such blowhards as my Uncle Sammy, all of that bitterness builds up inside a person, either developing into some kind of mental funk or even into a life-threatening disease. Or it gets displaced and redirected toward the wrong person, an innocent bystander, like siblings, wives, husbands, and children, the "kick the dog after a hard day at work" syndrome. My mother never needed to redirect her suffering toward me. I was suffering plenty all on my own having to be at my grandmother's every damn Sunday.

Uncle Sammy's appearance (or disappearance) at the front door is the start of a painful afternoon. As I climb the long, narrow staircase, which might take my eighty-eight-year-old grandmother ten minutes to accomplish, I consider racing back down, blowing past the android at the bottom, and launching out of the door. I'd run somewhere, anywhere, but somewhere other than here.

There is a cramped kitchen in my grandmother's apartment, made even smaller because there's a washing machine in it. I sit at an old-fashioned metal kitchen table, with two pull-out utility drawers, which I'm not allowed to open. (Clearly they know that if I have access to the utensils, I might pull out a knife and slit my wrists.) I'm with my mother, grandmother, and aunts. It's all women. No other cousins are there or anyone under thirty. It is all grown-up talk and gossip about people they know, and I don't. I understand even less of it than when my grandmother, who barely speaks more than fifty words of English, talks. I start fiddling with the salt and pepper shakers, drifting. I pretend they're gladiators and start slapping them together.

"Stop that!" my mother says, slapping my wrist. "Can't you see you're annoying everyone? Can't you sit still for five seconds?"

You must be kidding. I've been sitting still for nearly an hour. I'm an eight-year-old boy. I'm not genetically programmed to sit still for this long. It's a beautiful spring day outside and I'm cooped up inside with a bunch of old ladies. I got news for you: This is worse than school. At least there I'm bored with other kids who are bored. That's collective boredom. This is the solitary kind. Actually, I'd rather be alone. I'd settle for solitary confinement in prison. I think it would be an improvement. I'm getting rather used to that. Why don't you at least let me watch TV? A half an hour is all I'd ask. Daddy lets me watch TV when I'm with him. Okay, I know not to bring that up. That won't work to my advantage. And you never let me bring any toys, either. "It's rude," you say, playing with my toys or watching TV. It's about spending quality time "with your grandmother." Sure, she's a sweet, benevolent woman; a kinder soul can't be found on earth. But she's nearly ninety, obese to the point of immobility, and slipping into senility. She sits there smiling at me, and nodding her head once in a while, which is awkward and uncomfortable. I grin and nod back to her. She smiles and nods some more back at me. It's positively zoo-like. On occasion, she pats my hand. I bet she knows how awful it is for me to sit at this table for three or four hours. She's consoling me. Really, what's the point of my being here? Why can't I be with my friends? Why does everything have to be so unusual and uncomfortable for me? What did I do?

I stare out the window. Under the table, my mother pinches my leg, bringing me back to the scene of the crime. I'm not permitted to daydream either. It's the equivalent of playing with my toys or watching TV. I'm required to be interested in what's being said around the table, even if I have to fake it. I wish it would rain. I wish it would rain like hell, hellish rain with howling winds that would blow the roof off the house and carry us all into the flooding streets. It would break the monotony. I stare out the window again. Not a cloud in the sky. No chance of Armageddon this week. My mother taps my foot with hers a couple of times. She has an array of weapons. I don't need to look at her. I turn my attention to the table, smile, and nod my head at my grandmother, who does the same.

There's always a bowl of pasta with sausage and meatballs sitting on the stove for any visitors. I have some. Everyone teases me about how I really came for the meatballs and not to see my grandmother. I don't have the heart to tell them, "Neither." The meatballs are tasteless mush-meat. Because of my grandmother's through-the-roof high blood pressure, and some of my aunts' predisposition toward colitis, they're made with no herbs and little, if any, salt and pepper, as is the sauce. It's nondescript red and brown stuff. (How many Italian-American families make meatballs and sauce like this? Even the traditional fare is blandly offputting.) I chew on the cardboard. I grin through my stuffed mouth and swallow, although I could use some liquid to wash it down, except I'm not permitted to drink anything while I'm eating—it'll spoil the flavor of the food and my appetite. As if my appetite—for any of this!—could be any further spoiled.

"The meatballs *are* good," I say. They all laugh. "Ma," someone says, turning to my grandmother, "David isn't really here to see you. Here's here for the meatballs." I'm still grinning. She smiles back at me. She probably didn't understand what was said other than "David," so she strokes my face. Despite her tender gesture, I want to say, "I'm only here because I was forced to. For God's sake, you're the matriarch of the family. Do something!" I turn to my mom, hoping to impart a look of anxious weariness: "Let's go," my face begs. If we leave now, part of the day might be salvaged. There might be some daylight left when we get home. If it's an overcast winter afternoon, the day is already lost, so I don't bother shooting her the look. I'm resigned to my fate. I know this as soon as we arrive. We typically stay at my grandmother's until nearly five, later if right before we're leaving someone else shows up to visit. My mother always feels compelled to stay, to be polite. If I roll my eyes or show any signs of impatience I hear about it on the ride home. While she scolds me, I barely listen. Another Sunday has vanished.

I have vivid memories of those Sundays at my grandmother's, as I do the Saturdays with my father, and the weekdays with whoever was forced to watch me. I can even recall some of the finer details of the homes I went to only once. Much of my childhood can be replayed lavishly and clearly in my mind, like hitting the rewind button on a VCR. It probably has a lot to do with my outsider status. I became a vigilant observer at an early age. Wherever I was—even when playing with my friends—I always felt as if I were on the outside looking in, as if I were viewing my own experiences even while taking part in them. I became an involuntary recording device as a child. Left behind are trace elements for me to examine now, much of it in high definition and resolution.

On the other hand, I remember almost nothing about school, except for the trouble I started getting into. The rest is a blank. I had a lay teacher in third grade named Mrs. Delaney. She had dark hair and an aquiline nose. I remember nothing else. I can't call up a single memory of sitting in her classroom. Fourth and fifth grades are no different. It's like I wasn't there. In many ways, I wasn't. I learned nothing. That much I know. I became more withdrawn in school than in the strange homes I visited. I wasn't a troublemaker—at least not until the seventh grade, following a handful of harmless missteps in the sixth. For the most part, teachers leave me alone because I'm academically incompetent. It's the script they all seem to follow. They will pay greater attention to me when I begin to get into more serious trouble. I'm practically the center of attention in eighth grade, when I become a leading troublemaker, not coincidentally the year my father returned.

As with the later robberies, I'm really not looking for the attention. I don't know what I'm looking for. And I don't know what's come over me. I'm still not learning anything, except by eighth grade I have a sense that what I'm supposed to be learning is a bunch of B.S. anyway. The teachers don't know what they're doing. It's all rote and regurgitation and mindless busy-work, topped off with healthy doses of punishment. What we learn is used to measure us, to separate us from one another. Because I don't add up academically, I feel like I'm on the outside looking in, as I often do. From my point of view, the entire process reeks of ridiculousness. How can anyone expect fifty ten-year-olds, half of them boys, to sit still for four straight hours, eat lunch, and sit still for another two and a half hours, all the while having nonsense shoved down their throats? I began to take notice that at St. Charles instruction occurs to expose our ignorance and illiteracy rather than to facilitate our learning and advance our literacy. Sometime around sixth grade I began to actively resist the spoon-fed material rather than blindly accept it. I didn't even fake interest or show signs of uninterest. I was probably, in fact, on a mission to demonstrate just how goddamned idiotic I thought it all was by flaunting my indifference. As a result, I fell further and further behind my classmates. Unwittingly, I began to resent my own inadequacies, without understanding why. I certainly didn't take responsibility for them, as I should have. Instead, I acted out more and more by talking back to my teachers, to the point of telling Sister Marcella, my eighth-grade teacher, that I wasn't doing her "stupid" in-class reading because it was "boring junk" and "not worth my time." She sent me to the principal's office. In minutes I was suspended for either the second or third time.

Many of the teachers at St. Charles had no business teaching, especially the nuns. Our senile, borderline demented sixth-grade teacher sometimes fell asleep behind her desk, her false teeth rattling around in her mouth. She looked simultaneously helpless and preposterous. She wore her wimple too tightly on her face and it pressed her wrinkled skin together like a deflated, shriveled balloon. Sometimes she snored. Nobody woke her up. We welcomed the break from the dreary routine. Besides, she likely would have punished the person who did because doing so would have violated her rule that we were never to come to her desk without being invited. I was maturing, but only chronologically. I began to lose respect for teachers by the sixth grade, authority figures and adults generally. In addition to my being a poor student academically, the stirrings of misbehavior kicked in. It was the double whammy. It was bad enough that my parents had to hear from my teachers about my academic deficiencies. Starting in the sixth grade they began to hear about a handful of behavioral misdemeanors, which escalated in the seventh grade and grew into full-fledged misdeeds in the eighth. Neither one of them knew what to do or say. By the middle of eighth grade, they're back together, so they devote their time and energies to working things out between them, as they should have. Unlike in the further past, when I was unconsciously overlooked, I was consciously disregarded, perhaps a lost cause. My confusion about myself, leading to awful grades and bad conduct, must have made them wish they could separate *me* from the family.

As far as my schoolwork went, I don't know what my parents expected under the circumstances. When they were separated, my father spent zero time going over my schoolwork with me, not with what little time we had together. He wanted to make it as fun as possible, not have our few hours saddled by boosting my vocabulary or helping me know the difference between the numerator and the denominator. During the week, my mother was too exhausted every evening from working all day to assume any kind of instructional role. I also think she was worn down by the pressure and societal implications of being a single mother in an uptight, intolerant family, community, and, quite frankly, nation. I can't recall a single instance when she insisted I work with her on my school assignments. I don't remember her checking to see if I had done my schoolwork. I never once remember my sister's helping me either. I'm sure on occasion she did, as did my mother. But here again I may have been too distracted for their help to have made a dent in my academic development, let alone in my memory. I usually sat in my room pretending to do my schoolwork or I lied about already having done it at So-and-So's house earlier in the day. My mother had the luxury of not needing to coax my sister into doing her schoolwork because she was a proficient student throughout most of her youth and teens. She had been left to her own druthers and it had worked for her. Maybe my mother believed the same could be done with me.

But my track record indicated that being left on my own wasn't a winning strategy. My mother had to have noticed, especially after my nearly getting left back in the second grade, that I wasn't anything at all like my sister, unless I simply fell under the radar because my mother became too busy and too distressed working out her own issues to help me with mine. Honestly, I wish there was a more delicate way of putting this, but there isn't: I think she had limited, if any, faith in my intellectual abilities. She may have even started to believe, throughout my youth, that I was far from being a "gifted" student. Perhaps she even had reached the ultimate critical conclusion: I may have been seen as good old-fashioned dumb. In my youth and much of my adolescence, I did very little academically to dispel her opinion of my woeful mental abilities. After the second grade I wasn't failing subjects, but neither was I doing well in any of them. I was barely getting by. "Barely getting by" was enough for someone like me. It was better than "not getting by." Whether she was more depressed than she led on, causing her to ignore my formal education, or she simply believed I didn't have what it took to be successful in school, or a combination of the two, she gave up on me as a "good student" at a rather young age, long before the behavioral stuff kicked in.

I have no idea what my father thought. As usual, he was a sphinx. He rarely expressed his opinions about anything, and a person couldn't tell what he was thinking. Maybe being a cop all of those years had taught him to be emotionless in the face of consequential events and decisions, so there was nothing to express anyway. He never said anything one way or the other about my early schooling, either when he was living apart from us or when he was living with us. That reticence continued throughout my life, except once when he strongly objected to my accepting a scholarship to graduate school to study English. There was a time when I was a senior in high school when it seemed he favored my desire to attend a four-year college. He drove me to a local New Jersey school to check out its campus, before the decision had been made to send me to Johnson & Wales. Perhaps that trip was his way of telling me he supported me, without having actually to tell me (which he didn't). It made no difference. Apparently, the decision was in my mother's hands, because off I went to a two-year college after graduation from high school. Throughout my life they discouraged my academic ambitions. It pains me to think of my parents that way, how dismissive they were regarding my academic development. At least one good thing came out of it. It has guided my teaching practices, in a reverse psychology sort of way. I avoided treating my students apathetically in their academic development, whoever they are, "gifted" or "nongifted." In fact, I think I've inspired a few of those "nongifted" or underachieving students to realize their intellectual potential. Because of my parents' destructive views about mine, maybe I became a better teacher as a result—or in spite of it.

Regardless of my parents' perception of me academically, I take full responsibility for my succession of early school failures. Clearly, I was unmotivated and unfocused. While this is particularly true of my years at St. Charles, it wasn't much different during my first two and a half years in high school. I can't recall a single thing about my freshman year, except

for my fears, and absolutely nothing at all about my sophomore year. I'd
have to look at my transcripts to know what subjects I took. I haven't a
clue who any of my teachers were. I was on the academic, Regents track
rather than the non-academic one. (I think New York state remains to this
day the only one that awards a Regents diploma.) I know I was on the
academic track because I wasn't taking "shop" classes, assigned to students
who weren't. I'm guessing children who came from private schools were
automatically placed in the academic core curriculum, perhaps because
administrators assumed anyone who attended a parochial school must have
received a good education. I certainly didn't deserve to be in such a fast
academic track, based on my history at St. Charles.

To stay in the academic program a student had to pass all of the Regents exams, equivalent to mini-SATs for each subject. I scored a 65 on
the biology test and was always in danger of falling out of the academic
program because of my poor test scores—that is, until I got shot. I think
if I hadn't been shot, I eventually would've found myself making nap-
kin holders and fixing carburetors. Something tells me my parents were
unaware of the dual tracks because they saw me as a primary candidate
for those shop classes rather than for the academic ones. As they saw it,
my destiny involved working with my hands, not with my head, a rather
common belief among most in my working-class circle about the "fate" of
males. That ideology was even more ingrained after I was shot. It became
official doctrine.

It's not as if before the shooting I was this horrific student, drooling
into my workbooks, or a passionate troublemaker, planting stink bombs
in the nunnery, although the thought may have occurred to me more
than once. In high school I was mostly a ghost. I never got into trouble
there. Socially, I was neither a popular nor an unpopular kid. I was simply
passing time and passing through. Granted, until my junior year, I didn't
give two shits about the place academically. But neither was I considered
an ignoramus. I was the classic underachiever. I think both my social and
intellectual apathy had much to do with all of my friends' attending a
different high school. I was supposed to be there, too, but my parents lied
about where we lived in order to send me to the newly built high school
ten miles away, rather than send me to the one within walking distance
from our house. Somehow, they convinced school officials we lived on
the opposite side of Guyon Avenue, the geographical dividing line that
determined where a child went to high school. Kids living east of Guyon
attended New Dorp High School while those living west of it attended
Tottenville High School. My parents either used someone else's address or

my dad pulled a few strings, a practice not uncommon among New York City cops. Dougie, who lived around the block from me, and all of my friends went to New Dorp, as I should have based on the criteria. But my parents believed I needed to be separated from them, especially Dougie. According to my folks, the two of us were devolving into a highly problematic and volatile pair. Based on the robberies we committed two years after we were separated, it's evident it was a very effective plan.

The old Tottenville High School was a modest-sized brick building that looked like a nineteenth-century textile factory. It was so overcrowded that half of the students attended morning sessions and the other half attended afternoon sessions. The new school was built to house the tidal wave of kids who had moved to Staten Island from other parts of the city right after the Verrazano-Narrows Bridge was built. The new school was massive. Nearly 5,000 students attended it that first year. My freshman class, which was the first to graduate, comprised nearly 1,200 students. In an attempt to be modern, bureaucratically efficient, and economically prudent, the building was architecturally ugly as all hell. The entire structure was constructed out of cement, including the seating areas. It looked like a prison from the future. In fact, it looked like the ghetto housing complex that the sinister Alec lived in from the film *A Clockwork Orange*.

My best friend at Tottenville High School was Stephen Malloy, a St. Charles classmate, who was too wild even for my tastes. We hung out together between classes smoking cigarettes, which was about the extent of our relationship. Stephen started palling around with a rough, older crowd as soon as he set foot on the school's grounds—cutting classes, doing lots of drugs, and being a full-time "Juvie." Truant officers and undercover narcs were always pursuing him. He was one of the most popular kids in school, despite his troubles, or possibly because of them. He wasn't much of a bully, even though he had the strength to be one, and he rarely picked on other kids. He did more harm to himself, just like me. Maybe that explains why we got along so well. He was naturally athletic and extraordinarily good-looking. In seventh grade the girls passed around a note asking which of all of the boys in the class they would most want to kiss. All but one of twenty-five wrote Stephen's name. I think one wrote Dougie's. Stephen was even more desirable in high school. But he was a lost soul his whole life. (I've often wondered if he was gay, an impossible position to be in at that time considering Staten Island's fanatical homophobia, and the nation's.) He was the closest thing I had to a friend in high school, which I guess isn't saying much. Sharing cigarettes and a few laughs with someone isn't terribly evocative. But maybe that's about as profound as it gets with most male teenagers, or males generally, the extent of our emotional connections with one another being threadbare. Unless it was just me, wandering through my first couple of years of high school, content to be anonymous and disconnected. It was, after all, what I was accustomed to.

It was easy to get lost in such a large school. I made no new friends there. Other than Stephen, I mostly talked only to old St. Charles class-mates, like Jay—Pooh-Stain—Ruane. I went on only one date, right after I was shot, which went horribly. In a school of 5,000 students I was a lonely outsider, not identified in any way with any particular clique. I did float in and out of a few. I played football in my sophomore year, but I wasn't a jock; I smoked weed, but I wasn't a stoner; I wasn't into any particular genre of music, so I wasn't a Dead Head or a Glitter Queen (rabid David Bowie fan); I didn't belong to any clubs or organizations because I wasn't a joiner, and I sure as hell wasn't smart enough to hang around the various gaggles of smart kids who kept to themselves. I guess I didn't know where the fuck I belonged because I didn't know who the fuck I was. It didn't help that I didn't feel as if I belonged there at all, and technically I didn't. Once again my parents had shuttled me to somewhere other than where I was supposed to be. Other than a fleeting memory or two of getting high at the handball courts or in a wooded area near the school, I have no idea what I did there. I can't even picture those kids whom I smoked jays with, faceless and nameless, just like the nameless and faceless teachers I encountered. But that all changed in a hurry when I was shot, for the better. At least it did for me. For those closest to me, it cemented their worst impressions of me or deepened them.

In my senior year at Tottenville I had a 98 average. As mentioned before, I was enrolled in an AP Calculus class and hit a homerun on my physics Regents. I was even impressed with myself—but not for long. No one in my family acknowledged the transformation or how far I had come from that rainy night in just a few months. I didn't help my own cause, either, when it came to honoring the distance I already had trav-eled. It never occurred to me to celebrate, let alone embrace, the degree of time and effort I was putting into my school work and putting into my*self*, to find some self-worth and value in just how much I'd changed in a few months. I had almost died. I was "lucky," so I thought, to have had a second chance and to be doing so well. Part of my epiphany that night in the ER involved recognizing the need to re-educate myself, and I knew that a major piece of that undertaking would require books, and lots of them. Lying on the gurney that night, I actually saw them stacked in rows piled ceiling-high and spilling out the windows and doors. It sounds crazy, I know, as if I'm making it all up because it fits the *Shot Story* arch, the thug-turned-professor. I know all about poetic license, even when it comes to nonfiction. It's not that either. The vision of books in the ER is true. About that night, I remember *everything*. I also remember thinking that while I would be the greatest autodidact in the history of the world, I wanted to be more formally educated too.

I had had three synchronic revelations that night in the ER, one of which involved my re-education. I knew that if I ever came out the other side alive I would immerse myself in books like a medieval monk. I would join the Order of the Word all on my own, and pull myself up by my intellectual bootstraps. In addition, a *very* formal education of some kind was also a big part of the vision. I saw myself attending college for a long time, even though up until then I was anything but college material. When I did come out the other side, I was willing to do whatever it took to obtain the best formal education possible. I knew in my heart and soul I could thrive in the best colleges and major in any subject and succeed. My first thought was to become a medical doctor, to some day save lives, just as my doctor had saved mine. From then on, my formal education was never about acquiring a piece of paper, of moving up the socioeconomic ladder. It's never been about that. It's always been a matter of life and death.

But it wasn't to be, at least not right away. I was discouraged from going to college. My parents dissuaded me from attending four-year schools and instead persuaded me to attend a trade school. They even called in reinforcements to convince me. History repeated itself. I was discouraged from pursuing my formal education throughout my life. My earlier track record marked me as academically inferior to those who knew me best and who had the most influence over me. The countless hours I sat day-dreaming in class and toying with staplers and pencils in my cousins' rooms caught up to me. My past prevented me from reinventing my future, which altered my present plans. Casting a giant shadow over all of it is my having been shot during an attempted robbery. The shame of being shot during a hold-up made me vulnerable to how *they* wanted me to turn out. But coming so close to death was the very thing that changed me. However, it was the Great Unmentionable. I couldn't raise the specter of that night as the driving force behind my seeking to become someone other than who I was. And what I wanted to be. To my family, my life was already over. They spent the next twenty years trying to dictate how it was, right up until I was months away from obtaining my Ph.D., when my mother urged me to take the New York City Sanitation Department test.

7

It's a Mad, Mad, Sad World

I share the ICU room with two other patients. The one next to me is old and shriveled. He's skeletal, including his head, which looks like a skull on a cadaver. He reminds me of the Crypt Keeper. I'm thinking he's suffered a massive coronary, after a protracted illness. He looks hideous. He's never conscious the two days he's here, although my peripheral vision is limited, so for all I know he may have opened his eyes a couple of times. I still can't see much more than the ceiling and directly in front of me, my bed tilted upward at about a 45-degree angle. I'm immobilized. It's like I never left the old woman's lawn. Across from me, the bed aligned perpendicular to mine, is a mummy. He's so wrapped in bandages I can't tell how old he is. He was in a horrible car crash—multiple vehicles, gnarled metal, twisted bodies, flames, the works: a real Hollywood production. He's more carefully monitored than I or the Keeper.

After being here for two days I can finally turn my head enough to see a glass-enclosed nurses' station back toward my left. Sometimes two nurses sit there. One is present at all times. Before I could see it, I knew something elaborately medical existed behind me. I can hear the repetitious bleeps and irregular gulps of machines tracking our bodies, and once when a steady mechanical screeching woke me in the middle of the night a nurse rushed past me to take care of the old guy. The next day he dies. Periodically, the nurses come in to adjust the tubes jutting out of the Mummy. Far more tubes stick out of him than me. The Keeper has a lot too, but I can't see him well enough to know who's got more between the two of them. I count three attached to me: the IV fastened to my left wrist, the thin tube poking into my upper sternum, and the plumbing-sized tube inserted into the middle of my right ribcage. On the morning of the third day, the day before I'm moved from the ICU to a standard room, the doctor has to distract me when he pulls out the large side tube.

"So," he begins, inching closer to the bed once he's looked at my chart, "how are you this morning?" He has a foreign accent. I'm guessing eastern European. I tell him I'm fine. There's a long pause.

Out of nowhere, he asks, "Tell me, what kind of girls do you like?"

"Girls?" I ask, unsure of where this is heading. There are two younger doctors with him and one of the nurses from the station. They look at me and smile.

"Yeah, girls," he continues, now taking hold of the tube. "You know, what's your variety, your type: blondes with big breasts—excuse me, nurse [she waves him off]—brunettes with long legs. Maybe you're a man of the buttocks. You tell me."

What the hell is a "man of the buttocks"? Is this guy for real? One of the other doctors laughs. "You mean an 'ass man,'" he corrects him. "Oh, yes, of course," the older doctor says, "an ass man. Are you one of them?"

I decide to play along. It's actually becoming quite amusing. "Well, let me think," I begin, "I don't think I'm a 'buttocks man,'" I say, smirking at him. "Maybe I'm more of a . . . ." But there's no chance to complete the sentence. Subtly, without my noticing, he has placed his left hand on my chest. In an instant he presses down with it as if I need to be restrained. Then, with as much force as someone yanking the cord on a lawn mower that won't start, he pulls out the tube with his right hand. I feel as if I've been kicked by a horse, but not just anywhere. It feels as if it's kicked me everywhere, from head to toe. Pulling it out creates such a body blow it renders me incapable of even crying out. I utter something approximating a thunderous moan.

The distress is so pervasive and rapid it takes a while for my brain to comprehend it and catch up to it. When it does, the pain is so severe I wish I could pass out, which I almost do. But I don't. It goes away after a couple of minutes. Suddenly, I need to sit up, as if my diaphragm is compelling me, as I take big gulps of air. As I do, I see the doctor smiling at me, holding on to the tube like a prized sausage. He's tricked me, and he's proud of it. I can't really smile back at him. I'm still undergoing a hefty coughing fit, but he can see from the expression on my face that I'm grateful he made me contemplate whether I was a man of the buttocks. As the panting subsidies, I notice the Mummy, motionless as a corpse. He hasn't moved one iota through all of this. Sure, I'm suffering, but at least I can feel pain.

That poor soul hasn't stirred once the whole time I've been here. He seems as good as dead. It's different for me, I tell myself. I'm certain I'm going to make it out of here alive.

Every time I look at the Mummy I think of the concluding hospital scene in *It's a Mad, Mad, Mad, Mad World*. It's a marathon comedy with a marvelous cast of vaudeville and Borscht Belt comedians, such as Milton Berle, Buddy Hackett, and Sid Caesar, as well as a hilarious performance by the Broadway star Ethel Merman. It also includes a host of better-known jesters in cameo appearances, like Jerry Lewis and The Three Stooges. It's a laugh-fest for sure. It's such a long movie—a three-plus-hour running time—that when I saw it as a child with my parents and sister there was an intermission. It was a big hit, the kind of movie that created cultural buzz. When it appeared on TV a few years later, broadcast over two or three successive nights, millions of Americans stayed home to watch it again. But what I most remember about seeing it was the impact the final scene had on me. While I laughed at the slapstick silliness geared for kids, as my parents laughed at the kind of puns that went over my head, seeing the characters in the hospital ward was frightening. Even when I watched it again on TV and was older and more prepared for the scene, it still freaked me out. One minute the characters were clowning around, dangling from the top of a fire truck ladder and hanging off of a collapsing fire escape, and the next minute they were in body casts held together with pins the size of knitting needles. Learning about the precariousness of life may have terrified me more as a boy than seeing Spencer Tracy wrapped in bandages with his legs and arms suspended in slings above the bed.

But I'm not horrified now staring at the car-crash victim. Maybe it's because I know I'm in pretty bad shape too. It also could be that I'm gaining insight into how sorrowful life is for everyone, even for those living inside a smash-hit comedy. None of us can escape it. Only one letter separates *cosmic* from *comic*, after all. Strangely, I find this comforting. At the most basic level of human existence, we're all in it together. I'm no longer terrified by life's fickleness, as I was when I was a child. If anything, I feel relieved. For the rest of my life I am not in the least bit afraid to die, or afraid of death. I even begin to embrace the gruesomeness of living as part of the whole, the darkness on the other side of the light. One minute you're driving around cracking wise in a packed taxicab and the next minute you're laid up in a hospital bed with a tube sticking out of your mouth. Go figure. But not everyone can stomach all of the little ugly pieces, especially in our sanitized, packaged society. When Billy "Pops" visits me later that day, he nearly faints when he sees me. He has to be helped out of the room. By then, the nurses were all complimenting me on my progress and on how good I looked. What in the name of hell did I look like when they wheeled me into the place? I wonder.

In the early evening hours, the Mummy dies. The Keeper died the day before. Of the three of us, I'm the only one who makes it. Their deaths make me more determined to make a better life of myself, now that I have one, and to be a better human being compared with the shitbag they wheeled in here a few days ago.

After visiting hours are over, it's eerily quiet. Even the machines behind me are silent. I'm in the room alone. No one else is brought in to replace my dead roommates. As I try to fall asleep, I am strangely blissful. I'm getting another chance at life. The next day, I'm told, I'm being moved to a regular hospital room. Now it's official: I'll live. But there was never any doubt in my mind. The entire time I am in the ICU I know I will. Perhaps the doctors and the medical staff viewed my condition as touch-and-go. Not me. I was thinking green light all the way.

The belief exists beyond anything mental or visceral. There's no single word for it, maybe because it's all-encompassing in its own right. "Mystical" or "supernatural" might apply. But I was never a big believer in otherworldly phenomena. I didn't "convert" when I was being administered the last rites. If it didn't happen then, it never will. I know I'll live because I've convinced myself I have a lot of unfinished business. I simply have to go on, to live longer and accomplish things defined by honorable behavior and right action. It's a cliché-ridden thought process, but clichés exist for a reason. They often aptly crystallize what takes a generation to explain. As soon as I found myself in the ICU following the surgery, I knew it was the beginning of my new life. I am on a new path.

The world is all before me.

While past wrongs and injustices can never be rectified, I believe in redemption, in forgiving myself for what was done and preparing myself to do better. I'll be in training for the rest of my life, to live a better life. I promised that to myself in the ER: *If I awaken after this, there will be a reawakening.* Waking up in the ICU proves to me there will be more to come. *There is no way I am going to die,* I thought throughout my stay there. I have too much to do, and too much to discover, maybe even too much to answer for—at least in my own head. The next time I'm about to kick the bucket, which Jimmy Durante literally does right before he dies in *It's a Mad, Mad, Mad, Mad World,* I want people to think well of me, from those who know me to the checkout girl at the supermarket. I plan on killing people with kindness and generosity instead of killing myself slowly with ill feeling and ill will, which nearly led to my killing myself quickly. There's a rush of energy coursing through me. I think I get it: Really, what more is there to life than to be good and to do good for others? What else should we live for other than to make life less difficult for others, thereby making life more meaningful for ourselves? As I lay there, I knew I'd been far from being that kind of person before I was shot. I will remedy that in the future. I've been given a second chance. Being shot was the worst and the best thing that ever happened to me.

The morning I'm released from the ICU, I'm left alone for most of the time. The emergency-care nurses and doctors don't need to fuss over me anymore. That will be left up to the regular crew when I'm moved into a regular room. No one comes to visit me, either, knowing I'm being relocated soon. They'll visit me later in the day when I get there. Like the night before, I'm overwhelmed by the moment. It's spontaneous. An indescribable rush of infinity and temporality washes over me. I feel as if I'm going to live forever. I also feel as if I could die at any moment, and that every moment will be my last. Impermanence and eternity combined in a single vision. I can't help but think there is something special about this, brought on by my proximity to death and the startling revelations that followed. Will I feel this way forever? I wonder. Who else knows these things or has known them? Can it be articulated when I'm having trouble making sense of it in my own mind? Am I foolish for thinking this way? Is it brilliance or blindness, genius or madness? Should I tell someone about it? The answer to the last question will arrive in a few days when my parents advise me to remain as silent as humanly possible about being shot, as if it never happened.

But it did happen. And it will live *only* inside my head. Nobody else will know what I "saw" (at least not until now, until whoever is reading this "sees" it too). I don't know this as I wait to be removed from the ICU, how being shot will have to be kept a secret, including the illuminations. Many things pass through my mind as I lie there, especially what transpired a few days before in the ER. As I muse away the morning, I recall one of the other three consequential impressions I had: a vision of a fortress of books. It is, admittedly, an odd thing to think of before you believe you're going to die. Remembering it feels strange and awkward. I grin with private embarrassment—and conviction. Despite its oddity, I know I'll build it. If I build it, I will come. I will come to the house of books, a fortress of books, of my own creation and design. Later, after reading Frederick Douglass's slave narrative, I will learn what it was I must have been seeking: liberation. Douglass was on the verge of death, too, literally and figuratively, and books saved him. Of course, it was merely the color of his skin that brought him so close to death. That isn't a crime, unless you're living in the American slave South. He also obviously had more obstacles to overcome for books to "save" him, although his innocence may have had its strange advantages. I guess what I'm trying to get at is that it has occurred to me recently that literacy can "save" even a scoundrel. It can be a potent force in anyone's life.

On the sixth day, my sister brings me a book, the first book I will read on my own, without its being a required schoolbook, which I rarely read anyway. She didn't know about my vision of books stacked skyscraper-high, so it is a timely and fortunate gesture. Perhaps it's more opportune than accidental. She must have noticed that I wasn't reading the *Sports Illustrated* and *Playboy* magazines my friends had given me, and I simply couldn't bring myself to watch TV. As in the past, I stared out the window trying to figure things out.

For storytelling purposes, I wish I could claim that the book she brought held great emblematic value, some apt male *Bildungsroman* like *David Copperfield*, *The Red and the Black*, or *The Adventures of Augie March*. Even something like *Huckleberry Finn* or *The Catcher in the Rye* would have been more metaphorically suitable than the actual book she delivered. Her book wasn't remotely like any of them. Instead, she pulled out of a small brown paper bag, which included some chocolates, a bestseller. It was a blockbuster, really, one of the biggest-selling books in U.S. publishing history. When the Steven Spielberg film version of *Jaws* was released a couple of years later, a few more million copies were sold. Despite its lack of symbolic import, my sister had chosen wisely. A more complex book might have been too much for me to handle. I was a slow, feeble reader. In class, whenever I was called on to read aloud I could hear myself stuttering. (Yet I was known for *telling* funny stories.) I probably would have struggled and suffered through almost anything else. In the end, Peter Benchley's novel served as a valuable hook (I apologize for the obvious pun) because it was an effective introduction to the most important component of any good book: It was an interesting read.

When I recently assigned it in my undergraduate Senior Seminar course, "Popular Fiction in the Post-War Years," I re-read it for the first time since then. At first, its simple prose made me cringe. But that second reading followed a couple of decades of inhaling books. That has included several rather beefy, sophisticated volumes, books I suspect only a tiny percentage of the population has read, let alone has even heard of. So it's no wonder I found *Jaws* simplistically written, after pounding away at Proust,

Foucault, Tolstoy, Wittgenstein, Eliot (George), Thucydides, Ricoeur, Marx, and Hegel. During my quest, I had stumbled across Mortimer Adler's "Great Books" list. It wasn't enough for me to read the half-dozen works of Plato included on it, for instance. I read the entire extant oeuvre, including the nearly unreadable *Laws*. When I recently returned to *Jaws*, I was therefore light years removed from those days when I'd stumbled along in the classroom as a buffoonish reader.

Nevertheless, at some point while re-reading it I got sucked right back into the story, and the book turned into a page-turner, in spite of its familiarity. That's what I remember most about my reading the book for the first time in the hospital. Once I picked it up, I couldn't put it down. And once I did, I wanted to pick up another one, and another, and continue reading until the stories ran out or until I ran out of time to read them all. As strange as it seems, that was one of three pivotal thoughts I had that night in the ER. If I had time, I saw a future constructed out of books.

When my sister handed me the book, I grasped it as if I were holding the Holy Grail, or that I'd trumped Jason and captured the Golden Fleece. It meant that much. Days before in the ER, I'd concluded that I had missed out on something big and important, something wonderful and edifying. By not having been a reader, I was an incomplete person, or so I believed. I wouldn't overlook it the next time—if there was a next time. And there was. And there still is. In fact, there is a whole series of next times. *Jaws* represented the future. Holding it, I was certain that its pages contained the promise of discovery, perhaps even self-discovery. Sure, it was only *Jaws*, the kind of novel critics would call pulp fiction and my academic colleagues much worse. But to me it was a first step, a baby step.

Admittedly, I was susceptible to an exuberantly romanticized vision of what books offered, and I likely still maintain that idealistic view, but who can blame me? I was alive! I had every right to believe that the book's pages contained valuable material, aiding me in acquiring the kind of useful literacy I didn't possess before I was shot. I wasn't a reader then, and look where that had gotten me. If I became a reader now, it might take me to entirely different places. I would make as much use of every book as I possibly could, toward my restoration and toward knowing the world with greater insight—at least with multiple visions. I knew I wouldn't consume them as they had been handed down in school, as a yardstick with which to evaluate my academic progress and shortcomings, or with which to measure me against my classmates. I wouldn't become bookish, either, as the means to propel me out of the working class. (And possibly resenting them later for what they'd done to me, as so many working-class academic narratives reveal.) Nor would I turn around as a teacher and use them as weapons against my students. I would read books for their use-value, not for their exchange value. It's probably why I read *Jaws* as if my life depended on it.

After *Jaws*, then what? While my sister introduced me to the world of books, I couldn't expect her to be my guide. She was engaged to her childhood sweetheart and had her own life to manage. Besides, as good a student as she was, she wasn't a reader. Also, she'd dropped out of Marist College after one semester, mostly because she missed that childhood sweetheart. When she moved back home, she eventually enrolled in a Katharine Gibbs secretarial program, soon working on Wall Street. Years later she did obtain her bachelor's degree, while raising two exceptional daughters, which likely increased her sense of achievement. But that was years in the making. After high school, she was expected to attend college and she was expected to excel. My parents encouraged her to apply to some of the finest smaller liberal arts colleges in the area. I'm sure they were disappointed when she returned home from Marist done with her studies.

Perhaps her decision to leave had something to do with their decision to dissuade me from going to college. Maybe they figured if she couldn't cut it then how could I, a historically impoverished student who'd started amassing behavioral problems to boot. And then there was "the accident." That confirmed their worst fears and solidified their worst impressions of me. Even though I had diligently begun to rewrite my academic story after I'd been shot, that wasn't enough to convince them I was worthy of higher education. Nor was sitting in the local library during my spare time and bringing home cartloads of books. I don't think they understood what I was trying to do and how it all stacked up against that night in the ER. I certainly never told them. I wasn't supposed to talk about it. Besides, they likely were unimpressed with my new-found interest in books anyway. Not being readers themselves, they weren't interested in them, other than to acquire a skill or learn how to make money. Books had no use-value; they functioned purely as exchange-value. This outlook likely had a lot to do with their working-class background. To them, my books were, as Richard Hoggart points out in *The Uses of Literacy*, "strange tools."

Overall, books weren't part of my upbringing, not in the larger or smaller scheme of things. In the homes of my many "day care" providers, there were no books. None of the Oakwood Heights homes I was ever in had books either. I don't recall seeing even a single library book in any of the households of my friends or in the homes I was infrequently invited into when collecting for the paper route. Members of my extended family weren't readers either. Even an older cousin who became a grade-school teacher lived in a home devoid of books. There certainly were no books in our house—at least not ones my parents read. The ones that did exist were for "show." The year my father rejoined the family, he built a wooden dividing wall, half the length of the hallway, to separate the hallway entrance from the living room. The living room side included three bookshelves. In addition to placing a clock, photographs, and various knick-knacks on it, he supplied the empty shelf space with a few books he'd found left on someone's curb. They were maroon-colored, hardcover editions of historical biographies from the same press, none of which my parents read. Almost forty years later they sit on their fireplace mantle in the New Jersey condo they own. My mother of late regularly visits her local public library and reads lots of popular contemporary fiction, with an occasional "classic" thrown in. When I was growing up, though, her reading habits were like my sister's. She read only magazines and usually did so to extrapolate from them decorating or food tips.

As expected, we weren't terribly close with my father's side of the family during their separation, so even if any of them were readers I never noticed. I would sometimes be watched by one of my dad's sisters during the week or have a sleep-over in the summer at one of my cousins', but that was a rarity. In all that time I never saw any books in their homes either. One of my cousins received a half-academic, half-athletic (football) scholarship from Princeton. Like my sister, though, he dropped out, after one semester. He had attended a really rigorous all-boys Catholic high school run rather heavy-handedly by the Brothers. While there he was a top-notch student, an academic star lauded with all sorts of honors. His academic success may have been driven more from the constant coercion of the "whip" than from his own interest in learning. When he too was left on his own he couldn't quite bring himself to succeed without pressure from the outside.

In my youth, I thought he was the coolest guy on Earth. He started dating a gorgeous redhead who lived around the block from us, so I would sometimes see him in the neighborhood. He was one of the most well-known athletes on Staten Island, a speedy, powerful outside linebacker, who *also* garnered a host of academic awards. I used to drop his name around like he was a celebrity, which, in the small world of Staten Island back then, he was. But he didn't strike me as an "independent reader." I don't recall seeing any books in his home or in his room, other than schoolbooks. His academic successes in high school stemmed largely from hitting the *school*books as hard as he hit a tailback. As I learned during my quest, as well as inside the academy's corridors, as both a student and as a professor, being successful in school may have little to do with acquiring knowledge or possessing a profound desire to learn. Lots of students can be "good" students simply by playing the game and going through the motions of pulling the right levers, blowing the right whistles, and ringing the right bells. (The same can be said about teachers.) Neither students nor teachers need to be particularly interested in real learning in order to go far in the educational establishment. Pressing the right buttons can sometimes be enough. Whether or not my cousin couldn't continue doing that when he was at Princeton, I don't know. I do know that despite his "scholarship boy" credentials, he was like other members of my father's side of the family, not much of a reader for readership's sake. As such, when I was released from the hospital with my finished copy of *Jaws*, his name didn't appear in my brain's Rolodex as a person to ask for academic or intellectual advice.

On my mother's side, my cousin Andrew was the only member of my family who might have been "bookish," but there was still some uncertainty about that in my mind growing up; more important, circumstances dictated that the condition of our relationship didn't extend to books or matters of the mind. He had turned himself into a Big Brother of sorts during my parents' separation by doing such things as taking me to the airport to watch the planes take off and land or drive me to Fort Wardsworth to watch the ships and tugboats slip in and out of the harbor. He and his wife, Pat, who had turned herself into a Big Sister of sorts, sometimes came by our house at night to spend time with all of us as well. Their benevolence didn't include "schooling" or instruction. They correctly recognized that simply spending time with me, without passing judgment on how well or how poorly I was doing in school, was more than anyone else was doing and more than I could ask for. I vividly remember those trips to JFK Airport with great fondness. At that time in my life, being happy for a few hours was a treat. Andrew did a lot for me, although I still saw him too infrequently to consider him my book guide. More important, right before I'd been shot he had recently returned from the University of Illinois in Champaign, where he was studying for his doctorate in Comparative Literature. He stayed only one semester and never bothered enrolling in another program. At that time in his life he seemed dispirited and cynical about the usefulness of books and the value of intellectual development. He had crash-landed. It just so happened to coincide with my takeoff. I needed a true believer. Besides, I had learned plenty from him and his wife through their magnanimity. That was more than enough, and more meaningful than any school lesson or anything I've ever read in a book, quite honestly. Maybe I didn't want to ask any more of Andrew than he'd already given.

The dissociation between books and males in my family was typical of the general male population in Oakwood Heights in particular and on Staten Island in general, and probably in the nation as well. Book reading was strictly taboo. Guys who read books were either certifiable nerds or raging homos. Real men didn't read books. There was something suspect about anything too closely aligned to the mind or to the emotions. Books might distance a true man from reacting to life's challenges physically and viscerally. Certainly no real man would read a book in his spare time. Any man with spare time on his hands needed to be using his hands, not his brain, to weatherize a porch or turn an attic into a playroom.

Once *Jaws* had set me on my way, there were no men to model myself after as I prepared to begin my quest. If anything, I hid my passion for books from them. I wasn't close to any female, except my sister, so no female could act as my principal agent. Besides, book reading was already aligned with the feminine. I would have been doubly mocked taking on a female mentor. I might as well have said I was moving to San Francisco. I could have sought direction from teachers, but at that point I hadn't met any who didn't push books solely as a way to gauge a student's academic worth, to use books as a disagreeable means for testing illiteracy, by spotlighting it and identifying "poor" students, rather than as an agreeable means for promoting and advancing literacy. Reading, generally, was treated as a blood sport by almost all the teachers I knew. In addition, few of them seemed to enjoy what they were doing. It was as if books were ponderously weighing them down, almost as much as they were trying to weigh us down with them. There was nothing joyful about it. After I'd nearly been killed, I expected—and needed!—books to enliven me, not to deaden me. It seemed teachers were part of the problem, not part of the solution, as one popular slogan still in circulation then might have characterized it. I was on my own when it came to my education, to that part of me that believed a formal education would make me a "better" person. It was also my way of "getting out." And I don't necessarily mean getting out of the working class, more like getting out of what I was and used to be and getting into something "more."

8

"It's not too late to take the Sanitation test"

On parent–teacher night, my fourth-grade teacher, Sister Stephen-Marie, told my mom I'd do better in school if I simply tried harder. My mom wasn't surprised. She knew I wasn't much of a schoolboy. I was reading lots of comic books, though, in Dougie's basement and Tommy Malloy's attic. That was the extent of my reading habits. In school, I could hardly finish the shortest of assignments. I was a junior in high school before I read a book on my own, an accomplishment that required three bullets. Some of my teachers used to say I had to have a gun pointed at my head before I'd read anything. That was only half true. Someone obviously needed to pull the trigger.

Periodically, other teachers echoed Sister Stephen-Marie by describing me as a perennial underachiever who rarely applied himself. I just didn't take to books, unlike the working-class academics who fill the pages of such anthologies as *This Fine Place So Far from Home* and *Working-Class Women in the Academy*, along with better-known individuals such as Richard Rodriguez. Even more famous figures from the past refer to books as stepping-stones in helping them climb out of the working class. Apprenticed to an engraver at a young age, Jean-Jacques Rousseau recounts in his *Confessions* that he "did nothing but read." His "enthusiasm became a passion and soon a kind of madness." He had grown "bored with [his] fellow-apprentices," and then with "everything." He literally sold the shirts off his back to purchase more books from printers. Books provided a distraction, a way out, eventually leading to fame.

More recently, the chroniclers of working-class academic narratives also boast about their youthful obsession with books, their means of escape, and their increasing cultural capital. As they describe it, books supplied the sheen on their early academic achievements, frequently establishing them as "gifted" among their less academically inclined (and far less bookish) working-class peers. Books called attention to their extraordinariness, and teachers noticed. They stood out and were encouraged to get out of the working class. Reading lots of books in their youth made them bright stars in a rather dull constellation. I was one of those dullards who burned dimly.

I never shone academically in my youth. I certainly was never mistaken for a prodigy. Rather than successes, I had catalogued a steady history of academic shortcomings, and books played no part in my life until I had nearly graduated from high school. As a consequence, books didn't feed an urgency to leave the working class or fuel a simmering desire to enter higher education, whereas books are what most working-class academics flaunt as the wings giving them flight and as the totems proving they belong in the academy.

I therefore never attributed to books the same kind of exchange-value as most of my working-class academic colleagues. I never wanted that from my books; maybe it's been a backhanded advantage to have come so late to them now that I am a teacher—a professor of English, no less. For me, books furnished something different (a difference reflected in my teaching). Admittedly, I was probably too shortsighted in my youth to think of books as supplying social mobility. I didn't see them as my great escape. Besides, throughout my schooling books were deployed to keep me down. I didn't think they could be used to pick me up. To the nuns and lay teachers at St. Charles, a bad reader equaled a bad student and a bad student equaled a bad person. And whether I was being characteristically foolish or overly optimistic, I became a reader because I believed books would make me a wiser, better person, but not in the sense of being righteously better than others. As I lay in the ER, I thought if I made it out of there alive I'd be better off with books than without them. That's how I came to books. Or maybe that's how they came to me. I thought my (new) life depended on them. To put it more simply, I believed books could help me figure out stuff about myself and about the world. Maybe they could be a beacon *and* an anchor. Sure, there may have been no correlation between being shot and the absence of books in my life. There were plenty of other forces involved. Nevertheless, there's no denying I was troubled and lost in my youth. The absence of books may have made finding my way rockier and darker. I was nearly blown away without them. Maybe I could do better with them.

One of the first things I did after being released from the hospital was to walk to the New Dorp Public Library, located about a mile from our house. On my way there I saw a neighbor raking leaves in her front yard. It was a beautiful mid-October morning, similar to the kind of sunny, crisply dry day New Yorkers now associate with 9/11. I remember wearing shirt-sleeves as I left the house for the library. Our neighbor was also dressed for Indian summer. She seemed surprised to see me. It had been less than two weeks after I was nearly shot to death. Yet there I was, like an apparition, walking past her house. Her astonishment quickly changed into contempt, frozen on her face like ice. She stared at me for a few seconds, apparently disgusted that I had the nerve to show my face ever again in the neighborhood. She deliberately turned her back and resumed raking. It had its intended effect: It cut me like a knife. I would carry that encounter with me for the rest of my life. In some ways, she did me a favor. Her reaction further motivated me to rise above whatever image she had of me that made her react that way. It also further inspired me to stay steadfast in my quest, for I was certain that books would be the instrument of my transformation. After that day, whenever I walked past her house I hoped she'd see me lugging my books, a witness to my labors. I only wished I was carrying a copy of *Fuck You: It's Never Too Late to Change*. Maybe, I thought, walking past her house, I would write it someday. Maybe this is it.

Inside the library I was smitten—and overwhelmed, despite its being an extremely small library. The entire adult and children's collections were contained on a single floor, the total square footage covering not much more than the floor space of our modest home on Flint Street. The adult section had perhaps as few as ten rows of bookcases, roughly four feet high, along with floor-to-ceiling shelves along the entire back wall. The "Fiction & Literature" section was located there. I had no idea what the difference was between "fiction" and "literature" (even as an English professor I still don't, aside from the official canonical declarations). I headed straight for the back wall anyway. I think the "literature" half of the category appealed to me. It sounded robust, and a requisite place to begin if I planned on undertaking my mission seriously. As I slowly walked along the back shelves, my eye was drawn to a series of similarly bound, hardcover editions that appeared repeatedly along the wall. Below each of the sometimes recognizable titles was inscribed "World Classics." "Literature" had first drawn me to the back wall. "World Classics" sweetened the deal. I wanted to read those books—all of them!—in no small part because they announced themselves as "worldly." I needed a good dose of *worldly* if my mind were to free itself from its provincialism and my failure to live an examined life.

Some authors in the series warranted multiple volumes. I recognized some of them, like Dickens and Twain. Many others I didn't. I moved through the stacks in alphabetical order and nearly halfway through I decided to stop. At eye-level I spotted an unrecognizable author, Thomas Hardy, who warranted the "Classic" heading for several books. I grabbed the one with the most interesting and germane (to me) title, *The Return of the Native*. For some reason, I started reading from the second chapter. I was immediately captivated by the first passage:

> Along the road walked an old man. He was white-headed as a mountain, bowed in the shoulders, and faded in general aspect. He wore a glazed hat, an ancient boat-cloak, and shoes; his brass buttons bearing an anchor upon the face. In his hand was a silver-headed walking-stick, which he used as a veritable third leg, perseveringly dotting the ground with its point at every few inches interval. One would have said that he had been, in his day, a naval officer of some sort or other.

But as I continued reading I understood less and less, especially following a block of colloquial dialogue. I didn't know the meaning of every eighth or ninth word. I knew I couldn't begin with that book, or any of the "Classic" volumes. It wouldn't be a "good read" if I couldn't understand it. I would have to return to Hardy in the future, along with his worldly textual family. I eventually did, but not before being rerouted through action-adventure thrillers and mysteries.

After returning the Hardy volume to the shelf, I continued gazing at the other titles along the wall. "Can I help you?" a woman's voice asked. I was too engrossed to notice that a librarian was standing beside me. She was smiling.

"No," I said automatically, as if we were standing in a department store. "I'm just looking."

"Okay," she replied. "If you need any assistance, feel free to ask."

"Wait," I said, as she began walking away. "Maybe I do need some help."

I explained that I was a poor reader and had read little, but I wanted to start reading a lot more. I had enjoyed reading *Jaws*, I told her, and I wondered where to go from there.

"I was reading some of this," I said, sliding back toward the lower part of the alphabet, and pointing to the Hardy novel. "But I can tell it's too hard for me—for now."

She led me to the "New Books" section and picked out a recently published book by Alistair MacLean. "Here," she said. "I think you might like this." I can't exactly recall which MacLean book she handed me, in part because after reading it I read everything he wrote. A recent Google search revealed that *Breakheart Pass* came out in 1974, and so that might have been it. I was shot in the autumn of 1974. MacLean mostly wrote lean, muscular World War II spy thrillers, such as *The Guns of Navarone*, *Ice Station Zebra*, and *Where Eagles Dare*, many of which were turned into successful movies.

When I finished reading the MacLean books the library had, I headed over to the Staten Island Mall and bought the first of many missing MacLean works at the now-defunct B. Dalton bookstore. It was *Force 10 from Navarone*. It was the first book I bought in my life. After reading it, I treated it like an icon, as I would the remaining MacLean books I purchased. Piled on the small desk in my room, they were the bricks I had envisioned, and I would sometimes stare at them as if they held all of the world's mysteries and its answers. I wanted so badly to believe in their potential for my own sake that I invested in them far more merit than they likely possessed. Nonetheless, similar to Benchley's shark tale, they were the building blocks to increasing my literacy, which is why as a teacher I continue to object to forcing students to read Great Works of Literature because it's "good" for them when they may be barely literate to begin with. If anything, by suffering and struggling through *The Scarlet Letter* in school an adolescent or a young adult may end up learning the wrong lesson: to hate reading and to find books boring. Based on nearly twenty years of teaching experience, most of the students in my college General Education courses are about as "literate" as I was then. As "tasteless" or "popular" or "simplistic" as many cultural critics or English teachers might view MacLean's books and others like it, they did launch my personal literacy campaign and inaugurate my tactile fascination with books.

If I were to re-read MacLean today, I'd have the same initial reaction to him as I did with *Jaws* when I re-read it for my Popular Fiction senior seminar. I'd wince at the simple prose—and then get sucked into the stories. However simplistic the prose may seem now, back then I was occasionally bogged down with the words I didn't understand. I repeatedly consulted the dictionary, growing frustrated when I needed to look up the same damn words more than once. How stupid was I, for heaven's sake! I began to fear that my misspent youth had permanently wrecked my mind. My unschooled and untrained brain apparently required special treatment. I needed a plan. I bought a small, sky-blue, 3" × 5" spiral notebook and started creating my own dictionary. When I came across a word I didn't know I wrote it in the notebook along with its dictionary definition. I assumed that the physical act of writing the definition on the page would help me remember the word the next time it appeared. For the most part, it worked. I wasn't constantly looking up the same words, although whenever I "reviewed" the list I would sometimes find a word written down twice. When I did, I would turn to the back of the notebook and write a couple of sentences using the word, in hopes I might be able to commit it to memory. When I abandoned the project, sometime around my senior year at Boston University, I had filled it up entirely. I held on to it for years, as a keepsake and as a reminder of my progress. If I saw it now, I'm sure I'd be embarrassed by the words contained in it. But when I was compiling the list it consisted of difficult words. At the start of my reading adventure, even popular spy thrillers posed a challenge to me from time to time. I had a lot of catching up to do. As do many of my students. Now, I keep those early experiences of my advancing literacy uppermost in my mind as a teacher, maintaining Zen-like patience with my "nongifted" students. It's not my job to point out their debilities and create additional frustrations with their learning. I have to hope for the best and for progress in all of them, however fleeting that potential may seem from time to time. Otherwise, there's no point in my presence. I hand them some straw and mud and *maybe* they'll start making some bricks with it too, just as I did.

After finishing MacLean's adventure novels, I tried reading similar books, but none appealed to me. Perhaps MacLean was king of the genre, or perhaps I was exhausted with it. I again asked the librarian for help, the same one who'd offered it on that memorable day. I made a beeline to her as soon as I walked into the place. She was busy with someone else, but that didn't stop me from going to her, probably causing her to feel un-comfortable as I impatiently waited for her to finish talking to an elderly woman. I wanted to shove the old woman aside, I was so eager to start down another path. Finally, *my* librarian led me to Raymond Chandler and Dashiell Hammett, recognizing that I shouldn't stray too far from the field just yet. From there, I was off and running. Soon, I was able to revisit the back wall and begin reading those classics I'd had my eye on. But before then, I had to deal with the more dense Chandler material. I was inserting many more words in my dictionary and the plots were thicker to wade through.

I was completing my summer of reading Hammett and Chandler when I entered Mr. Larson's English class in my senior year. On the first day, he went around the room asking us who our favorite authors were. I didn't have many authors to choose from, clearly. When it was my turn, I said Chandler, and I meant it, unlike some of the other students who seemed to tell him what they thought he wanted to hear. I was expecting "The English Teacher" to scoff at my lowbrow selection. Instead, Mr. Larson was impressed with it. "Chandler, you say! Excellent choice! My boy, he is, in my humble opinion, one of the best, under-appreciated modern American writers. A real stylist—a great one, to be precise. And I dare anyone to find another author who deals so honestly, and so consistently, with the subject of class." I didn't know what the hell he was talking about. I would, in time, but at that point I read the guy to unravel the murder mysteries and be intoxicated by the snappy prose and witty dialogue. What I did understand, though, was that someone had praised me for my reading habits.

Chandler and Hammett came to a fast end. I plowed through both during the summer months. The dust jacket of one of Chandler's detective novels left a clue for where I might turn next. It noted that not since Doyle's Sherlock Holmes had a writer invented such an intriguing detective as Philip Marlowe. It was all I needed. I raced through Arthur Conan Doyle's short stories, then devoured in quick succession the detective novellas *The Sign of the Four, The Hound of the Baskervilles*, and *A Study in Scarlet*. Reading Doyle was different. Because he was "foreign" and not a contemporary writer, I became interested in learning about Edwardian England—its history, politics, and culture—to see if that might lead to a more enriching reading experience. I also began reading about Doyle "the writer" and the construction of his famous fictional character, eventually learning that he'd likely based Holmes on another fictional detective, perhaps the first of its kind, Edgar Allan Poe's Dupin. The game was now truly afoot. Authors and texts were building on one another. The bricks were beginning to resemble a structure of sorts, not spread out willy-nilly, and the expanding edifice owed its existence to that first brick. I've found that as a teacher, it's essential to distribute bricks to students rather than insist they inhabit *our* buildings right from the start. They need to assemble their own places, just as I assembled mine. It's more interesting and amusing that way, and it also means they have to make their own decisions about which bricks they want to use. If teachers make all of those decisions for them, they won't bother building anything for themselves. They'll remain uncritical renters. In time, I'd reach similar conclusions about student writing. They need to own that too, even if it begins as a dilapidated shack.

I devoured Poe like a gourmand, but he was the most challenging author to date. I seemed to be looking up a lot more words. I typically had to re-read a story after compiling its dictionary. I'd pore over the words and "test" myself before the second reading. In doing so, I began to appreciate the stylistic devices and "tricks" that infused the tales, often informing the story and adding to its richness. I remember thinking how cool it was that style and substance were so happily wedded and how singular Poe's writing "voice" was. In looking ahead (far ahead) I wondered if I could ever write like that someday. In the meantime, I knew that reading Poe was better than reading *Jaws*. Compared with the latter, the former was masterly. I felt ready to return to Hardy.

I was partly mistaken. I finished *Return of the Native*, but I slogged through most of it, and I didn't understand half of it, but neither disadvantage prevented me from enjoying it and admiring it. Like Poe, it was heady stuff, but on a grander scale and there were breathless passages that perfectly captured the mood and the sentiment of a scene, with the characters leaping off the page as if they had a pulse. The summer between Johnson & Wales and enrolling in Boston University I was going through my "Russian phase," reading the usual suspects—Tolstoy, Dostoevsky, Pushkin, Chekhov, and Gogol. At the same time, there was a good deal of press about Vladimir Nabokov's recently published essays, taken from his class notes when he was teaching at Cornell, one volume entitled *Russian Literature*. I sat in a Providence library reading it and recall being struck by his commentary about the genius of Tolstoy, his ability to draw characters as if they were walking beneath our windows. Invention could be that artfully imaginative. I started wondering if the reader required as much imagination as the author and whether when I picked up *Jaws* three years before I would have had enough imagination to have read *Anna Karenina*. If so, would reading more complicated material increase my imagination? Do some books tap into my imagination more deeply and therefore foster its growth? As a teacher, I hope I am encouraging my students to think more imaginatively and critically, but that old debate hasn't been settled yet—on whether certain kinds of books do that better than others. For me, the jury is still out. Increasing my students' literacy seems like a pretty tall order these days anyway. Maybe that's enough—or maybe I'm not doing enough.

More instinctively than deliberatively did I return to Hardy and the "classics" after MacLean and Poe. At the time, I wasn't concerned with advancing my cognitive skills by reading headier material. I wasn't planning on building a better brain. I wanted to build a better person. If increased imaginative powers were its byproduct, I could certainly live with that. But that was an afterthought. Correctly or not, I assumed that the "classics" contained the best chances for my conversion. That was my main reason for starting to read them. I was additionally drawn to the "classic" brand because it included such authors as Plato, Gibbons, and Freud. In the back pages of Hardy, I saw a list of additional "classic" books that weren't stacked along the "Fiction & Literature" section. I started with literature because it made more sense to segue from *Where Eagles Dare* to *As I Lay Dying*. But if I could someday get through *The Leviathan* and *The Origin of Species* then I'd have proved to myself I had traveled a long way from sticking up pizza delivery drivers with an empty water pistol.

In the beginning, however, I focused on the titles shelved on the library's back wall. For some silly reason, I dismissed the ones that had been made into films, such as *The Hunchback of Notre Dame*, *War and Peace*, and *The Three Musketeers*. As movie adaptations, I equated them as less serious than the other texts. Whether or not I read *Crime and Punishment*, *The Red and the Black*, or *Madame Bovary* first, after *The Return of the Native*, didn't make much difference. I had trouble wrapping my head around all of them. But I stuck with it and my dictionary was filling up faster than Webster's. Despite my bumpy, sometimes incoherent start, these classic works of literature did adhere to the basic element that had made *Jaws* such a good book: They were good reads, even if gaps existed in my fully understanding them. (Many I've re-read since, but it's like reading them for the first time considering how little I remember.)

I was nearly a high school graduate, then, before I could safely call myself a reader, and still a relatively poor one at that. Academically, I was gaining ground, but I was certainly nowhere near being "gifted," like other working-class academics, which explains why my parents dissuaded me from attending college, followed by discouraging me from attending law school and then graduate school. Talented working-class academics write about their parents' encouraging them, in some cases shoving them off to prestigious schools, scholarship in tow. But they were kids who excelled in school and who were bookish at a very young age. Even for some who weren't terribly "gifted" in their youth, family support remains a commonality among working-class academic narratives. We learn in *Lives on the Boundary* that Mike Rose didn't really get going academically until he attended Loyola University in southern California—thanks to the help of a high school teacher—but his "parents [still] used to say that their son would have the best education they could afford," and that maybe he "would be a doctor" some day. When I told my mom I wanted to be a doctor right after I'd been shot, she practically laughed in my face. Unlike me, though, Rose had been bookish as a child, so at least he had that going for him in the eyes of his parents. As impoverished as his family was, Rose managed to wheedle "enough change out of [his] father to enable [him] to take the bus to the public library." With his "back aching" from reading his plentiful supply of books, which he'd "sometimes read through the weekend," Rose appeared to family and friends the way other working-class academics appeared to theirs: bookish, and therefore unlike most working-class kids, who weren't. As he tells us, while "reading opened up the world" for him, he also became "a skinny bookworm drawing the attention of street kids." If I drew the attention of any street kids in my youth it sure as hell didn't have anything to do with books.

In *Hunger of Memory* Richard Rodriguez admits that he began grade school speaking barely fifty words of English. But books propelled him forward, all the way to Stanford. So quick was his rise that he had read hundreds of books by the time he entered high school. I had barely read a few dozen by the time I graduated from it. I had grown into a better student, but compared with other working-class academics, no one was handing out scholarships to me, as happened to Keith Gilyard. As he explains in *Voices of the Self*, both Notre Dame and the University of Connecticut offered him scholarships—and he was a junkie from Harlem, for heaven's sake. But he and other working-class academics had established themselves academically long before they graduated from high school. Despite his rough-and-tumble history outside of school, Gilyard was still considered college material inside of school. Based on his long, impressive academic track record, teachers and family urged him to join the ranks of higher education. No one in my circle did for me. Given my long, unimpressive academic track record, I would've been lucky if my family and teachers had urged me to attend Hamburger University in Illinois.

Now that I am a professor, my bookless childhood of school failures makes me wonder if I share much with other working-class academics, the majority of whom admit to feeling uneasy about their place in the academy. I don't. I earned my stripes the hard way, and I'm proud of it. If anyone wants to turn their back on me, like my neighbor who was raking leaves that day, that's their problem, really, not mine. Furthermore, many working-class academics aren't terribly gung-ho either about allowing their working-class roots to show. I couldn't care less. I've made no attempt to color mine. I still prefer the direct, matter-of-fact style of working-class speech, as opposed to the verbose, meandering style of academic discourse. More important, my sputtering education, which differs sharply from those in "gifted" narratives, mirrors the conditions of many of my own nontraditional students, who often are from the working class. No "genius" history operates as a barrier between students and me, and I've never felt uncomfortable about coming from the working class.

I started thinking about this a few years ago when I obtained my doctorate and landed my first full-time job at a community college in the Bay Area. I also had begun reading working-class academic narratives. I read as many as I could get my hands on, and there were plenty. It all came to an episodic head during the winter break when I went home to Staten Island, the same borough that spawned Melanie Griffith's character in the film *Working Girl* and was the butt of jokes for those Manhattan socialites in the TV series *Sex and the City*. It's a place where cops, firemen (trust me, *they* don't call themselves firefighters), nurses, construction workers, beauticians, secretaries, mid- to low-level corporate types, elevator maintenance mechanics, and other trade unionists reside, along with a good number of organized-crime foot soldiers, some of whom I likely grew up with. Even the criminals on Staten Island are bossed around.[1]

While home, I went with my mother to see two of her sisters, two of my former Russian Roulette, day care providers, if you recall, Mary and Donnatelle, eighty-year-olds who shared a two-family house their entire adult lives. Aunt Mary and Aunt "Do-Do" were the kind of working-class housewives who often outlive their husbands by ten or twenty years because they incessantly lug baskets of laundry up and down stairs like Sisyphus and scrub tiny kitchen floors so clean that protective eyewear is required. I was quickly seated at the kitchen table, they being the Italian half of my Polish-Italian heritage, to drink kegs of coffee and eat stacks of homemade zeppoles, holiday staples around my mother's family. As I wiped powdered sugar off my chin and dusted it off my shirt, my Aunt Mary complained that her sister-in-law wouldn't stop bragging about her daughter who'd married a surgeon. "For Christ's sake, he's not even her first husband."

Stuffed with zeppoles and soaring from caffeine, I lowered my eyes, compressed my mouth, and nodded my head, proof of my profound understanding and enduring sensitivity—and as a deft way to glance at my watch. Sometimes these "quick visits," as my mother liked to call them, might last for hours. I had already "done my time," I told myself, when she and my father were separated. Such visits reminded me of when I sat at my grandmother's kitchen table as a child. If I didn't respond to my aunt, maybe the afternoon would go faster. My mother, who sat across from me, didn't remain silent. "Well," she began, rising stiffly in her seat, "why don't you tell her about David, that you have a nephew who is a doctor of ... of ... of?" She was struggling. "Of philosophy," I calmly said. "Right," she hurriedly resumed, "that you have a nephew who is a *Doctor* of Philosophy." She placed as much emphasis on the "doctor" part as possible. Aunt Mary, who sat at the far end of the table, slowly and mechanically swiveled her head toward me, like a gunner's turret. She peered at me, but only for a moment. Suddenly, she barked: "For all of the time you spent in school you coulda been a *real* doctor." My mother slouched into her chair, diminished. "Oh, Mare," she screeched, "what'd you have to say that for?" followed by a gushing celebration of my vocation as Doctor of Something-or-Other. But it was evident she hadn't the slightest idea what I'd done to acquire my doctorate or what I was doing with it now. For my part, I again nodded and said nothing, thinking: *Yes, for all that schooling I could have been a real doctor—as opposed to the fake one I did become.* But I had another thought, less sarcastic and more theoretical. I retreated into the kind of abstract decoding typical of any incisive Phony Doctor of Humanities worth his or her keep: This scene surely must fit into any number of working-class academic conflicts in those narratives I'd been reading.

One such conflict is categorized by editors Jake Ryan and Charles Sackrey in *Strangers in Paradise* as the "imposter-syndrome," the sense that working-class academics, like those *Saturday Night Live* characters from "Wayne's World," are "not worthy" of being in higher education. When it comes to genuine intellectual timber, many working-class academics believe they just don't cut it, and it'll be only a matter of time before the authentic scholars figure it out. That's what Louis Potter in *Strangers* worries about—exactly when will his working-class past and his colleagues' present perception of him collide? "When will they find out I'm a fraud?" he wonders.[2] John Koonings holds similar views, considering himself an "interloper" who does "not belong in the academy."[3] Julie Charlip shares their fears. In her testimony in *This Fine Place*, she admits that "despite my accomplishments—awards, fellowships, teaching assistantships—I still have the sneaking suspicion that someone will shout 'Fraud!' and send me away."[4] In *Working-Class Women in the Academy*, Donna Langston substantiates the trope established by Ryan and Sackrey by describing herself outright as "an imposter."[5]

But feeling like a charlatan has its flip side, turned on its head when

Aunt Mary said I was no real doctor. Evidently, the imposter-syndrome can hit from below as well as from above. The families we come from can see us as "fake" doctors just as surely as can the colleagues to whom we climb up. In my case, my immediate family didn't think I had even the intellectual wherewithal to attend undergraduate school. They couldn't imagine my graduating from college, let alone imagine my becoming a fake doctor. Perhaps, then, I could see myself in those narratives, so long as I focused on feeling humiliated, even if the humiliation was driven from the bottom rather than from the top.

After all, I had every reason to feel inadequate "from below," considering how frequently my family doubted my intellectual abilities. In fact, what I most remember about that day at my aunt's is how my mother impulsively celebrated my alleged doctor-hood, as if all along she had persistently supported my efforts to obtain a Ph.D. If anything, the exact opposite was true. While listening to her unexpectedly proud defense, I remembered that the year before, a few days after I'd submitted the first three chapters of my dissertation for review, she'd mailed me an article from the *Staten Island Advance* reporting that the New York City Sanitation Department was conducting a citywide test to fill hundreds of openings. For years, a hiring freeze had existed because of city budget cuts. She highlighted a passage which warned that the test must be taken before an applicant's fortieth birthday. I was fast approaching that milestone. At the bottom of the page, neatly printed in red ink for maximum visibility, she'd added, "You'd better hurry."

A few days later, she phoned. Right before hanging up, she asked, "Oh, by the way, did you get what I sent you?" Needless to say, I knew "what" she was referring to. That's really why she had called. The miscellaneous chit-chat was pretext for the primary message. "Yes," I replied. "Yes, I did. Thank you. I'll look into it," I lied. I could hear the relief at the other end. "Oh, good, do that. It's not too late, you know. Really, Dave, it's not too late to take the Sanitation test." I didn't respond. There was a long pause at the other end. "You know, it would be a good backup plan," she continued. "How much security will you have with your degree, if you ever get it, and then what are your chances of getting a job anyway?" I didn't feel the need to tell her there was no way in hell I planned on taking the Sanitation Department test a few months shy of receiving my Ph.D. After all my schooling, and all those books, what did she want me to become, Lord of the Flies?

As a matter of fact, she did. Being a college professor didn't make sense to her. It wasn't real work for a real man. Her brother, Sammy, the World

War II veteran auto mechanic, was a real man who performed a man's job. Her attitudes about what constituted appropriate work for a man were similar to those of most people in our working-class community, especially males. There was, and still is, a lot of pressure on working-class males not to be bookish or overly educated. It's uncool, for one thing. For another, only wimps, nerds, and fags are into books. As Richard Rodriguez admitted, he "suspected that education was making [him] effeminate."[6] (Imagine if he had admitted back then that he was gay, rather than leave it out. It would have confirmed to other working-class males that books indeed did turn boys into sissies. Maybe that's why he withheld that very big truth from the book.) My mother held the same opinions about the usefulness of books and higher learning as did most of the men in her circle. Sissies read books and escapists went to college. My Uncle Sammy never went to college and he never read books. As part of the Greatest Generation, he almost singlehandedly saved the world from fascism—well, at least according to my mom. Moreover, what did books and college do for the next generation, except turn them into campus protesters, draft dodgers, hippies, and dope smokers who turned on their parents, the Greatest Generation no less? Compared with them, my mother's brother was more than a hero. He was a saint by taking care of his parents their whole lives by living downstairs from them. Reading books might not only turn boys into homos, but they also might learn about faraway places or find out about things and decide to move away.

As close as I was to completing my doctorate, my mother couldn't help herself when she insisted I take the Sanitation Department test. She wanted to stop me before it was too late, before I acquired my Ph.D., and became ... what? What if it was something less than "a real man"? In her estimation, picking up trash far outweighed picking up *Middlemarch*. For all practical purposes, I understood her reasoning. The unfamiliarity of receiving a higher degree in the humanities distanced her from why I valued it. To me, I wanted to get ahead, or should I say, "a head," at least one better than the one that had been missing a few screws. For her, it all came down to dollars and cents. Getting a doctorate in English made absolutely no sense to her. If nothing else, it seemed highly improbable that some poor schnook growing up in Oakwood Heights who'd been gunned down by a cop could become a professor of English at some for-lorn university. Actually, when I enrolled in a doctoral program I wasn't even thinking that far ahead. I just wanted to keep on learning. I had no plans to parlay my education into professional success. Only near comple-tion did it occur to me that I could.

I finally applied to graduate school while teaching high school English, a job I was happy doing. I assumed that by taking graduate classes part-time I'd end up with my doctorate about when my first Social Security check arrived in the mail. Only when state budget cuts forced the school to fire me (which they euphemistically called being "R-I-F'ed," a "reduction in forces") did I take advantage of the opportunity to attend graduate school full-time. But a lot had changed in the university since I'd last been there, especially within English studies, and not for the better in my opinion. Under the theoretical weight of poststructuralism, specifically, and postmodernism, generally, learning had shrunk to its smallest components. Fifteen years earlier students in my undergraduate English program were encouraged to read such sprawling works as Eric Auerbach's *Mimesis: The Representation of Reality in Western Literature* and Gilbert Highet's *The Classical Tradition: Greek and Roman Influences on Western Literature* to hone their own comprehensive analytical chops. A decade later, in the new theoretical world order, Jacques Derrida and deconstruction were all the rage, and students were celebrated for writing literary analyses focusing on a single word in a text, tracing its unstable meaning and shifting signification. It was all well and good for scholarship (and I enjoy it as a "parlor game") by establishing minutiae as an endless stream of supposedly important esoterica. It thereby creates an infinite supply of finite cultural capital. But what did that have to do with the students I was teaching at various CUNY colleges, the tens of thousands who could barely read and write?

While I was enrolled there, I began earning a less-than-part-time salary as a more-than-full-time adjunct professor. This reinforced my earlier impressions that I had a passion for teaching. And I was pretty darn good at it, too. (I would learn later that that can be a serious impediment in the academy.) After a year at the CUNY Graduate Center I sensed I was staying largely to be as well prepared and as well informed as I could be—for my students. It's why I became interested in Composition and Rhetoric, because of the field's interest in pedagogy, discourse analysis, and literacy, rather than in the narrow specialization that had taken root in the literature program. While I was there, a part of me realized that obtaining a doctorate in the humanities was in fact not the most practical thing to be doing, other than as a means to help others learn. At least that's how I saw it. Had I not seen it that way, I likely would have dropped out. My mother didn't see *any* benefit in what I was doing. According to her, getting a doctorate in English was a *complete* waste of anyone's time. Even now, after all these years, I can't quite bring myself to blame her for thinking that way. After all, once I was enrolled in the program, we were only quibbling over fractions of its value.

My mother's more general views about the uselessness of books and the futility of pursuing higher education were reinforced by her personal views about me. I had done little to demonstrate I'd benefit from even a college education, let alone from graduate studies. I had squandered my youth academically, compounded by my having put the family through hell by getting shot during a botched holdup. It didn't matter how long ago it had occurred, or how far I'd come academically since then. I was not one of those "gifted" children present in the narratives I'd been reading. The shooting solidified her sense of life's devastating disappointments and the fragile human condition, especially among those she was closest to, like her husband. For her son to have carried out such a terrible act confirmed her suspicions that ours was a fallen world; what was the point of trying to improve it by improving yourself? The world's defects and disgraces began with her spouse and her own flesh and blood. She therefore had little faith in redemption generally and almost none in my chances of improving myself specifically. For her, there were no second acts in life. I was nongifted in my youth and I'd be overstepping my capabilities by enrolling in a doctoral program, going nowhere fast with my doctorate in hand. She probably pictured me becoming a stereotype, the Doctor of Something-or-Other who drives a cab for a living. It didn't matter how far I'd come from almost bleeding to death on the old lady's lawn, doing really well as an undergraduate at Boston University, and all those books I'd read. She thought I should drop out of graduate school to become a Sanitation worker. Even after all this time, I have the same reaction now as I did then: Should I laugh or cry? I might laugh at the absurdity of the notion and cry at its implications. Urging me to take the Sanitation test was her way of "looking out for" me. What she saw, what she was looking at, wasn't enough and wasn't going to be much more.

She'd made that clear to me from the start. For a long time I believed her. I didn't have enough faith in myself to resist. I was still Robin to someone else's Batman. Soon after I was shot I learned about the enormous mess my body was in after taking on three bullets. Nearly all my blood had leaked out. I was in worse condition than some of the sports cars my father drove. As bad as my condition was, medical science saved me. As much as I believed my unawareness of being shot with real bullets, and the epiphany that followed helped, I survived primarily because of the scientific knowledge and nimble skills of the surgeon, Dr. Rose. The minor miracle that kept me alive amazed me. Sure, nothing short of an actual miracle can save people like the Crypt Keeper and the Mummy, but I was so intrigued by the medical magic Dr. Rose practiced I thought I might one day become a doctor. That would be a clear path toward turning my life around if I could help others turn theirs around.

"*You* want to be a doctor?" my mother replied in total disbelief, as if I had said I wanted to build the world's first time machine. Her dismissive tone provided the answer to her own question. In case there was any doubt about its unsoundness, there was "the accident" to dangle over my head. "Considering what you just put us through," she added, "I'm surprised you'd even think of such a thing." But there was one more nail to put in my coffin. "You have to be smart to be a doctor," she added, "and you have to be really good in school." Then there was a pause. Finally, she asked, less stridently, and almost soothingly: "Do you really think it's for you?" as if she were seeking my opinion. The question at the end of her observations became a pattern throughout my life. It punctuated her resistance to whatever aspirations I had, set up like Plato's Dialogues wherein Socrates gets to ask all the juicy questions to demonstrate his cleverness and expose the shriveled acumen of others.

But this was no book. Her words struck harder and reached deeper. It was an anti-motivational ground-to-air missile. It often proved lethal, as it did the first time. Once she shot the idea down I never gave it another thought. *She was right*, I concluded. End of story. I could never become a "real doctor." What was I thinking? In fact, she was convinced I shouldn't even attend a "real" college. On that I put up some resistance. But it didn't last. She threw too many obstacles at me. First, she sabotaged my meeting with my high school guidance counselor. When that didn't completely work, she called in reinforcements, a cousin who was a school principal who convinced me of the brilliancy of going to a junior college to become a court reporter. Before then, though, I continued thinking that my life had been spared (not in any cosmic way, just pure and simple logistics). I wanted to do important things with it, with what I felt was a second chance.

Okay, I thought, *so I can't be a surgeon and restore people's fading lives, as my surgeon had done for mine.* But maybe I could be a brilliant scientist or mathematician. The off-the-charts upswing in my academic performance suggested that I could. In the back of my mind I knew I'd acquire a doctorate. I might someday help solve such vexing problems as hunger or more small-ball ones like championing better personal health. It may have been unrealistic to think I could do those things. I might never have gotten to any of those places, even if my parents had supported me wholeheartedly. Nevertheless, I happened to be in a certain mental place then that might have taken me to those places. I wanted to save the world instead of destroy myself. I didn't tell them that. Maybe I should have, but my mother wasn't even willing to wrap her head around the idea that I wanted to attend college let alone that I wanted to rescue some piece of humankind.

In my senior year I started sending out college applications, all of them in the Northeast and all of them either second- or third-tier schools. I was applying later than most kids. But what did I know? Nobody was helping me fill them out or offering advice. I was on my own, doing it ad hoc and probably with little skill. What I did know was that my overall record in high school wasn't so great, despite the recent upturn. I didn't have a chance of getting into any top-tier school. But I had a plan. First, I'd work my ass off at Anywhere U., just as I had been doing, turn my newly acquired laser beam focus up to maximum setting, and prove my mettle. After my freshman or sophomore year, I'd transfer to a top-tier school. My mother thought otherwise. I wouldn't be going anywhere. Second-, third-, or last-tier four-year colleges weren't in her sights for me. She'd been pleading with me to take New York City's battery of civil service tests, especially the Sanitation one. It was the safest bet. Dealing with garbage was better than dealing with fires and bad guys (like me). Instead of seeing me take those tests, she saw the "Thank you for applying to our school" postcards arriving in the mail.

"Why don't you set up an appointment with your guidance counselor?" she suggested one day. "Maybe he can help you." I thought she meant he could help me decide what college to attend or help me fill out the applications. Only years later did it occur to me that she suggested it for another reason.

"Can I help you?" the Counseling Office's secretary asked when I walked into the main room. She sat at the base of a T-shaped configuration of sprawling offices and rooms, a portal to the dozen or more counselors on staff. My counselor occupied the first office behind her to the right. "I'm here to see Mr. Sorensen," I said.

"You must be . . ."

"David. David Borkowski."

She didn't bother looking at any chart or schedule book. She took me at my word, who I was and that I indeed had an appointment with him. "He's with someone right now, but as soon as he's done he'll be right with you."

I sat down and waited my turn. Within minutes, a student walked out of his office, with Mr. Sorensen trailing behind. He stood in the doorway, looking at me and then back at the secretary, waiting for one of us to say something.

"This young man is here to see you," she said. "He has an appointment." She didn't give him my name.

His office was a mess. Folders, papers, files, and books were everywhere, piled on his desk, piled on the floor, and piled on top of filing cabinets and shoved into metal bookcases. It wasn't surprising. Tottenville High School was enormous. Nearly 5,000 students went there. My graduating class was 1,200. If Mr. Sorensen was responsible for counseling only the students whose last names started from A to E he must have been overworked.

"What can I do for you?" he asked. I immediately launched into my story, how I hadn't exactly been a model student for a few years but that I'd gotten my act together, starting especially in the second term of my junior year. I hoped it wasn't too late to get into college, I "asked" rhetorically. "I'm in AP Calculus right now," I added, "and my math teacher thinks I should take AP Algebra next semester."

"AP Calculus!" He sat up in his chair and unruffled his tie. "That's pretty impressive. I bet we're only offering one. I bet you're among ten students in the class, tops. Am I right?" I nodded. "Nice," he said. "Who's your math teacher?" I told him. "Well, she knows what she's talking about. If she's high on you then you must be a good student." I talked about my plan, to get into a decent school and then apply to a better one.

"That's a good idea," he said, "but you should still apply to one or two of those better schools you're interested in, now. You never know. Maybe your math teacher can write you a letter of recommendation." He fumbled through the material on his desk. "What's your name again?" He didn't remember that he hadn't been given my name, nor had I introduced myself. I told him. "David. David Borkowski."

I might as well have said "Charles Manson." His expression completely changed. He slumped back into his chair, taking his eyes off me completely, and somberly said, "You know, college isn't for everyone." *Where did* that *come from?* I wondered. "Have you considered taking the civil service tests?" he asked. "They make good money. I wish I made as much as them." I was stunned at the reversal. I don't remember what I said, if I said anything. I don't think he said anything more, either. He had given me two pieces of advice, the polar opposites of each other. The first he based on my profile; the second, on my name. Only years later did I realize that my mother had called him in advance, explaining her side of the story and undermining my own, perhaps even telling him I'd been involved in a robbery. After hearing my name he made the connection of who I really was rather than who I was trying to become.

I left dejected—and less certain of my goal—but not without grabbing off the wall racks a few brochures for what I believed were the weakest colleges in the area. I set my sights even lower, considering what he'd told me, that college wasn't for everyone. But I figured maybe there were some colleges accepting just about anyone, not just the chosen ones. Even a nobody might still have a chance of survival. Hell, it worked for Odysseus.

My father mostly stayed out of the picture. He said little to us and rarely shared his opinions about anything. He seemed doubly reserved among me and my sister at the time because he'd been back for only a couple of years. I imagine he felt more like the way a stepfather might feel in a new household among children not his own. There also was an additional distance between the two of us as a consequence of the shooting. As I learned several years later, he thought that leaving us had led to the robberies, which led to the shooting. *His* guilt silenced him further than the silence he already was predisposed to, virtually stifling whatever influence he might have had concerning the direction of my life when it mattered most. But maybe that's why he waited so long to tell me. It was safer that way.

We were driving back to Staten Island from a golf outing in New Jersey when he brought it up. I had recently enrolled in graduate school, so it was more than fifteen years since the shooting. For all I know, he might have been looking for years for the "right" time to raise his concern. Then again, this was the same man who had advised me days after being shot not to talk about it, ever. No wonder it took him so long. He wasn't in the habit of expressing himself, especially when it came to that subject. Not surprisingly, he did so in a roundabout way. At first, I had no idea what he was talking about.

"Does it bother you to swing a golf club?" he awkwardly began.

"Bother me? No. Why?"

"Oh, I don't know. I was just asking." He had to slow down as the traffic slowed ahead. We hadn't timed the day well. We were returning in the middle of rush hour and as we approached the exit for the Outerbridge it began to look like a parking lot. "I guess I was asking," he resumed as the car came to a standstill, "if, well, you know, if there's any lingering pain or discomfort making that kind of motion, twisting your body like that, you know, still, after the accident?"

"You mean *after being shot*?" I asked, in the most weightless, matter-of-fact tone possible. "You can say it, Dad: 'After being shot.' It wasn't an *accident*. It didn't just happen."

"No, of course not." There was an uncomfortable pause. "Speaking of which, sometimes I blame myself."

"What? Really? For what?"

"Well, yes. I blame myself for, you know, for you being shot. That maybe you did it because of the separation, the robberies and all. That maybe if I was there it wouldn't have happened."

"I can't answer that," I said. "Maybe it had something to do with it; then again, maybe not. A large part of me thinks that whether or not you were there I still would have done it."

I'm sure that didn't sound reassuring to him. If anything, it must have seemed I was suggesting that his presence would have provided as much guidance as his absence. I didn't mean it that way, not entirely. From the moment it happened, and for the rest of my life, I never blamed anyone other than myself for it. It had to be that way. I *needed* to take full responsibility for bringing myself to that "bad" place in order to be accountable for taking myself out of it and heading toward a better one. I had to accept all of it to fully recover, to find redemption, however privatized it had become.

Whether his presence during my childhood would have altered anything was irrelevant to *me*. If he needed to come clean about how he felt, it might have been better if he'd done so sooner. If anything, I may have found fault with his behavior *after* he'd come back into our lives. He had physically returned to us, but he stood in the shadows. He said virtually nothing to me about anything significant, except to advise me to keep quiet about having been shot. He had given me the impression that important subjects weren't to be discussed, by either of us. Whether he expected me to go to college or not, he never said. My mother did all the talking, and strategizing. She held strong opinions about my future, and she zealously expressed them.

When I said I was thinking of becoming a doctor, my mother clearly thought it was one of the most ridiculous things she had ever heard. She wasn't prepared to send me to even a four-year school, let alone somewhere where I would enroll in a pre-med program. When she quashed my idea of becoming a doctor, I removed it so fast and so far from my mind that only now, writing about those days, do I recall the exchange. What she most wanted me to do was take as many civil service tests as possible and become a train conductor or a sanitation worker. It's funny that she never completely abandoned her dream, right up to the time I was obtaining my Ph.D.

But I wasn't signing up to take those civil service tests. Instead, I was filling out college applications. As much as she disapproved of my going to college, she liked the possible "going away" part, my being at a safer distance from Dougie and other bad influences that had led to the "accident." But sending me to a four-year college wasn't worth that. As I continued to fill out college applications, even after I'd talked to my guidance counselor, she grew increasingly worried. If Mr. Sorensen couldn't stop me, and neither could she, then she'd have to wage a two-front war. Sure enough, she sent for backup, now someone who'd try to sell me something other than civil service tests. The romance and practicality of attending a trade school or a community college appeared on the scene, including one in particular that would require me to live away. If I wanted to leave Staten Island so much, finding such a school could only enhance the scheme, making it easier for me to accept it and therefore drop my own plan. A cousin was summoned to "advise" me. But as had been the case with my meeting with the guidance counselor, the advice he offered had been prearranged.

In truth, my mother probably overreacted to my chances of getting into those four-year colleges, especially without anyone's help. Sure, I had a plan, but I didn't know how to execute it properly. Also, much of my crappy academic past wasn't far behind, casting a shadow on whatever very recent progress I had made. Furthermore, I'd bombed the SAT. My scores were abysmal. I didn't take the PSAT in my junior year because I was recovering from gunshot wounds when it was first administered, and I was too ignorant about it overall to know what it was. I was so nervous taking the SAT I might as well have been drunk. I was unaware that it could be taken more than once. I thought it was like all tests, a one-time-only deal. Nobody suggested I try again. My SAT scores only confirmed what my family already knew and what my counselor had advised: College wasn't for everyone. And it wasn't for me.

I probably made a mess out of the applications too. Not knowing any better, I may as well have filled them out in crayon in my attempt to make them more colorful. I didn't know how to type, so in my nearly illegible handwriting I submitted a personal statement that was undoubtedly riddled with mistakes and likely incoherent. Most of the schools rejected me, but a couple didn't, probably the ones with near–open admissions policies, the schools I hurriedly applied to after visiting my guidance counselor. Which ones accepted me, I don't remember. Once I'd been persuaded not to attend any of them and apply to Johnson & Wales Junior College to learn to become a court reporter, I stopped caring one way or the other. I think I threw out the last couple of responses without even opening them, something I'd repeat when I was offered scholarships to graduate school six years later.

My cousin-in-law John was married to my oldest cousin, Ann-Marie, on my mother's side. John and Ann-Marie were nearly as old as my parents. John had risen through the ranks of the public school system, first as a gym teacher, eventually reaching as high as superintendent. While teaching gym, he had worked evenings and weekends on his Ed.D. He was the most educated member on both sides of our family. In addition, during my parents' separation John had taken a personal interest in my well-being at our frequent family gatherings. For anyone unfamiliar with Italian American families, "frequent" is an understatement. Not only did we have family barbecues on Memorial Day, July 4th, and Labor Day, but if there was any food left over (and there always was) we would get together the following day and finish it. Religious celebrations rivaled the Vatican's pageantry, and we consumed as much food and drink as Rome. We even celebrated St. Patrick's Day. If there had been some way to work in roasting a groundhog, we would have celebrated that day too. Any excuse was found to bring the family together, to eat for eight to ten hours. On such occasions, John made it a point to play with me, tossing a football around or playing an improvised game of handball within a chalked-out miniature tennis rectangle. They were generous gestures, and not anomalies by any means; I welcomed them and appreciated him for it. Between his degrees and his closeness to me, my mother saw him as an ideal ally in her campaign to prevent me from attending a four-year school.

One Saturday evening during the winter of my senior year, she invited him over for dinner. My sister was out preparing for her upcoming wedding, auditioning bands. While I'm sure my father was present, I can't picture him there. I clearly remember John and my mother, though. They did all the talking.

As if it were last Saturday, not more than thirty years ago, I vividly remember the preparations and what my mother cooked. She treated it as if it were a holiday. To her, it was a special event. To me, it seemed like the end of my dream. For everyone, it was a blueprint for the future. She served roast beef, mashed potatoes, and stringbeans. We all drenched the meat and potatoes with the thick gravy poured from a white ceramic watering pitcher we passed back and forth. Dinner conversation involved the usual topics about favorite TV shows, popular movies, and family gossip. When she served dessert—apple pie à la mode—my mother introduced John as if he were a public speaker. "Well, you know why I invited John here, to discuss your plans," she said, nodding at me, "and where you might go to school. He has a couple of ideas in mind. So, why don't we turn it over to him: John?"

He had only one thing on his mind, not "a couple of ideas." John was well aware that I wanted to leave Staten Island, along with the benefits of ridding me of the people, places, and things interfering with my "rehabilitation," as the recovering substance abusers I'd teach years later would say. He must have felt he'd found the perfect solution. He handed me a brochure from a two-year college in Providence, Rhode Island, that specialized in culinary arts and had a business school. Within the business school, a number of associate degrees were offered in accounting, finance, and management. He and my mom must have agreed that such subjects were too difficult for me to handle, or that I wouldn't bite at someday managing a food franchise. Instead, they settled on a program that was, not coincidentally, the most "hands-on" degree available, short of becoming a cook if I enrolled in the culinary school. He pointed to a section on the brochure that touted the benefits of majoring in court reporting. It was a rare white-collar skill to master. I'd be working with my hands, but they'd remain clean—no dirt under my fingernails. I wouldn't be embarrassed, like Pip in *Great Expectations*. I'd be a "respectable" member of the middle class. It wasn't working-class work. ("They make good money!" John and my mother euphorically reminded me several times throughout dessert.) Everything about it was a plus. "Providence would be a great location to go to school," he declared. "You'd have a lot of fun there," he added, making it sound more exciting and exotic than the run-down industrial city it was back then.

I examined the brochure. There were a few sentences pitching the advantages of becoming a court reporter: taking dictation during important corporate meetings, playing a significant role in important court cases, and working with some of the most powerful people in the country. Like John's remarks about Providence, the brochure made it seem more glamorous and interesting than the tedious, intellectually dreary work it actually was. Nothing about it appealed to me, except the opportunity to leave Staten Island. As if I were a boy back in Andrew's room daydreaming, or sitting in my grandmother's kitchen, I stared out the window. I imagined myself sneaking into Providence College or Brown University and hiding in the back of a classroom—acquiring some kind of covert education there. After I arrived at Johnson & Wales that vision never left me. I often walked alone through Brown's leafy campus wondering what it would be like to be a "real" student.

My mother went to the kitchen to put the softening ice cream away and returned with a pot of coffee. She poured three cups and passed them around. She was using the "good china," as she liked to say, so the cups rattled a bit on the saucers they rested on because she was nervously unaccustomed to using them. I wasn't drinking coffee then so I had a glass of milk. I pretended to be studying the brochure carefully. I felt trapped. When I looked up, the two of them were staring at me, smiling, pleased with themselves for the clever way they had handled the situation. My father said next to nothing the entire time. Like the day I learned he was leaving us, his head and eyes were buried in his lap.

"You know, Aunt Julia," John began, "this coffee is a little too hot for me. Could I please have an ice cube? That'll cool it off."

"Why, sure, John," my mother said, getting up. She could practically stretch her hand out and reach into the refrigerator from her dining room seat. "I'm so sorry," she continued, returning and carrying several ice cubes in a small dish. "I guess I should have let it cool first."

"Oh, no, it's perfectly fine. I'm just not a fan of really hot coffee," John informed us, scanning the room. "Let's make a bet," he said, plopping a cube into his coffee, "to see how long it will take for this to dissolve." He looked at his watch and pronounced his prediction. The rest of us played along. Of course John had the correct time. He probably had done it before. It was a calculated experiment with a predictable outcome. Maybe that's how he viewed suggesting court reporting to me. He meant well, but it was exhausting enough enduring my mother's low expectations of me. John's presence and impact had squared it. Once the ice cube melted I couldn't help but see it as representing my own dissolving desire to become formally educated.

Despite my recent academic accomplishments and my epiphany, I didn't have the wherewithal or the guts to fall back on myself. I continued to rack up other academic victories that demonstrated I had come a long way from the stickup. In addition to spending a semester in AP Calculus, I scored a 91 on the state's Physics Regents exam, a feat likely shared by a tiny fraction of the tens of thousands, if not millions, who've taken it over the decades. That happened at the end of my senior year. By then it probably was too late to prove anything further to anyone, if it would have even mattered anyway. My bags already were packed before that test was administered. I was heading to Providence to become a court reporter. Similar to how I purged any ideas of becoming a doctor, I rid myself forever of studying math or science. Even when I was accepted into Boston University two years later, neither subject occurred to me as study options. I had moved on, and I did so as swiftly as when I abandoned a career in medical science.

When my AP Calculus teacher asked me why I would be dropping that subject in the spring and not enrolling in AP Algebra to prepare for the exam, as she advised, I casually told her I would be taking typing and stenography instead.

"Why are you doing that?" she asked with alarm.

"I've decided to become a court reporter," I proudly explained, sounding as if I were fulfilling a lifelong dream.

"Really?" she said, more surprised than alarmed.

"Oh, yeah, it's a good career, and it's what I want to do," I assured her. I said the words with such conviction they further convinced *me* of what a great idea it was. No sooner had the idea been planted in my head than I'd started believing in its soundness.

"Well, okay," she said, "if that's what you want to do."

It was, I told her, it definitely was.

I hated Johnson & Wales. I sat in typing classes and learned how to decode the court reporting machine's Byzantine system, when what I most wanted to be doing was studying Aristotle or taking Organic Chemistry. Whenever I came across a relatively challenging course or project, I sank my teeth into it like a pitbull, such as the compulsory business law course. One of its requirements involved summarizing a prominent court case. I decided that wasn't enough. I spent hours inside the state's Supreme Court library researching the landmark affirmative action case *Regents of the University of California v. Bakke*. When the instructor returned it, he had written at the bottom of the last page only "Please see me." There was no grade.

"You wrote this?" he asked.

"Well, yes. Of course I did. Why?"

"I can see it's in your own words. The writing, quite honestly, is very unpolished and weak in a few spots, but you could have rewritten an article to make it appear your own."

I didn't know what he was getting at. "Plagiarism" probably wasn't part of my vocabulary at the time, and it never would have occurred to me to skip the process of learning about the subject by piggy-backing on someone else's accomplishment. When I was a helplessly indifferent student I wouldn't even have bothered trying to figure out how to plagiarize a writing assignment. I was quite comfortable either doing it half-assed or not doing it at all.

"I didn't rewrite any articles," I said. "I read a bunch of law books, if that's what you mean. The stuff I pulled directly from them I underlined," I added. I didn't know how to properly cite from other sources because I'd never written a research paper before. I assumed that a law paper required some special treatment, so that's what I'd given it. "Look, I did a lot of work on this," I said, as I pulled a notebook from a cluster of books I was carrying in a small canvas duffle bag. "Here are my notes."

He thumbed through the notebook's pages, pausing once in a while to read over the material. Nearly the entire book was filled with details about the case and material dealing with affirmative action, college admissions policies, discrimination, and quotas.

"You didn't supply a bibliography and you didn't cite the material properly. More than anything, you didn't need to do all of this; so, I'm sorry, but I thought maybe you didn't do it. I guess the real question, then, is why would you? You didn't need to go through all of this trouble."

"I wanted to. It seemed interesting."

He looked at me strangely. "Again, the writing has its flaws, but other than that it's almost as good as what my law students do." We stared at each other for a couple of seconds, the encounter growing increasingly uncomfortable. I didn't know what else to say. "What are you doing here?" he finally asked, breaking the silence. "I mean, at this school." I knew what he meant, but I still didn't know what to say. What was I supposed to tell him, "My mother made me"? He might have thought I was joking and laughed. Really, though, if I told him the real reason why I was there I might have broken down in tears right then and there, having to listen to those words come out of my mouth. Talking isn't always a cure.

I did my time at Johnson & Wales. For me, at least, the most intellectually rewarding experience occurred outside of school. That experience also influenced my decision to get a well-rounded liberal arts education when I attended Boston University, as did the influence of my girlfriend's family (but that's truly a whole other story).

At the beginning of my first semester at Johnson & Wales, I stumbled across a beat-up hardbound copy of Mortimer Adler's *How to Read a Book*. I spotted it sitting on a "Free Books" portable book rack in the Providence Public Library. Finding the city's public library was one of the first things I did when I arrived. After taking the book back to my dorm, where I hid it under my clothes in the dresser, I avidly began reading the "Great Books" listed in the back pages of Adler's manual. I wasn't entirely antisocial at the school by any means. I attended my fair share of dorm parties and took my fair share of hits from the bong. They grew like weeds in every dorm room. Most of the time we played cards or backgammon while listening to Led Zeppelin or to Peter Frampton's *Live* album. On some nights a person didn't need a bong to get high. You could simply inhale the smoky air and get a buzz while playing blackjack.

I managed to sneak off frequently to read *The Odyssey* or Xenophon's *Anabasis* once I discovered Adler's list. I decided it wasn't enough to read only the Greek classics he listed, or the two or three "especially" plays by the Greek playwrights he recommended. I read all the extant ones available and whatever else I could find written during that era. I did, however, heed Adler's advice to have a "conversation" with the texts by underlining passages and writing responses along the margins. I still have many of those texts. In reading the margin notes now I must admit I'm rather pleased with myself. Several keen insights survive, in a sloppy handwriting that doesn't seem to be my own. I wasn't quite as insipid as my family thought I was.

I wasted two years at a school that was barren of the intellectual stimulation I craved. Its library was as small as my bedroom back home and it contained only business books. I knew plenty of wonderful people there, but no one was serious about learning anything serious: Get the two-year degree in finance and get the hell out. That was fine for them, but not for me. I wanted something else, something more. I felt the same way about becoming a fireman or a sanitation worker. It wasn't what I wanted to do. Don't get me wrong. Such work is honorable and important. I've never once believed that my books or my advanced degrees make me better than friends and family who did become firemen or elevator repair mechanics. In our celebrity culture, we mourn the deaths of unimportant people in our lives who really don't matter much to us, like Lady Diana or Michael Jackson, whereas the truly important ones, the people who keep our streets safe and clean, go largely unrecognized (until politicians want their vote). I never felt disdain for any of my classmates at Johnson & Wales. Nor did it ever occur to me that I was better than they because I was reading Aristotle's *Poetics*, and they weren't. Being bookish doesn't automatically confer moral or social superiority on a person, or even intelligence for that matter (knowledge, yes). Hemingway was one of the most widely read men of his day but that didn't stop him from beating the shit out of his wives or blowing his brains out with a shotgun. Many

Nazis were thumbing through the pages of Goethe and Schiller, while listening to Bach and Brahms, as they turned up the gas on their victims. Books can do as much harm as good.

But in all honesty, most of my schoolmates at Johnson & Wales were as suspicious of books and "education" as the Staten Island kids I'd grown up with and my family. They memorized their textbooks for exams and forgot the material as quickly as possible to prepare for the next one. But I never faulted them for that, just as I don't fault my own students now. Over time, what I began to question was a school system that largely used books as a gauge while simultaneously touting their value as a way to get ahead materially. Both ultimately diminish their real value as a way to advance literacy. In many classrooms, books are agents of social discipline rather than agents of personal liberation. The biggest lesson many people who pass through our educational institutions learn is realizing how uninterested they are in the very subjects they are being taught. My classmates at Johnson & Wales were all bright, decent kids, but they were typical of the "average student" who consumes knowledge and learning according to how the typical factory school system produces it. They were by-products of an intellectually dispassionate environment, as was I. Johnson & Wales existed to turn out worker bees, not thoughtful citizens, as do many institutions of so-called higher learning. Perhaps that's why what I most remember about the place were the things I learned outside of school, the joy and satisfaction of reading Thucydides and Sophocles while moving around Adler's list.

I received an Associate Degree from Johnson & Wales in court reporting. I learned to type as fast as 280 words per minute on the steno machine. I could have started working in the field immediately, earning more back then, twenty-five years ago, than I'm earning as a college professor now. But I couldn't imagine myself sitting in a courtroom listening to testimony or squirming in a boardroom listening to depositions. I never practiced court reporting professionally. I foresaw this as soon as I began studying it. But I decided to complete the program because I didn't want to go down in flames as a quitter. More important, I believed if I stuck it out I could shake my family off of my back and enroll in a more earnest academic program.

Once again, I filled out college applications. This time, though, I could type. And this time I didn't tell my family. Only my girlfriend knew. Because I wanted to stay near her, I applied strictly to colleges in Boston. Tufts University and Boston College rejected me; Boston University accepted me "on probation." I had to maintain a 2.5 GPA my first semester, which I did easily. I wouldn't say my parents were upset I had abandoned court reporting to attend BU, more like in shock. For years thereafter my mother often asked why I didn't dust off the machine and earn some real money. She did this even while suggesting I take the Sanitation Department test as I was preparing to complete my doctorate. I guess I could've combined the two skills and taken minutes during all the trash talk. Once I declared my major after one semester at BU, English, and minor, history, my parents went from shock to batshit, especially my mother. She and my sister repeatedly urged me to switch my major to something more practical, like business administration. For three and a half years I kept hearing the same stereophonic tune. There were additional refrains. "You could at least take some computer science or business courses," they'd both say, as if a couple of computer science classes would secure a position in the field. Really, they didn't know what they were talking about. But here's the thing: I listened to them. I'd take such courses, resent being in them, and not do well in them. (Okay, sure, possible passive/aggressive behavior at play, but I was also uninterested and bored.) In all my other courses, including a couple of graduate courses I'd slipped into, I was receiving A's, with an occasional B+.

In such courses I *had* become a gifted student. I shone in class, less lustrous in my writing at first, although I did better at compiling heavy-handed research papers for my history classes than I did writing standard literary essays for my English classes. I must have sparkled enough in all of them because at least two of my professors, without any solicitation on my part, contacted colleagues at three different graduate programs about me. One was in history. All three not only invited me to enroll in their programs, they also all offered me scholarships. It was better late than never, as the cliché goes. True, the scholarships came six or seven years after most working-class academics were offered theirs, but I was six or seven years behind them intellectually so I didn't mind. To me, the invitations and scholarships demonstrated how far I'd come, no matter how late they had arrived. I felt liberated. But not from the working class, or from my working-class family: I finally felt free of that jerk carrying a water pistol that rainy October night.

I hadn't been gifted in my youth, but there I was being offered the same prize as those who were. By fudging the years, I might begin to see myself in all those working-class academic narratives I'd been devouring. Even if my Aunt Mary was right, that I was only turning into a fake doctor, I had become a "Scholarship Boy." In the tradition of the narratives, I'd be undergoing the most significant chapter in a bootstrapper's journey, except for one significant detail. I let my family and my girlfriend, Madeleine, talk me out of pursuing those programs and scholarships. Within months, I'd broken up with her, a woman I'd dated for five years and whom I'd planned on marrying. I didn't realize it then, but I must have been subconsciously resentful that *she* hadn't at least supported me. Her I could get rid of. Family is different. I didn't accept the scholarships and go to graduate school at that time. Given the chance, I turned down the opportunity to cast myself in the classic role established in nearly every working-class academic story. I didn't become a Scholarship Boy, just as I didn't become a doctor, or a scientist, or a legal scholar, a prospect opened up to me at Boston University by a man who had argued cases before the Supreme Court. Similar to all those other opportunities, I heeded the unsound advice of my parents. I turned it down and did nothing.

After being shot I became, like Odysseus, "the man of twists and turns driven time and again off course." After receiving his wound, it took him ten years to return home. It took me a little longer after receiving mine, finding a home in the classroom. If I had become a Scholarship Boy, starting out all the way back to when my math teacher had implored me to take AP Algebra, I might not have found that home. All those setbacks made me who I am; not a Scholarship Boy but a Teacher Man.

9
Witness

Smelly Capelli watched them pack me into the back of the ambulance. But he didn't recognize me. He had no idea he was seeing someone he'd known practically his entire life. I had lost so much blood by then that I no longer looked like myself.

Paulie lived around the block from where I lay bleeding. At some point he had to see for himself what all the fuss was about. The general commotion, which lasted more than an hour, already had aroused most of the neighborhood. Once the cops on foot finally found me, they called for backup, and eventually an ambulance arrived. The police cruisers tearing up and down Guyon Avenue looking for me quickly converged at the corner of Isabella Avenue and Leeds Street. There were dozens of them. The place was lit up like an old-fashioned grand opening for a Hollywood movie. It was a spectacle. It undoubtedly was the only one the area had ever had before and likely the only one it would ever have.

Paulie was watching TV in his basement when the ruckus forced him to turn off the set, put on his jacket, and walk around the block to see what was going on. He told me that the steady drizzle nearly stopped him from going. "I almost went back inside and didn't bother walking to the spot." By the time he did, the cops had finished interrogating me and I was unconscious. When he arrived they were rolling my limp body onto a collapsed gurney. Others had emerged from their homes as well to see what was happening. Paulie had to nudge through the small semicircle of neighbors and cops surrounding me. Only days later when word spread that I'd nearly been shot to death did he know it was I he'd seen being placed in the ambulance.

The ride to Richmond Memorial Hospital from Oakwood Heights took nearly half an hour. With today's increased traffic it might take twice that long. On the way there I flatlined. For a few moments I was officially dead. I was stabilized long enough to reach the hospital. Soon after I arrived I flatlined again.

For another hour or so while I was further stabilized, I remained firmly unconscious, until I briefly snapped out of it and saw the nurse fiddling with whatever liquid-filled bags were keeping me alive. For nearly three hours I was as close to death as anyone can be without actually dying. I would remain perilously close for several more hours and alarmingly close for a couple of days. In their extra-professional estimation of those first few hours immediately after I'd been shot, nurses and doctors spoke of how it was "a miracle" I hadn't died, with one doctor casually informing me, "You really should be dead, you know." Others mentioned how "lucky" I was. More like dumb-luck. Lucky because I was too dumb at first to realize I'd been shot by a real gun loaded with real bullets.

But it was no miracle either, as the medical staff well knew. It was a convenient turn of phrase for them, and a way of highlighting just how much my being alive was an aberration. There was nothing divine about any of it for me. Of those two hours while on the verge of death I remember nothing. It's a void because I was in one. I was blanketed by complete and utter darkness. Recently, in preparing to write this, I searched the web for "near-death experiences," hoping to find a group or organization where people discuss their experiences. I thought it might be useful and interesting to learn from others what they went through, finding out about the similarities and differences of having come so close to death. After scrolling through more than ten computer screen pages of listed sites, I gave up. Nearly every one featured contacts of people who had undergone a spiritual or religious vision. And almost all of them mentioned a bright light coming at them, or their moving toward one, or their being engulfed by it. Others claimed momentarily joining dead loved ones, greeting them in blazingly bright rooms or floating with them like cumulus clouds along a tranquil haze. A few discussed seeing Jesus or the Virgin Mary, usually in some magnificent setting, like standing at the base of a glorious sun rising on the horizon.

I saw nothing. And I think what others saw is what they wanted to see. They envisioned what already existed in their minds. I'm sure if I were to locate a website devoted to Hindus who've had near-death experiences, they'd claim they saw Vishnu rather than Jesus, Joseph, and Mary, whom the Christians saw. And those who saw the deceased were likely grieving about their loss long before they encountered them in "the afterlife." Something tells me those repetitious recollections of rock 'n' roll light shows are manifestations of the withering physical body. I truly wish I could claim I saw such splendidly brilliant lights rather than the total darkness I experienced.

So, no, my near-death experience didn't produce any rapturous lights of transcendence or spiritual figures guiding me to glory. Nor did I see any dead loved ones, probably because no one I loved was dead. When I was unconscious I saw nothing. The same was true of my epiphany. In fact, that *was* my epiphany—the absence of time, place, and thing. I had a series of revelations when the priest was administering me the last rites, and the one that most mattered, and has no other equivalent in name except "an epiphany," took place when I did see the light. But not an actual blaze of light, more like the metaphorical kind. It was enlightenment. It lasted for only a minute or two, but it was so powerful that it felt as if the energy of the universe were coursing through the fabric of my being. I can't say for sure whether that's what saved me the most from death, the "miracle" or "luck" of that vision. All I know is that I felt the sheer concentrated force of life in those few moments. I've relied on that imprint ever since, as a way to exist in the here-and-now. Consciously aware of being so close to death transformed how I would live the rest of my life: *One* glorious *moment* at a time. As Blake wrote, eternity is in love with the productions of time. In some respect I had wed my hell with heaven.

10

Re-Gifted

I tested the possibility of attending graduate school on the four people closest to me. I informed them separately. On four separate occasions, I heard four different reasons why I shouldn't.

"The University of Kansas?" my sister hollered in disbelief when I told her about the first school that had contacted me. We were sitting in her TV room, waiting to watch a movie I'd rented. My brother-in-law was in the kitchen, pouring a couple of beers and tending to the popcorn they always made for me when I came over. "What are you going to do way out there?" my sister wanted to know. From the kitchen, my brother-in-law twisted the famous line from *The Wizard of Oz* into how I *would* be in Kansas, forevermore.

"It has one of the best graduate programs in English in the country, especially in American Literature," I explained, saying it loud enough so both of them could hear me.

"Who cares?" she said. "It's in the middle of nowhere. Oh, Dave, please don't tell me you're thinking of moving to Kansas."

To my father it didn't matter if the school was located in our back yard. "Don't you think you've been in school long enough?" It was the classic rhetorical question. Perhaps he'd been taking lessons from my mom. He was sitting on the porch in a wicker chair doing the *Daily News*'s crossword puzzle. I had sat down next to him in the other wicker chair, divided by the matching wicker end-table, when I interrupted him with the news. "Don't you think it's about time you get a job?" he added, returning to scratching letters in the tiny boxes with his pencil.

Get a job? Was he serious? I'd been working thirty to forty hours a week in a warehouse and then a supermarket to pay for my schooling. While I had strung together a number of Pell Grants and taken out a couple of extremely low-interest student loans to cover my tuition at Boston University, I still needed to pay for books, food, clothing, and the occasional night out with Madeleine, which seemed to cost nearly a week's wages. I didn't have a car. I didn't own a TV. I couldn't even afford a telephone. When I called my parents I did so from a pay phone in a laundromat across the street from my dingy studio apartment. We had it worked out that I'd call collect for "David," they'd refuse the call, we'd hang up, and then they would call me back. My father did send me $100 every month to cover my rent. As an older transfer student I didn't have to live on campus, which was what I wanted. My freshman year I lived in a rat- and roach-infested apartment building in Boston and then moved to Franklin, a town close to where Madeleine lived with her parents. After experiencing Johnson & Wales's dorm life, I wanted to avoid any distractions from my studies. I preferred the real roaches to the ones piled up in ashtrays in most dorm rooms.

When I was accepted to Boston University my parents didn't offer to pay my tuition, and aside from the rent check I received in the mail every month, they didn't provide any financial support. I didn't care. I was attending a top-notch university, I knew where every used-book store in Boston and Cambridge was, and I was in love with someone I had met the year before at Johnson & Wales. (Okay, there were *two* terrific things that came out of my time at Johnson & Wales: Adler's *How to Read a Book* and my relationship with Madeleine.) I was a hundred times happier than I'd been at Johnson & Wales, and that had been paid for.

I still went home whenever I could and remained close to family and friends. I often was made fun of for acquiring a "Boston accent," although that's not what happened. I was loosing my working-class accent. I began shedding it shortly after kids at BU mistakenly made fun of my "New York accent." There were lots of kids from New York at BU and they weren't accused of having "New York accents." People who live on the Upper East Side of Manhattan or in Park Slope, Brooklyn, don't have a "New York accent." What the BU kids heard was a *working-class* Staten Island accent, the same kind that Melanie Griffith's character in *Working Girl* wanted to shed. What my family and friends heard after a year of my being at BU was the inevitable erosion of it.[1] To family and friends, it sounded unfamiliar. When I went away this time, unlike when I was at Johnson & Wales, I came back a different person. Tellingly, none of my friends ever visited me the entire time I was at BU or Johnson & Wales, or the fifteen years I lived in New England for that matter. Other than the trip my family made for my BU graduation, they never did either. Madeleine's parents once asked her if my family didn't like me. They liked me well enough, although it remains a mystery to me why, in the fifteen years I lived in New England my family never came up just to see me, other than once when only my father visited me when I was at the University of Massachusetts. Staten Island was a rather provincial place back then. People rarely left the Island, other than to go to New Jersey malls (no sales tax) or to its beaches (cleaner water). Some never bothered taking the ferry ride to Manhattan (too cosmopolitan). My parents didn't like the idea that I was attending Boston University in the first place, and they sure as hell weren't thrilled that I was studying English and history either; that must have been an additional reason for them not to visit me. At least I wasn't wasting their money, which is why my father had no business confronting me about getting a job instead of going to graduate school. For once, I would have welcomed his silence.

"What's this?" my mother asked as I handed her the letter from the University of Kansas. It was a two-page letter, not only inviting me into the program and offering me a scholarship but also praising the work I'd done as an undergraduate. Based on the highly laudatory recommendation—etc., etc.—of Professor X (I wish I could remember for sure, but I think it was Distinguished Professor Millicent Bell), I was an ideal candidate for graduate studies. Kansas was confident I'd succeed there as much as I had at Boston University, practically congratulating me in advance for becoming a successful scholar some day—in the tradition of the professor who recommended me, of course.

"Read it," I said. I had walked into my mother's bedroom one morning when I was home from school, a long weekend that seemed to last longer as my entire family, one by one, criticized the idea of my attending graduate school. She was folding her clothes, placing them delicately in an open bureau drawer. I delivered the news to her first, figuring I might as well get her reaction to it over with as quickly as possible. I expected she'd be unimpressed. Encouragement seemed out of character. Congratulations were completely out of the question. But I hadn't anticipated how vehemently dismissive she'd be. She was facing the bureau as she read it while I stood behind her. She practically threw it onto the floor once she finished reading it, thrusting the letter at me without turning around.

"Yeah, so?" she said testily.

"So, so what do you think?"

"What do *I* think? I think you're nuts. Graduate school? Graduate school? Now it's graduate school." To her, going to Boston University and not becoming a court reporter demonstrated that I couldn't make up my mind about what I wanted to do with my life. "Oh, please," she said, stretching the word "please" out as far as it could reach. "You aren't really thinking of going to graduate school, are you?"

"Well, why not?" I said, already uncertain. "I didn't contact them. One of my professors did. I don't know, it's quite an honor," I added with greater conviction.

No response. She was thinking. It *was* an honor, all right; there was no escaping that. There had to be a way, in her mind, to sidestep that while destroying the idea of it altogether before it got too far off the ground, just as she had done six years earlier when I wanted to attend a four-year college.

"First of all, Kansas seems a little far, don't you think?" she said with calmer firmness. "Second of all, do you know how long it takes to get a graduate degree?"

"Sure. Quite a while, I bet."

Not the level-headed answer she might have been hoping for. I wasn't romanticizing it. She was thinking it through.

"Andrew didn't finish, and he's pretty smart. What makes you think you can?" She stopped abruptly. Maybe that was too harsh. She didn't wait for a reply. "If you want to go to graduate school, why not get a job first and get it while you're working, like John."

John, the cousin-in-law mentioned previously, was her role model, a practical academic who'd obtained his Ed.D. for professional, social, and financial advancement. He also had been her ally when it came to my (her) career choice a few years earlier. I hadn't picked up the court reporting machine since leaving Johnson & Wales. I know that irritated her no end. For some reason, she believed I too looked up to John just as she did. "After all he's done for you," she'd often say. There was no doubt that John's advancement through the educational system was impressive, from gym teacher to school superintendent, while never missing a paycheck. Unlike him, as I considered graduate school, I had no real job. Furthermore, she knew I'd be taking my studies in English or history, working, in her opinion, toward an advanced degree in futility. I would have become a fake doctor sooner than I did. Still, I must say, she was more disapproving than I'd imagined she would be.

As I'd done six years earlier, I backed down. It never occurred to me to tell her what I wanted, how much I wanted to be a scholar or at least to complete formally the intellectual journey I'd seen before me in the ER. My silence and lack of resilience followed a pattern. I often remained silent on smaller issues as well, such as not telling her she was crazy to think that while I was enrolled in BU a couple of computer science courses would prepare me to become a computer scientist. Instead, I signed up for the damn things and hated them, just as I had signed up for court reporting and hated it. For all my academic successes at BU I still lacked the self-assurance and the resolve to make decisions about my life, let alone express them. And there was still the "accident" looming over almost every important conversation, the guilt of having permanently and prominently put a scarlet letter above our house's doorframe. Or maybe it was simply hanging around my neck, an albatross for sure.

"Let's say you get a degree in English. What will you do with it?" she asked.

"I don't know." (And I didn't.) "Maybe I could become a professor."

It was the answer she was looking for. After the few years she spent working at a bank, she became a secretary at a local community college and often came home with stories about the haughty, absent-minded professors she had to assist all the time. To her, they didn't know anything, at least not anything that was practical or useful. They lacked common sense. Without her, they couldn't operate the photocopier or make an outside phone call. Some of them lived "alternative lifestyles," commuting back and forth into Manhattan or Brooklyn Heights, living with "partners" or "significant others." For all their egg-headedness, she considered herself smarter than they were, and morally superior as well.

"A professor?" she said, blowing out a mocking stream of air through her lips. "Being a professor isn't a real job. I work with them all day. They don't really do anything, and what they do isn't real work."

She wasn't alone in her thinking. That's why I didn't exactly view her snap judgment as an insult, or take it personally. As one of the more famous lines in *The Godfather* informs us, even when it comes to whacking a friend or a family member, sometimes "it's not personal; it's business." This wasn't personal either. Among most members of the working class, certainly those within my extended family and community at that time, working with your head rather than with your hands wasn't real work, certainly not for a real man. My mother's working-class roots were showing when she scoffed at my chance to attend graduate school on a scholarship. It wasn't personal; it was business. It's why years later her sister would claim I wasn't a real doctor when I finally had my doctorate in hand. At least the real doctors work with their hands. What did I do with mine—flip the pages of books?

I never informed my family about the other two schools that contacted me. I didn't see the point. The second invitation showed up in the mail as unpredictably as the first. It was from a school in the vast Ohio state system, the University of Akron or Cincinnati, I think. It was from the History Department. Where the third came from I can't recall, other than that it was from an English graduate program. By the time it arrived I'd decided not to go to graduate school. I glanced at the letter and quickly chucked it into the garbage. While I showed my family only the first letter, I decided to show Madeleine the second, hoping to convince her of my "destiny" after she had dismissed the first one. She wasn't exactly thrilled about seeing me head off to Kansas. Akron or Cincinnati didn't alter her opinion. They seemed just as far from Bellingham, Massachusetts, as Kansas. It wasn't "Where?" It was more like "Why"?

"Don't expect me to be waiting here for you when you get back," she said. She was standing by the stove in her parents' kitchen, heating up soup. Like me, she was a late bloomer. When we met at Johnson & Wales she was pursuing an Associate's Degree in finance. She was working at a cosmetics counter at a local department store. She was planning on remaining in the beauty industry, perhaps some day advancing within the field. She likely could have done that without an Associate's Degree. She was quite a beauty herself. Many people commented on her striking re-semblance to the young Natalie Wood. Her father was a rather prominent local lawyer. He had run for Congress in 1956 as a Democrat and was resoundingly whooped when Republicans across the country rode the coattails of President Eisenhower's popularity when he ran for and won a second term. Despite the loss, Madeleine's father remained a well-known figure in the community. To his credit, the family lived modestly. His liberal, French-Canadian demeanor created a more ascetic than materialistic atmosphere in their home. I often stayed there on the weekends, even after leaving Boston and living only a few miles away in the next town. Madeleine's older sister, Constance, was a French Literature professor and Madeleine admired her for her accomplishments. She would have traded her looks for her sister's smarts in a heartbeat. Madeleine had less confidence in her intellectual abilities than I did in mine. A year after I enrolled in Boston University, she enrolled in Northeastern University, majoring in history. We had a lot in common, which is why I was so surprised when she reacted to the letters of invitation no differently from the way my family had. But considering what I'd put her through a year earlier, when we'd agreed to get married, it shouldn't have been surprising.

"What if you moved out there with me?" I asked. She didn't like that idea at all. And why would she? She wouldn't be going to Lawrence, Kansas, or Akron, Ohio, to become a "Scholarship Girl." She'd be tagging along, and I'd be taking her far away from her family. She also had another year to finish her undergraduate degree. She'd be giving up a lot. A year earlier she had agreed to give up even more, to attend school part-time and work full-time after we married and I enrolled in law school. In addition to her own reluctance to move away, now as the Scholarship Boy's companion she had every right to be suspicious of *my* plans, which she knew first-hand weren't always firmly in my grasp.

In the spring term of my junior year at Boston University I started working at BU's Center for Law & Health Sciences through a work-study program. I had no plans on attending law school when I took the job. Of all the jobs listed in the program it seemed the most interesting. I half-hoped to find myself duplicating the arduous law paper I'd written at Johnson & Wales. It wasn't like that—I wasn't doing legal research. It mostly involved filing and typing. But when a junior lawyer asked me to find some information on nosocomial infections (hospital-borne illnesses) and their legal ramifications, I pulled another Perry Mason. I went to the law library of the state capitol and even went so far as to visit a hospital on the outskirts of Boston where a patient's lawsuit had reached the District Court. I showed up unannounced. The public relations officer was kind enough to grant me a quick interview, which I included in my report. A couple of days after I handed it to the junior lawyer, I was called into the director's office. At first, I thought I was in trouble, that I'd done something wrong or, worse, failed to do something entirely. He had my report on his desk.

"What are your plans after graduating?" he asked.

I didn't really have any. I was toying with journalism, after some of my articles in the college newspaper had received a fair amount of attention, but that was it. "You," he said, pointing his finger at me and nodding his head, "should think of law school." He kept nodding, as if that would convince me. "This is a very impressive piece of work," he added, tapping the folder that contained the report. "You clearly have a head for it, and an interest in it, in doing legal research." I didn't argue with him. He was right on both counts.

"I hadn't really thought of it," I said, "but I will."

"You should, seriously should." Behind him a couple of shelves contained a number of mementos and a bunch of photographs of him shaking hands with JFK, Martin Luther King Jr., and President Carter. Others had captured him with U.S. Senators Ted Kennedy and Edward Brooke at a luncheon or convention. A number of prints showed him standing alone on the steps of the U.S. Supreme Court. I later learned he'd argued a couple of cases before it. "I'd be more than happy to write you a letter of recommendation," he finally said. "Just ask."

Madeleine told her father about the encounter, and one evening during dinner he brought it up. He knew who the director of the Center was, apparently a bigger legal bigshot than I was aware of, someone who was well known not only in the state but also nationally, especially within the Democratic Party. "What kind of law would you practice?" her father asked. I hadn't really thought about that. The whole thing was new to me, so I mostly talked about how much I enjoyed doing the research, as I did when I looked into the *Bakke* affirmative action case at Johnson & Wales. I didn't really imagine myself "practicing" law, not in the sense of how I naïvely envisioned it, the way it appears in the movies and on TV. "It sounds to me like you're interested in being a legal scholar," he said. Why, sure, I said. I liked the sound of that, particularly the "scholar" part. "I could write you a letter of recommendation, too," he said. "Of course, if you want one from someone as lowly as me," he added, smiling.

So there it was. I was going to apply to law school. What's more, Madeleine and I would get married. We'd struggle financially, but we didn't care. We had part-time jobs and when she graduated from Northeastern, she'd work full-time. She was even willing to attend school part-time and work full-time to support me. She knew her parents would help us out. They had practically adopted me already, so it would make matters more official. We informed her brothers and sisters and they couldn't have been happier. It wasn't just her parents who had adopted me; it was her entire family. In fact, largely through their influence my dream of "formally" educating myself had rematerialized. They certainly played a major role in my decision to acquire a classic liberal arts education when I enrolled in Boston University. I probably even did it to impress them.

My real family, on the other hand, was appalled on both counts. Getting married before I graduated was a mistake, and enrolling in law school was possibly a bigger one.

"Do you know what we call lawyers?" my father, a New York City cop for thirty years, asked. "Cockroaches. They make a mess of things and they're everywhere."

My mother agreed. "A lawyer, you want to be a lawyer? Are you kidding? You dropped being a court reporter in a flash, so what makes you think that'll work out? Besides," she continued, "lawyers are a dime a dozen. Any idiot can be a lawyer."

Initially, my sister was more influenced by my decision to get married than by my decision to attend law school. She thought I was too young, even though by the time of the anticipated marriage I would have been a year or two older than she was when she'd gotten married. In time, though, she too joined my parents' chorus of denouncing law school.

For weeks, my mother and sister kept hammering away at the sheer lunacy of my plans to wed before I went off to law school. It would be the first and last thing they'd bring up whenever we spoke on the phone, often repeating, verbatim, what the other had said days before. It was a tag team. My father spoke out against it, but he'd had his say and didn't harp on it as they did. Sure enough, I was worn down. I didn't apply to a single law school, and by the time I started my last year at Boston University I told Madeleine it would be best if we waited to get married after *both* of us had finished college.

It's no wonder Madeleine didn't encourage me to become a late-blooming Scholarship Boy when I showed her the invitations to attend graduate school. I already had left her high and dry. She couldn't be faulted for having such feelings and for not encouraging me to go to the University of Kansas, or to some other far-off place. Back then, though, that didn't stop me from penalizing her anyway—and her alone—for not supporting me. I punished her by breaking up with her.

But what strikes me now, after all these years, is that no one suggested I look into *local* graduate programs, including me. It also never occurred to anyone (again including me) I could get in touch with the professors who'd contacted those distant schools and ask if they could help me secure scholarships at local institutions. Ultimately, everyone's response to the letters seemed less about location and more about the very concept of graduate school. Perhaps that's why nobody brought it up, and why I didn't think of it either. It wasn't so much that the University of Kansas was so far away; it was more that enrolling in graduate school seemed like such a far-fetched idea in the first place. To my family it was as silly as my wanting to become a doctor or a lawyer. We'd been down this road before, so perhaps their rhetoric had become an art form. It didn't take long for their words to get inside my head, to convince me of what a bad idea attending graduate school was, whether it was a three-hour plane trip or a half-hour car ride. Attending graduate school—scholarship be damned!—was a stupid idea in the first place. So I told myself, after being told.

Despite my being turned away from the idea of attending graduate school, it was what I wanted. I knew it, viscerally, and maybe I always reminded myself of what I had wanted to become after I almost became nothing. Apparently, I hadn't driven a stake into the heart of my dream. I guess you could even say I didn't entirely give up on myself, not entirely. Years later that undying dream of attending graduate school was resurrected. In time, I obtained my doctorate, enrolling in a program ten years later. I flitted around professionally during those ten years, working for four years as a staff writer/editor in John Hancock's Group Marketing Insurance division. I hated that job almost as much as I hated being at Johnson & Wales. When I quit John Hancock and entered a post-baccalaureate teacher certification program at the University of Massachusetts, Amherst, my parents went batshit. They couldn't believe I'd left such a promising job, expecting me to retire from there after rising up the corporate ladder and earning a hefty salary. The problem with rising up the corporate ladder is that it requires someone who actually wants to do that and to reap the rewards of the big bucks. Most people aren't terribly passionate about sitting in a cubicle all day doing whatever it is they do. I sure wasn't, not writing copy for dental brochures. There were clear paths toward promotions and furthering my career, as I watched some of my colleagues glide into executive positions. But I didn't like the work and I wasn't interested in gaining promotions and therefore making more money. It was pointless to stay.

But instead of going all-out and enrolling in a doctoral program, I copped out by not even enrolling in a Master's program. I thought by becoming a teacher I'd get that much closer to obtaining my Ph.D. I might have let it enter my head that I *could* be just like my cousin-in-law John. Whatever the reason, I'm glad I did become a teacher. I discovered how much I loved teaching and how predisposed to it I was. I was even good at substitute teaching, which is hard to imagine. The students took to me almost immediately. After a couple of days of my subbing at a school, the secretaries were calling me almost every day. I was often asked to fill in weeks at a time for teachers who were injured in accidents or were sick. I worked practically five days a week the entire time I was in the certification program. And I was having a blast. It was as if everything about my life that had come before had prepared me for teaching, especially being giftless in my youth. Even being shot produced beneficial results for what the profession required. I don't mean that sarcastically or ironically. ("It's a war zone in there, kid. You might as well be armed!" some of the more jaded teachers would warn me along the way.) I spent four years as a public school teacher honing those skills before enrolling in a doctoral program. By the time I did, I was too old—not just in years, but also temperamentally—to be a Scholarship Boy. Instead, I was on course to become something else—a Teaching Man.

Not being a true-blue Scholarship Boy likely explains why I didn't feel disconnected from my working-class family and friends, or why visiting Aunt Mary and Aunt Do-Do wasn't uncomfortable. If anything, coming home was actually rather special. I wasn't embarrassed or unnerved by that scene sitting around my aunt's dining room table, or the times I would go to bars and clubs with my friend Jimmy and we'd run into guys I'd known growing up in Oakwood Heights. ("Ya gotta be fuckin' kiddin' me! You're a college professor? No shit. *You* became a professor. That's fuckin' unbelievable. That's great.") Yes, I guess it was pretty great. I enjoyed coming home, pleased with just how unbelievably fuckin' far I'd come. I liked the feeling. But I didn't think, *Hey, look at me, I got out and you didn't. I became a professor and you're still an asshole, stuck in this shit-hole.* No, that was never it. I never felt superior to anyone. I got "out" because I got shot. Really, who's the bigger asshole? Ending up as I did after nearly ending up dead didn't seem to warrant bragging rights, no matter how far I'd come compared with others who'd stayed close to home. Besides, whenever I did come home, I wasn't remembered as the gifted bookworm, different because of my astonishing youthful academic talents. I was remembered mostly as that stupid kid who was shot during an attempted robbery.

It became official doctrine. I'll always be remembered for it, no matter if I have as many degrees as a thermometer. While teaching as an adjunct professor at the College of Staten Island I ran into a high school classmate whom I hadn't seen in twenty years. The shooting was the first thing she mentioned when she remembered me. I was walking out of a cubicle where the photocopier was located (I made sure I knew how to operate it *and* how to make outside phone calls), when we bumped into each other. In high school, she was a slight, pretty girl with stringy, dirty-blond hair who sat next to me in homeroom my freshman year. She hadn't changed much, except for the lines on her face. For months she was the only girl I spoke to. I often thought of asking her on a date. But she turned out to be quite a tough girl. She was in a number of fights with other students, some of them quite vicious. In one that I witnessed, she grabbed a girl's hair, after distracting her with a swift kick to her shin, dragged her to the ground caveman-style, and started punching her in the face with her free hand. By then I had decided she wasn't my type. When I saw her at the College of Staten Island she still looked a bit rough around the edges, now more beaten-up by life itself. CSI was part of the City University of New York's vast collegiate system and she was among the hundreds, if not thousands, of adult students who attended CSI hoping to get their lives back on track or were returning to school after raising a family (most of them were female). She stood near the cubicle as I walked out, apparently waiting to use the machine next. I recognized her immediately. I could tell she thought I looked familiar but couldn't quite place the face.

"Well, hello," I said. "You probably don't remember me but we went to Tottenville High School together. We sat next to each other in home-room." She looked at me more carefully. "Oh, yeah, right," she said. With-out missing a beat, she added, "You're the one who got shot." I wasn't shocked or troubled by the association. "Yes, that would be me," I said, smiling at her slightly. "So," she said, "what are you doing here, taking classes?" "No. I teach here. I'm finishing up my doctorate." She was vis-ibly stunned, moving her head and torso back as if I'd taken a swipe at her, revealing just how jarring the news was. "Wow, you've come a long way," she exclaimed. Yes, I had. But my having done so hadn't altered her recollection of me, no matter how far I'd come. I was "special," all right, just like other working-class academics, although for different reasons.

What made me "special" weren't my books or the accolades I'd re-ceived in grammar school or the scholarships I'd been offered in high school. Unlike other working-class academics who spotlight their schol-arships and boast about the classics they read as children, I *haven't* been able to share my "special" past. After all, what made me "special" while growing up can't be slipped easily into conversations with colleagues or brought up during staff meetings: "I propose we seek to reduce the cap in all of our composition courses, and did I ever tell you all about the time a cop nearly blew my head off during a stickup? Funny story...." Yet it's *the* story, the single most important experience in my life, the one that propelled me out of Oakwood Heights and eventually into the academy. Not the books or the scholarships. In fact, when I inform colleagues, and even students, that I was a juvenile delinquent (that's as far as I go) and didn't become a reader until I was a junior in high school, they scratch their heads, bewildered: "Really? Wow. So what changed you?" What am I supposed to say: "Oh, being gunned down by a cop and being admin-istered the last rites. You know, the usual"? Learning that I was a giftless, nonbookish child seems shocking enough to most of them. Keeping the shooting a secret has likely kept me distant from colleagues, including those who are from the working class, whereas the opposite is true "back home." In the end (but there is no real "end") there was never much distance between friends and family while I was home because I'll always be "the one who got shot." Try escaping that.

Those sentiments aren't shared by other working-class academics. Their pasts *are* marked by special academic excellence and achievements, and home becomes an uncomfortable place. The discomfort increases as they climb the academic ladder. After one year at Stanford, Richard Rodriguez had little to say to his parents and they had little to say to him—"One was almost grateful for a family crisis about which there was much to discuss."[2] And once John Edgar Wideman left his "poverty" and "blackness" behind in Pittsburgh by becoming a Scholarship Boy at the University of Pennsylvania, he built a "wall" between himself and his family, especially between himself and his younger delinquent brother Robbie.[3] I never felt that way, and I still don't. I'm certain it's because I emerged late and lame out of the academic starting gate and also was a bookish latecomer. I never viewed myself, or was viewed by others, as "gifted," as other Scholarship Boys and Girls are.

For my part, not only did I not become a Scholarship Boy but I didn't divine escaping from my family by becoming hyper-educated. It's true, if I had had a bit more sense and self-confidence I might have realized I needed to peel myself away from them in order to take a faster track to my Ph.D. But I didn't. And just like being shot, I have to live with such decisions (or nondecisions in this case). Not traveling in the fast lane has had its advantages all the same. For my family's part, because I had taken such a slow, circuitous route to becoming a fake doctor, they always saw me as "one of them" rather than as an overly educated stereotype, the arrogant, pretentious brainiacs who are a staple of our popular culture, like Diane Chambers on *Cheers*, Charles Emerson Winchester on *M*A*S*H*, and the *real* Dr. Gregory House on *House*. The uneasy feelings are mutual. If parents, siblings, and friends had access to the same rhetorical platform as working-class academics, they'd be spinning narratives filled with as much unease, rancor, and remorse. As it stands, in our one-sided versions, we learn from many working-class academics that practically from the time they became bookish in their youth they couldn't wait to get the hell away from their oafish families and intellectually vapid communities.

For me to fit into the tradition of working-class academic narratives, I'm supposed to recount how once I returned home with my doctorate in hand and was called a fake doctor the umbilical cord to my working-class past was severed forever. According to the editors of *Strangers in Paradise*, at this stage of family dissonance a "strain of disconnection from the past" occurs, especially from "parents and siblings." It's "a theme that resounds clearly in a majority of the narratives."[4] For example, Jane Ellen Wilson, the daughter of Pennsylvania farmers, acknowledges in *Strangers* that she kept "betting on education" because she "had rejected [her] family's way of life."[5] Narratives by a more ethnically diverse group of academics, compiled in the anthology *This Fine Place So Far from Home,* contain even more "disconnecting" confessions. In "A Carpenter's Daughter," Renny Christopher admits she "never really felt like [she] belonged" to her working-class surroundings in the first place. It's no wonder that after joining the academy she felt "ill at ease" whenever she went "back home."[6] For Irvin Peckman the "disconnection" became so complete that he "infrequently [goes] home," describing "the break" with his "family, parents and siblings" as an essential "erasure" for "incorrect" working-class professionals like him who must survive among the more "correct"-minded people in the academy.[7] In a separate account, Linda Brodkey reveals in "Writing on the Bias" that she "had to write off [her] father who read newspapers, automobile repair manuals, and union materials."[8] Unlike his young daughter, he did not read "literature," which constituted the "right books" in Brodkey's mind.[9] Richard Rodriguez concludes "a scholarship boy" like himself "cannot afford to admire his parents."[10] Eventually, "bewildering silence" confronts both parent and child.[11] Bookish, gifted children may no longer feel at home with their own families. In some respects, I had every reason to experience that as well.

All things considered, my mom's lobbying me to become a real garbageman to avoid becoming a fake doctor certainly gave me some license to feel apart from my own family. If, like the others, I felt the "strain of disconnection from my past," I might then see myself in those traditional working-class narratives; now I could connect with other like-minded academics, however abstractly. But there was one sizeable snag. I *didn't* feel that way. I wasn't a Scholarship Boy and I came late to the academic circle. When I did arrive I may have been older (not necessarily wiser) than the average Scholarship Boy or Girl and a bit less prickly about my past. Many of them admit to being overly sensitive about their working-class history once inside the Ivory Tower, only to have many of their academic trappings come crashing back down on them whenever they uncomfortably and sometimes agonizingly returned "home." Home was the living, breathing reminder of where those embarrassing traits came from that "legitimate" colleagues might detect. I didn't feel that way at home or in the academy. As such, I didn't feel detached, and a lingering comfort and connection with working-class life kept me in my family orbit, however linked it was to my own rather misguided conception of remaining the dutiful son. Therefore, much of that "connection" had to do with my family's preventing me from leaving when I wanted to, along with my complicity in that prevention. Nevertheless, not being a Scholarship Boy created a different kind of working-class academic and it has kept me tied to the working class. Perhaps that's why I wasn't angry with my mother for suggesting that I see sanitation duties as a career goal, nor was I bothered by Aunt Mary's remark. (I still think it's pretty damn funny.) I fully understood why either becoming a garbageman or becoming a "real" doctor (or marrying one, for that matter) is in working-class households considered the equivalent of winning the Lotto. Such work makes more sense to working-class people than studying a Shakespeare sonnet. Hell, sometimes it makes more sense to me too, and I do it for a living!

When it comes to the appeal of becoming a doctor or a sanitation worker, for folks like my mom and aunt it's largely because both use their hands, which is what working*men* largely do among families on that island. (They're not called Scholarship *Boys* for nothing.) Women, according to my family, generally shouldn't become real doctors. Staten Island women are vigorously socialized into "maternal-helping" jobs such as nurses, beauticians, secretaries or . . . teachers! And while "sanitation worker" replaced "garbageman," no sane woman, in the minds of the Staten Island working class I grew up around, would willingly become a "garbageperson"—or a police*man* or a fire*man*. So that career path was closed off in the division of labor. No wonder, then, that my aunt categorized the surgeon as the real doctor because *he* works with his hands, like an auto mechanic, except the doctor fixes bodies rather than cars. Moreover, a doctor attends school to acquire a very tangible skill, to learn a trade, so to speak (like court reporting), not unlike becoming a welder or learning to splice cable for a telecommunications company. All that education is ultimately manifested in the concrete performance of the work involved. There's nothing abstract about it. It also helps that in our hypercapitalist health care system real doctors earn a whole lot more money than nurses or garbagemen—or professors of English. In addition, my aunt, like anyone from the working class (or any class), comes into direct contact with doctors. Medical men are part of her social fabric. How often did my aunt go for her annual liberal arts checkup? ("Read two Byrons and call me in the morning.") In contrast, my own position as a doctor of letters is too steeped in the abstraction of book learning, revealing why my aunt considered it somewhat unreal, maybe even surreal. I suppose she saw me as an ultra-educated figment of my own imagination.

My mother obviously felt the same way. It was okay to send my sister to college, but that was different. She was a girl (and she had been a good, obedient student). For me, a college education seemed highly unrealistic, other than to gain "hands-on" experience. My becoming a real doctor would have supplied that kind of training, except it was a "trade" that also required top-notch academic experience, which I was in short supply of at the time. My eventually becoming a fake doctor was possibly even more ridiculous because it was more indefinable compared with becoming a "real doctor" or a court reporter or a sanitation worker, for that matter. Actually, the most uncomfortable person sitting around my aunt's dining room table that wintry afternoon was my mother. Aunt Mary was mocking me about something my mother had considered bogus herself. While she didn't agree with her at that moment, she believed my aunt was right, and she had for much longer. For all my schooling I could have been something other than an English professor instructing students how to read and write. (What kind of work was that anyway? Didn't people learn how to do that in grade school?) On the other hand, *without* all that schooling I could have been something *more* than an English professor. That day at my aunt's house my mother was essentially defending me about becoming something she had done her best to prevent me from becoming. No wonder she didn't have the words to express it. To her I was a "Doctor of . . . of . . . of . . . what?"

If I was uneasy that day it was because after I'd read so many working-class academic narratives the irony of the moment was agonizingly clear to me. In testimonial after testimonial, despite the encroaching distance between parents and children, narrators recount the stories of proud parents who saw their children "as inherently important and intellectually promising."[12] Parents often were asked how proud they must be of their gifted children, as Richard Rodriguez's were, while one Scholarship Girl recounts how her "mother pushed [her] toward a life of higher education very early."[13] Even though Mike Rose, in *Lives on the Boundary*, informs us he wasn't exactly "gifted" as a child, his parents still thought of him as someday becoming "a doctor"—the real kind.[14] My mother (and my father) was not one of those parents. And I was not one of those "gifted" children. That came later. It took a lot of time, effort, and patience for that to happen. I've got the scars to prove it. My mother's transformation into the proud, supportive parent was practically magical in comparison. All she had to do was simply change the storyline. She made it seem as if she'd supported me from start to finish. In altering the past, she had placed herself in the archetypal role of the parent of a typical Scholarship Child.

In effect, she was revising her real role in how I acquired my doctorate.

It was a rather abrupt about-face. She had, after all, only a few months earlier tried to convince me to put down the books and pick up the trash as a livelihood. Years later, when I wrote my first scholarly book, she asked me several times why I hadn't dedicated it to her and my father. It wasn't as if I were ungrateful or considered their parenting the epitome of recklessness. But it did seem disingenuous to reward them for erecting so many barriers toward my writing it. Unlike in traditional narratives, the disconnection between me and my family wasn't because I was ashamed of them. If anything, they were ashamed of me. There was therefore a disconnection between the past and the present, a revisionist account of family history. As a result, my mother did something I was incapable of doing after reading so many of the narratives. *She* found herself in them. She became the longstanding, approving parent who had encouraged me to become what she knew all along I could become. The backstory therefore underwent drastic restaging once I earned my doctorate, as if the very scenes I appeared in had never been performed. Of course, they had. In the actual roles established by central casting she hadn't played the part of the admiring parent.

In altering her part in my educational journey, she was completely rewriting *my* history, conducting her own form of "erasure," thereby negating the resolve it had required for me to obtain my doctorate and join the academy. More important, how I arrived has had a lot to do with the kind of academic I became and the kind of teacher that I would become. I took a different route from those of other working-class academics. My route involved tenaciously clinging to the ER "vision," along with a heck of a lot of perspiration, sweating it out in unbefitting places. Unlike gifted working-class academics, acquiring my doctorate and landing in the academy seemed epic—in the sense of how damned long it took Odysseus to return home. My mother never approved of my intellectual ambitions and scholastic goals, and I've always been fine with that—really. To this day I don't resent her for trying to figure out what would be the best career "fit" for me. She had her reasons, one of which was the botched robbery and how it tainted my character in her estimation. The other was my rather sketchy, if not pitiable, academic past. I wasn't exactly proud of either. I get that. But I also overcame both to "redeem" myself, starting immediately down that path when I walked to my local library the day after I was released from the hospital. There never has been any acknowledgment of any of that on my family's part. Instead, in my mother's version the task was made easier, perhaps made entirely, thanks to her and my family. By claiming to have been a source of encouragement and motivation when she historically had been a source of discouragement and opposition negated the authenticity of my journey and what I accomplished to become a professor. It was worse than an erasure. It was identity theft.

For her and for my family I became what they least expected. If anything, they seem more anxious around me than I am around them. Maybe it's because they got it so wrong. Still, if I had been they, I might have had as little faith in my competence as they did. Granted, I would have preferred less conviction about my shortcomings, especially on my mother's part. Yet in her own awkward way she believed she was acting like the concerned parent. Like many good-hearted mothers, she got it wrong because she was trying to safeguard me. She was trying to protect me from myself, from my own crazy notions that I was intellectually fit to succeed, first in college, then in graduate school, and finally professionally in higher education. That's why she sent me the announcement about job openings in the Sanitation Department, just a few months before I received my doctorate. Joining the Sanitation Department would save me from terminal and inevitable embarrassment and disappointment. It was a reason she never expressed then, or has owned up to now—certainly not now, when my success had so much to do in her mind with her support. Before now, she was certain I'd be a roaring failure in the academy. In short, I had no business being there in the first place, so acquiring a doctorate in English would be a tremendous waste of time.

If indeed the gifted child, replete with supportive parents, permeates working-class academic narratives, I didn't add up. A "shot story" is far removed from the traditional "gifted"-child versions. I couldn't add myself to the traditional story, after all. While not all the narratives contain accounts of prototypical cheerleading parents pushing for their children's academic success, they almost all contain the "gifted child" who would warrant such praiseworthy attention.

So pervasive is the "gifted child" in the stories of working-class academics that it has become a trope, just as the narratives became a genre. In *The Gatekeeper*, noted literary scholar Terry Eagleton considers "the scholarship boy" an archetype. Recounting his experiences growing up Catholic among Protestant England's working class, he stepped into "the process of becoming that most archetypal of post-war characters, as much part of modern mythology as the Mad Scientist or the Dumb Blonde, the Scholarship Boy."[15]

The recurring theme of the "gifted," bookish child originated in Richard Hoggart's "Scholarship Boy" in *The Uses of Literacy*, the granddaddy of all working-class academic narratives. In it, he describes a child (like himself) being identified as intellectually endowed, someone "marked out early" and therefore "set apart" from his working-class environment because "'e's got brains." Meanwhile, the books he brings into his home "look like strange tools" to other members of his socioeconomic caste.[16] In due time, his "brains are the currency" that pays for his ticket out of the working class. Similarly, Richard Rodriguez, who frequently cites Hoggart in his narrative *Hunger of Memory*, describes how the Catholic nuns in his California grammar school quickly earmarked him as a candidate for academic success. Rodriguez was unlike other children from his socioeconomic class because he loved to read at an early age—"So I read and I read," he explains. By the time he entered high school, not many years after entering first grade knowing only "fifty words of English," Rodriguez had read "hundreds of books."[17] Essentially assured that higher education loomed on the horizon, Rodriguez used his atypical talent to catapult him beyond his Chicano working-class background. For both Hoggart and Rodriguez, their childhood bookishness literally and figuratively removes them from their working-class environment. In time, like most working-class academics, they grapple with its psychological and emotional ramifications.

Another Hispanic from the working class, Victor Villanueva, was less assured than Rodriguez that he would advance beyond his roots. His story, like mine, was more circuitous. Nevertheless, in *Bootstraps: From an American Academic of Color* Villanueva reports that he "would correct [his] folks when an English rule was broken," just like Rodriguez, and at an early age he discovered "the Brooklyn public library's air-conditioned reading room," a place drastically different from the spaces inhabited by his working-class schoolmates and neighbors.[18] I was close to graduating from high school before I discovered my local library—and look what it took to get me there! Keith Gilyard, an African American who grew up in two different New York City working-class neighborhoods (Harlem and Corona, Queens), received scholarships from Notre Dame and the University of Connecticut. He proclaims in *Voices of the Self* that he knew "just how important [. . .] reading was" even before he entered the first grade. "In fact," he continues, he "had been doing a considerable amount of reading before [he] received any formal instruction."[19] For Gilyard, Villanueva, and Rodriguez, being bookish—all at *very* young ages—helped them to overcome not only the drawbacks of class but also the liability of race in a white-dominated society.

Scholarship Girls fall into the pattern as well. Linda Brodkey notes that she "literally read [her] way out of the children's library in the summer of the fifth grade" and immediately feasted on the "books in the adult library" section. "Only the best books,"[20] she adds, would do—a sharp contrast to my latecomer visitations to my local library. In the Introduction to *Calling Home*, Janet Zandy tells us, "I went to college on a scholarship. I studied literature. No, I embraced it like a lifeline." She expected her extraordinary passion, which starkly differed from that of the working-class world around her, would take her "across the great divide of class."[21] Like their male counterparts, Scholarship Girls were looking for a way out, and books supplied the means. Other Scholarship Girls throughout *Working-Class Women in the Academy* and *This Fine Place So Far from Home* also describe their bookish and gifted backgrounds.

On close inspection, most narratives duplicate Hoggart's and Rodriguez's accounts of the gifted and bookish child from the working class who rises above his (or her) station. This theme cuts across boundaries of race, sex, and gender, with class shared by all. The "child as intellectual prodigy" is a common feature in the narratives, whether written by a white male or an African American female, as are the "best books" they read, as if *their* lives depended on it.

For instance, Robert Brown, the son of uneducated Irish immigrants, notes in *Strangers* that his "library card became [his] most valued possession,"[22] and Robert Cole, a coalminer's son, writes, "I loved school, and I was in awe of learning."[23] In *Coming to Class: Pedagogy and the Social Class of Teachers*, Karen Fitts proudly informs us, "My parents, teachers, and friends saw me as inherently important and intellectually promising,"[24] while Patricia A. Sullivan recalls being "a star" in school and "[excelling] at it."[25] Writing in *Working-Class Women in the Academy*, Suzanne Sowinska discusses how she and her twelve-year-old classmate had the "highest scores on that year's academic achievement tests." At the same time, she "coveted the books" a neighbor owned, spending "most of [her] time" reading "(what most university English departments) referred to as classics."[26] In the same anthology, Donna Langston points out that her "mother pushed [her] toward a life of higher education very early." Not only her mother, but all the women in her family "indoctrinated" her "with the idea that [she] possessed extraordinary intelligence."[27] As bell hooks explains, "a scholarship girl," like her fellow male prodigy, frequently "lived in the world of books."[28]

However, working-class women in the academy face a "doubly-pronged threat," Pat Belanoff contends, because working-class male language "has a value" greater than working-class female language, which is "certainly a quality our society rates highly."[29] Overall, gender and race relations continue to privilege white, male, working-class kids over females and minorities in their class, while male prodigies have a leg up on their female counterparts. But we shouldn't forget that largely *within* the working class, bookish boys remain targeted as "pussies" and "faggots" or any other insulting term that questions their manhood. Lately it seems that sentiment has begun to creep into all classes. Any male from any class who is bookish often isn't a "real man," especially if he's reading more than his schoolbooks. It is one thing to be a boy from Palo Alto reading a required high school text like *To Kill a Mockingbird*, which helps certify entrance into a college commensurate with his class, but it's another matter altogether to be reading *Anna Karenina* just for the heck of it.

More specifically, among the working class being bookish potentially differentiates *any* child from other working-class children. It accounts for why the child is "discovered" as gifted and eventually guided toward academic advancement. By the second grade Keith Gilyard, for example, had reached "the so-called cream of [his] grade level," and he'd been "'identified'" by his teachers as academically special.[30] His family knew too, which is why his uncle reminded him while he was in junior high that he had "a good head for the books" and that all young Gilyard had to do was "stick with the books and they'll take [him] places."[31] Going places, for any child of the working class, regardless of the social disadvantages of race or gender, is made easier by showing early signs of owning cultural capital.[32]

Some of the most culturally diverse stories of the bookish, gifted working-class child occur in *This Fine Place*. Gloria D. Warren reports in "Another Day's Journey: An African-American in Higher Education" that she passionately read Shakespeare and Langston Hughes in grade school and announced to her mother at such an early stage that she was "going to get a Ph.D."[33] Rosa Maria Pegueros maintains in "*To-dos Vuelven*: From Potrero Hill to UCLA" that she seemed an aberration to the people around her: "To my family I was an oddball: bookish, self-absorbed, reaching beyond my family."[34] Dwight Lang, who grew up in Montana, felt equally unusual for the same reasons. He was an "anomaly in [his] childhood" because he "surpassed" his parents' already high expectations of his academic accomplishments.[35] Mary Capello, a self-described "Woman / lesbian / feminist / Italian American," realized at a young age that "studying and reading" would be her escape, certain that she "deserved" to attend Princeton and that it "would open up to" her.[36]

Escape! That's what they're after. For working-class academics, books were swapped for a tangible exit strategy, a way to get out of Dodge. At first, books may simply provide the means to mentally or metaphorically flee working-class conditions. Books might start out as symbolic flights of fancy, even for those who "love to read" for its own sake. In time, much more is possible. Real flight can be seen in the not-so-distant future. Books train working-class kids in the cultural practices of the elite, equipping them with information and discourses typically not circulating in their daily lives. Books, and their association with elite literacy, can sometimes supply upward mobility, the very real escape from a working-class environment seemingly at odds with the bookish child who has been singled out for being different from others in her class. Books are "strange tools" to many in the working class, Hoggart asserted, and the child who wields them may seem just as strange, "an oddball." This stage of the passage therefore involves more than a socioeconomic leap because the bookish child often desires to join a cultural setting in which such bookishness is not an anomaly. Moving from one class to another, Jake Ryan and Charles Sackrey point out in *Strangers*, involves "moving from one cultural network to another."[37] For some, the conscious exchange of cultural capital begins at a young age. Naton Leslie "used to wonder how [she] escaped the anti-intellectualism of the working class." Leslie observes that she "did not grow up in a house of books and intellectual aspirations." Nevertheless, because her mother noticed that she liked to read, she would be left at the local library "for hours" where exposure to privileged discourses could occur.[38] According to Suzanne Sowinska, "education was devalued in the white, working-class culture in which [she] was raised." As a result, her "deep passion for reading" became "intricately connected to notions of escape [and] survival." Seeking to escape the material *and* cultural conditions of [one's] working-class life is a "reality," she argues, "of almost all the poor and working class women in academia" whom she knows.[39] It's likely the "reality" for all working-class members in academia.

Out of the intellectual preparation for escape, physical flight typically becomes the next step. In some cases books therefore represent socioeconomic salvation, a way to rise above a family history marked by "extreme go-to-bed hungry" poverty, as Nathan Green recalls.[40] Books represent more than just cultural capital. They accrue bankable, real capital enabling some to find "a way out of" limiting economic circumstances, as Alice Trent recalls of her growing up in a "small town in the River Valley of Pennsylvania."[41] In "Nowhere at Home," Christine Overall tells us that when she was twelve she "decided that education would be [her] way of avoiding a future as a waitress, factory worker, or clerk-typist."[42] Writing in "Bronx Syndrome," Stephen Garger declares, "What saved my butt was reading."[43] George T. Martin also saw reading encyclopedias from cover to cover and excelling in school as "a path to a better life."[44] For several working-class academics, being bookish in childhood, along with the ancillary "gifted" label, rescued them from the material conditions of working-class life. Whether it develops unconsciously or deliberately, "a deep passion for reading" imparts to the working-class child a view that the culturally alien and economically restraining world of the working class can be overcome. "In a working-class milieu," Sharon O'Dair claims, "a child's desire to read books or to succeed in school signifies difference—not just emotional or intellectual difference but material difference as well."[45]

But the books present a double-edged sword for the working-class academic for two reasons. First, while offering salvation they likewise create estrangement. Books often are responsible for the intellectual, physical, *and* emotional split that occurs between working-class academics and their home culture. The closer Rodriguez gets to becoming "the prized student" who eventually attends Stanford on a scholarship, the more he "cannot afford to admire [his] parents."[46] Instead, he turns his admiration toward his teachers. In time, the break from his parents and family progresses from an intellectual one to a physical one, concluding in an emotional fissure as well. For him, the "closeness" and "intimacy"[47] with his family life are replaced by "a lonely community" of scholars.[48]

It's a jarring tradeoff, shared by others. For some working-class academics, little in their new environment reminds them of the familiarity of their past. Many may have to "leave behind the familiar validations of experience and community offered by [their] family and friends," as Suzanne Sowinska claims.[49] Karen Fitts and Alan W. France wonder how working-class academics, "nurtured in the bosom of [their] reasonably sane and loving families, emerge so disaffected."[50] It would seem that Fitts and France weren't listening close enough: The disaffection often develops because loving family and friends *have* been left behind.

This explains why "especially bright" Sharon O'Dair still feels uncomfortable with what she sees in her rearview mirror, even though she "vowed" in her youth never to "cross to the other side" of middle-class life. While she currently sees herself struggling to "resist" the academy's elitism, she's not exactly pining for those bygone working-class days either. It's "dual estrangement" with a twist, she tells us in "Class Matters." O'Dair mentions the "alienation and shame" she continues to bear for "what [she] left," no matter how hard she tries to defy "what [she's] become."[51] This alienation often can result in "diffused anger," according to Ryan and Sackrey in *Strangers in Paradise*, as the "strain of disconnection from the past—parents, friends, etc., those who you left behind" takes its toll.[52] For many working-class academics, overdeveloped bookishness bears a sobering irony: On the one hand, the books provided the means to leap across the divide of class; on the other hand, they also lead to an unexpected emotional separation from those "left behind."

On occasion, the emotional estrangement can progress into such a tremendous source of pain that the main "tools" in causing it are blamed, as occurred in Dorothy Bryant's semi-autobiographical novel *Miss Giordano*. In it, the main character, a lifelong English teacher who rose from the working class, undergoes a book-burning, book-exorcising crackup. In some instances, those who'll be left behind want to prevent the flight from occurring, as occurred in Willy Russell's play *Educating Rita* when Rita's domineering husband burns her books and papers because— emotionally—"the girl he married is gone."[53] Such dramatic (and "fictional") scenes illustrate the contradictory role books play in the lives of many working-class academics whose butts may have been saved by them, but who also face the offsetting anguish that books may have helped destroy intimate (if, at times, oppressive) ties with those from the past.

Books carry another unsettling irony for many working-class academics. While being bookish may signal an exceptional position for the gifted child in the working class, that quality is in bountiful supply within the academy. What makes the child so uncomfortably different in the academy is certainly not bookishness but, rather, the very thing that he or she had escaped: the working class! While being bookish is not remarkable among academics, being working class is. But there is an important difference between these "special" qualities. Among upwardly mobile working-class kids, books were special—particularly "the right ones"—because they advanced the gifted child's cultural capital and claim to higher socioeconomic positions. However, the uniqueness of being from the working class may be a source of embarrassment and even distress, especially if the academic displays or betrays markers of working-class identity. This situation may prompt some to feel "an urgent need to mask [their] working-class origins."[54]

Neither gifted nor bookish as a child, I held no great expectations of climbing out of my social situation. It never occurred to me that school could provide social mobility or that books could lead to my great escape. Even when I became a voracious reader, and even when I became a "good" student, I didn't take advantage of either to leave through the front door and return through the back. For me, it was more of a revolving door. My ascent to the academy came in fits and starts, hurdles jumped and jumps foundered. There was no quick exit that started in my youth as it had with so many other working-class academics. It was more like crawling along the way rather than clawing my way to the top. Perhaps most important of all, it began after I'd been shot. That rather shameful event fueled my bookishness and made me take to my studies. By the time I became bookish and began inching toward "gifted-student" status, most working-class academics had already received their scholarships and were attending top-notch schools. Because of these things, I knew too little to be embarrassed about my class origins.

As a giftless child, I failed three subjects in second grade (when, not coincidentally, my father left), spending that summer in a devilishly hot classroom making up the failures. Like any child in summer school, I thought I had died and gone straight to Hell. My school memories differ dramatically from those of many working-class academics who describe their successes. I certainly can't say that "I loved school," like Robert Cole, a coalminer's son.[55] Or that I had a great "belief in education," as did Gloria D. Warren, an African American from Detroit.[56] Never did I believe, like Keith Gilyard, that my "eventual prominence" would evolve out of my "academic progress in school."[57] In no way growing up could I relate to Laurel Johnson Black, the daughter of a handyman, who states: "I wanted to be like my teachers."[58] Nor could I see how someone like Linda Brodkey would actually "prefer school to home."[59] Maybe the typical Scholarship Boy, according to Hoggart, will make "a father-figure" of his teachers,[60] or, like Rodriguez, even go so far as "to idolize [his] grammar school teachers,"[61] but I sure didn't.

For the most part, I disliked teachers, especially the nuns, who seemed to enjoy belting kids, although the girls generally evaded their assaults. Any "bad boy" might be slapped in the face or have his hands whacked with a thick wooden ruler. Or he might be pinned against a wall and have his head bashed against it. Sister Louis Marie, the principal at St. Charles, roamed the hallways like a commandant, chiefly whenever a class spilled out into the corridors during bathroom breaks. Students weren't permitted to use the bathroom on their own. Entire classes would be herded to "the lavatory" right after recess. (The nuns and most of the lay teachers rarely said "bathroom." I guess it sounded too naughty, it being the room where people get naked to take a bath.) During potty training, Sister Louis Marie was known to corner boys she'd learned had misbehaved. She'd grab a wrongdoer by the hair with her left hand, hold his head in place, and slap him several times with her right. If she was having a particularly bad day she'd then pound his skull against the wall for additional effect.

Unlike the other nuns she was quite strong, and whenever we saw her in the hallways we were terrified. We all thought she looked like the Wicked Witch from *The Wizard of Oz*, which she did. Both possessed sharp features like a pointy nose, headdresses that crimped the face into creepy contraction, and remarkably similar ways of addressing prey by pointing a crooked finger at the victim, pulling him into sight with beady eyes, and threatening him with a high-pitched, menacing voice.

One time Sister Louis Marie slammed classmate Jay (Pooh-Stain) Ruane repeatedly over the head with a hefty geography book because he'd scratched his initials on its cover. She often popped into a class unannounced to "observe our progress," but her primary objective was to make us crap in our pants, which most of us did, on sight. She could strike any boy at any time for something as innocuous as not wearing laced black shoes or not wearing accompanying black socks. Jay's infraction of writing on his book was therefore akin to practicing Judaism. When Sister Louis Marie spotted the graffiti she practically hurtled to his desk. She picked up the book and started slamming him over the head with it. "What [*whack*] have [*whack*] you [*whack*] done [*whack*] to [*whack*] your [*whack*] book [*whack*], Mr. [*whack*] Ruane [*whack*]?" She could have at least spared him one wallop by not pausing between "Mr." and "Ruane." When he tried to explain he hadn't done anything, she started hitting him again. "Liar!" she screamed, really giving it her Whac-A-Mole best. At one point, she accidentally dropped the book and watched it crash to the floor. "Pick that up," she demanded, pointing to it with her bent index finger. When Jay did so and sheepishly handed it back to her, she continued pounding the piss out of him.

Less severe attacks from the general nunnery included having ears twisted, noses tweaked, hair pulled, or scalps wrenched by knuckles—the notorious "noogie." Evidently, the nuns borrowed their pedagogical practice from Moe of The Three Stooges. Perhaps St. Charles was harsher than most places and an abnormality, even among many parochial schools. After all, Richard Rodriguez, Linda Brodkey, and Mike Rose thrived in their seemingly nurturing Catholic schools, while other gifted working-class academics appear to have hailed largely from less oppressive public schools. Still, I don't recall any Scholarship Boys or Scholarship Girls in my school, just a few "do-gooders" or "brown-noses," as they were called, who behaved and did their schoolwork, even though they were just as apathetic about it as the troublemakers who failed to behave. For staying in line, they were rewarded with good grades and a pat, rather than a smack, on the head. The rest of us were called morons, idiots, stupid, stupid idiots, brainless, stupid brainless idiots, useless, vegetables, useless vegetables, and stupid idiots with vegetables for brains. Positive reinforcement was not a strong suit of the nuns.

I reacted to their cruelty and indignities, along with the boredom, by rebelling, especially from about the sixth to the eighth grades, as did many of my classmates. What the teachers dished out, we gave right back, including their indifference to our educational development. Most of our assignments were returned to us obviously unread, branded with nearly page-long checkmarks indicating we had completed our "busy work." Book reports, copied verbatim from the dust jacket, received passing marks. I should know. I did it all the time. I knew I didn't have to bother reading the book, so I didn't. Once, I wrote an assignment using microscopic print, way too tiny to read (to see if they were paying attention or to receive it?). I didn't know what to expect. Would my sixth-grade teacher, a senile, wispy nun, notice? She did. As I sat at my desk Sister Mellette returned it to me, pulling my nose with her feeble fingers. "Bigger, you silly fool," she said, throwing it onto my desk. The next day I handed her a ream of paper with one enormous word written on each page. (Really, what was I thinking? I wasn't trying to show off to my classmates. Did I do it out of principle, or a lack of principle?) After she boxed my ears, I ended up in the corner of the room for the rest of the day sitting in the garbage can. Whatever set me off, I wasn't alone. Other boys pulled similar gags.

As time went on, our rebellious behavior took the form of intricate, patiently planned pranks that attempted to disrupt the steady flow of tedium. By eighth grade, for instance, someone (sometimes me) would pass a note around the room that read, "At 1:15, cough." Sure enough, as we sat rigidly erect at our desks, our hands dutifully folded in front of us, nearly every boy (fifty of us) would begin coughing. After the failed seventh-grade experiment of pulling out the really "bad" boys from one class and putting them in the other, the school irrationally decided to place all the boys in one eighth-grade section. It was believed that we could be broken and corralled by the meanest nun in the history of Catholic school–dom, Sister Marcella. She also happened to be one lousy teacher who didn't know the first thing about creating a credible learning atmosphere, let alone inspiring kids to achieve. Even the Goody Two-Shoes disrespected her for that and participated in our hijinks now and then, like the timed coughing.

Such public displays drove Sister Marcella nuts. She couldn't single out anyone, either by hitting someone or by sending a boy downstairs to the principal's office where Sister Louis Marie might be waiting, yardstick in hand, ready to spank a kid like a dominatrix—except the outfit was all wrong. Instead, Sister Marcella would announce that the entire class had to serve an hour's detention as punishment. Was she kidding? We were just getting warmed up. Ten minutes later, right on cue, another note would float around the room: "At 2:00 sneeze." Simultaneous, near-symphonic sneezing would commence at the designated time. Predictably, an additional hour would be tacked onto the first. We'd all get home just in time for dinner, but few of us cared. Clearly, the nuns had the upper hand (literally!), but we managed to generate power through numbers, to undermine a school system that appeared hopelessly meaningless and obsessed with discipline and punishment. (Boy, did I appreciate Foucault when I first read him.) Over time, I became more intractable and got into even more trouble. In eighth grade, I was suspended four times (a record, I was told twenty years later), and Sister Marcella informed my mother she should prepare to visit me at Sing-Sing someday. I was in fact getting into some trouble outside of school, so the good sister was not too far off the mark, I suppose.

High school brought little change, except that now I was exposed to an even more diversely dedicated group of innovative delinquents, although most of the damage (to myself, mainly) was conducted outside the classroom, culminating in my getting shot. I was gaining a lot of ground in "Sidewalk U," as Keith Gilyard describes his own tumultuous teen years, except that no one had ever told me that I was as "bright as a star," as he was, nor was I ever accepted into a Special Progress Class, as he was.[62] As at St. Charles, no one I knew in high school was gifted or in love with books. For various reasons, Staten Island wasn't exactly home to the intellectually curious. As a result, I was never exposed to the kind of academic role models or intellectual mentors frequently featured in the narratives. In contrast, my mentors taught me how to hit a curve ball or spit great distances, as if it were an Olympic event. In some of the narratives, future working-class academics brushed against fellow bookish travelers, such as Mike Rose's high school English teacher Jack MacFarland, who became more than just an intellectual father-figure following the death of Rose's father. Then there's "the guy who lived two blocks from" Charles Finder, the son of a Boston fish peddler, and stimulated Finder to become an avid reader. Finder's nameless "guy" was simply described as an "underground Trotskyite."[63] If any such characters lived in my conservative neighborhood, they undoubtedly were so far underground I would have needed a backhoe to dig them up.

I'm convinced that my youthful nonbookishness altered my view of intellectual work as less transcendental and more tangible. I didn't think of books as taking me out of my social situation or even out of my "trapped" condition, the way many other working-class academics describe their books, permitting them to flee (however provisionally in their imaginations) from the vulgar around them. After I was shot, I started reading because it seemed that being an ignoramus had had its disadvantages. I wasn't heading away from anything, more like heading toward something, some unidentifiable (intellectually) brighter future. Furthermore, by being giftless I had avoided some deeply conflicting attitudes that escaping my working-class background could bring, as described by several narrators. For one thing, I never set out to escape, nor had anyone dangled that prospect in front of me based on my intellectual talents—even when I was months away from obtaining my Ph.D. My brain wasn't supposed to take me anywhere, and those who knew me best assured me it couldn't whenever I tried. I would be better off staying in place and forget thinking of going places.

But, then, how can I explain my near-absolute comfort in the classroom as a teacher? It happened the first moment I walked into a classroom, along with my own sense that of the few things I've ever done really well in life—short of hitting a fastball or catching a one-handed pass—teaching is one of them. All in all, being giftless, *and* being a late bloomer deterred from blooming academically in the first place, has shaped my attitude toward my students and my intentions as a teacher. Sometimes I think I connect better with "flagging" students than with "successful" ones. My attitude toward books and my approach toward students surely explains why many of the voices from the working-class academic narratives sound so different from mine, like that of Gary Tate, who describes his "love" for books as a child, along with the "scorn [he] felt for [his] past" as well as for "[his] students." But it "was nothing compared" with the scorn he "felt for [himself]" for so many years as a working-class academic.[64] My past didn't involve growing up gifted, but neither did I ever view it with disdain, nor have I thought of my students or myself with contempt. Maybe being giftless and succumbing so long to those who wanted me to think of myself that way rescued me from these feelings. Coming so late to the scene and never feeling like a star may be more of a blessing than a curse.

As it turned out, I've been unlike those working-class academics whose bookish and gifted childhoods led to estrangement from their working-class past, and different too from those like Louis Potter who admits that he "spent most of [his] career trying to live down [his] past."[65] Like Potter, Carol Faulkner once hid from her working-class past and tried to mask it, but she changed directions by eventually embracing and celebrating it. She regards the shift as amplifying her scholarship and, especially, her teaching. She writes in *Coming to Class* that she "saw [her] class background in the same way [she] saw" other embarrassing features, such as her youth, as "weaknesses, drawbacks, things to overcome." But, she continues, "it's taken [her] a long time to understand and accept how profoundly class has influenced [her] pedagogy, how inseparable it is from the way" she teaches. Faulkner was the classic "successful student" who struggled with her former identity and the conflicts associated with it. Once she accepted her working-class past and even "returned" to it, she felt better off for it.[66] In fact, this unexplored theme appears in a handful of other narratives as well. Despite being "wrenched from the culture of [her] birth," Sharon O'Dair finally realized that "the weight and significance of class" was not something she should "dissolve" or abandon because she had entered the academy.[67] Being a child from the working class could be worn as a badge of honor rather than be the cause of embarrassment.

However metaphorical the "return" was for O'Dair, Faulkner, and others, it typically influences teaching practices by spotlighting class inside the classroom rather than concealing it. Actually, Faulkner believes she has become a better teacher as a result of her "return"; perhaps it has even helped her negotiate the typical conflicts of academics from those of the working class. She writes:

> As I become more myself as a teacher, I find more ways to allow my own experience to shape the way I respond to students and to validate my place in the college classroom. In spite of its drawbacks, I feel fortunate that I grew up with a strong working-class identity. It gave me enough of a sense of what matters to me or enough discomfort with what doesn't that I had to find my own way, true to myself, true to my class.[68]

Now this was a position I could relate to, the idea that a working-class identity could enrich a teacher's life and inspire a more creative and rewarding classroom experience for the students as well. Finally I'd found some connection between me and other working-class academics. Once that cartoon light bulb switched on over my head, I thought more and more about how "the return" could explain how I practiced my own intuitive working-class pedagogy, maybe even allowing me to "become more myself as a teacher." The return concept revealed the value of working-class roots for a teacher negotiating his own class identity. Of course, what doesn't fit into that model is one's having been shot nearly to death. Something tells me there aren't too many academics (working class or otherwise) who were gunned down by a cop during a botched holdup. I can't say that having been shot has in any way helped me navigate through the academy as a giftless working-class academic among my "gifted" colleagues. If anything, it's made me more reserved than gung-ho (or should I say more gun-shy) compared with most, professionally speaking, in carving out my "rightful turf" during the inevitable turf wars. However, inside the classroom that experience has generated an everlasting, ever-present approach to how I conduct myself. When it comes to being "in the moment" (an altogether overused New Age phrase that has lost its meaning), I'm at my best in the classroom. The intensity is palpable, as some of my students have remarked. I think this intensity—a profound passion, if you will, of bringing to bear the importance of "the moment"—explains why I am so good at it. In fact, my near-death encounter overshadows my having always accepted my working-class past as a pedagogical tool, which probably comes as no surprise to anyone who's undergone such a traumatic, life-altering experience.

In addition to that, being "giftless" in my youth is certainly a significant component of my teaching DNA as well. It too strongly influences my teaching. Because I hadn't tried to escape from my working-class past, I didn't need to "return" to my past to become a teacher "true to my class" or to feel the "weight and significance of class." This is the condition of those of us nongifted who barely left. By the time I started my graduate studies I was already in my thirties, and by the time I started teaching college I was nearly forty. I was still closely tied to a world of Sanitation tests, real doctors, homemade zeppoles, and reminders that "you're the one who was shot" as I continued to go camping and play darts with childhood friends. I carried the weight of my class origins around with me. Despite the differences, of being giftless, and feeling neither especially estranged from my past nor terribly conflicted about my class identity, the importance of "the return" as a trope in teaching was the thing I most understood from the narratives. As a whole, the stories of Scholarship Girls and Boys armed me with discourses on the problems and anxieties of class, even if I wasn't an official returnee.

Several working-class academics discuss the advantages of retracing their past and its importance in enhancing their teaching practices, like John Ernest. He describes how his "background journey continues" to inform his understanding of how he and his students fit into the culture of the academy, along with how class overall fits into his classroom practices. His "understanding of class, and the role it plays in the classroom" began

with a retrospection of his own story, of what he "discovered" about himself.[69] Olivia Frey likewise reports how her "return" influenced her work
as a teacher: "My own teaching has changed to reflect my reconception
of knowledge—where it comes from and what it should do." Before
then Frey admits she embraced a more traditional approach, much of it
stemming from her development as a Scholarship Girl. "When I left my
small town in South Florida," she writes, "I knew I was bound for such
'greatness'—high aspirations, great books, the great tradition, everything
above and beyond that low, small, common place on the map that I called
home." Like others, being bookish and gifted propelled her beyond her
working-class origins, and the academy, which appeared in the distance
as an institutional Shangri-La, drew her into a new class identity: "I left
behind my working-class parents and their friends and my friends and all
they represented to me." She credits her students with reconnecting her to
that abandoned past: "[I]t has been my students who have compelled me
to come home to my working-class values." She claims that such forgotten
values resurfaced when she noticed how her students were steeped in the
"immediate" and "practical" experiences of working-class life. Over time,
such lived experiences were incorporated into her curriculum, and she
now believes all learning should involve the same principles. The "im-
mediacy of language and events" must be the cornerstone of a lively, rich,
and meaningful pedagogy.[70]

Janet Zandy argues in favor of a similar curriculum, which she adopted
for the same reasons. As a Scholarship Girl, she too had lost sight of the
importance of class. In her final remarks in the Introduction to *Calling
Home*, she states, "It took me twenty years to circle back." Growing up in
Union, New Jersey, across the street from a factory where the "whirr of
the machines" could be heard inside her family's tiny apartment, Zandy
was "determined to escape" the working-class life that engulfed her. Like
other working-class academics, she went to college "on a scholarship,"
convinced that the books she "embraced [. . .] like a lifeline" would bridge
that journey. But the great tradition and the great books, according to
Zandy, ignore working-class life and create "holes" in a person's formal
education. Part of circling back therefore involved "fill[ing] in a small part
of what has been left out of [her] education."[71] Eventually she discovered
the significance of a curriculum grounded in class. In a subsequent essay
in *Coming to Class*, "The Job, the Job: The Risks of Work and the Uses of
Texts," she claims that stories of "working people" need to be "at the center of study rather than at the margins of a syllabus or not on the page at
all." Teachers engaged in these activities will be pursuing a "working-class

democratic pedagogy." In doing so, the course she teaches at her school seems more "*real*" and "the 'real' world [is] not out there somewhere," which parallels Frey's creation of an "immediate" and "practical" curriculum after she "returned."

Frey and Zandy are right about the need for creating a less abstract curriculum, but they and others are wrong to assume it can occur only if "working people" are its focus. My not being a Scholarship Boy and never "determined to escape" my past may explain why I differ with them and others on this point. Oddly, I feel better about the usefulness of The Great Tradition than they do. Maybe that's because I didn't reach for it like a tow rope to pull me out of my "low" and "commonplace" socioeconomic waters. I reached for it in the very "real" and "immediate" sense of advancing my literacy. For me, at least, it worked.

Generally speaking—and I mean that literally, not just rhetorically; I'm *generalizing* excessively here—it seems that many working-class academics who now feel guilty about leaving the working class blame the very things that got them out: books. They especially regard the classics as the main accomplice in the "crime" they committed. First, the Great Books in their youth represented a step up from the kinds of improper or incorrect material someone like Linda Brodkey's father read. Now in adulthood they may feel bad about having identified the "inferiority" of their loved ones based on the books they did (or mostly didn't) read. Next, they associate books and the "right" books with their increased socioeconomic status and very real material gains. Books were the stepping-stones that permitted them to "escape" the working class and join the ranks of the academy. Many testify to feeling uncomfortable about that. In effect, they are correctly criticizing the way books are deployed in school: not to increase literacy but to evaluate and rank. Scholarship Girls and Boys are living proof of not only this practice's implementation but also its effectiveness. (The system is designed to detect and then skim off the cream at the top, eventually homogenizing the different classes of containers.) *Now* working-class academics resent what took place. But *then* they clung to the practice "like a lifeline." In the narratives, *nearly* every working-class academic acknowledges that he or she wanted to be measured. Measurement brought rewards for many working-class kids who measured up. The grand prize was social mobility, gained through the acquisition of cultural capital. They see now that they were judged "better" than their peers because of their bookishness, and they begrudge their books (now) for the inequality books created. But that was the name of the game, and it still is: Books in school mainly exist for exchange-value rather than for use-value. Nearly all the narratives contain testaments of Scholarship Girls and Scholarship Boys who banked on that system, bigtime.

Books were the great un-equalizers that working-class academics trafficked in. For them to feel ashamed today about being singled out seems somewhat disingenuous. Most admit they didn't want to be seen as "equals" among their working-class families, friends, and classmates. Their books, along with their academic successes, separated them from other members of their class, and they showcased their bookishness. They banked on them. Books are why they're no longer among the working class. Books made them different. As described in the narratives, many presently feel conflicted about that. And they appear to be taking it out on their tools when they should be taking it out on their teachers who marketed books as measuring sticks, or better yet on the system's inequitable structure. They want to "punish" books (or burn them as in Dorothy Bryant's fictional story) for facilitating their rise out of their socioeconomic position because after their "return" they realize schoolbooks often don't foster a "democratic pedagogy." As the "special" and "gifted," they are living proof their analysis is dead-on. There was nothing democratic about their departure.

This attitude is rather unfortunate. It's not the books that are to be faulted, no matter how "strange" they may seem to the average member of the working class. It's how most teachers use them—or in many cases misuse and abuse them. Used as benchmarks, books become hostile instruments to the nongifted, and even to the average student, as they were to me. At best, they exist in the abstract, intangible instruments at odds with a student's "real" life. In turn, they often breed indifference, causing no real harm and doing no real good. Books and the Great Tradition seem so vastly unreal and so disconnected from the student's "real world" that teachers like Zandy who "return" and study the problem want to create a more "*real*" curriculum. Perhaps for some Scholarship Girls and Boys the best means to that end is the establishment of "a working-class democratic pedagogy" with "working-class people at the center of study." I'm all for that, up to a point, so long as working-class kids aren't denied opportunities to read fascinating and edifying material such as Sophocles' *Ajax* or Shelley's *Frankenstein* or Eliot's *Middlemarch*. Incorporated thoughtfully into a classroom, such works can be very "real" for students from any socioeconomic stripe. And shouldn't our objective as teachers be to turn out conscientious, articulate, and literate students, whether they escape from their class or stay behind to repair elevators or clean streets? The pedagogical bridge that working-class academics should be building is one that connects the concrete, "real" world of the working class with the abstract, "calculating" world the academy has made out of books. Let's keep in mind, too, that in letting the pendulum swing too far in one direction we may end up with an "intellectual" landscape dominated by *Real Housewives of New Jersey*.

In the "return," working-class academics largely ignore the "tools" that catapulted them out of the working class and focus instead on the class conditions of those "left behind." Zandy does that through her "working-class pedagogy," which she argues owes itself to the influence of "the return." While she "can't go home" per se (most of her immediate family is dead), she, like other returning working-class academics, returned home metaphorically. During her career, she writes in "The Job, the Job," "something happened" that transformed her thinking and she "came to understand that [her] circumstances were classed circumstances." What she "experienced was not so much a change in consciousness as a recovery of consciousness," in what she describes as "a reclamation of working-class epistemology."[72] Gary Tate reached the same conclusion. In "Halfway Back Home" Tate recounts how, after thirty years of teaching, he finally became "comfortable" with himself and found a more "meaningful" way of teaching by reclaiming his working-class origins. He tells us that encountering *Strangers in Paradise* for the first time "served as a catalyst" for him to think more fully about social class, which also acted as a portal into his own buried working-class background. This journey back involved an understanding of his "past," which enabled him to understand his "present"; as a result, he started teaching "more effectively" and "more imaginatively." Before that, he admits, he felt disconnected and bitter, and he frequently took these feelings out on his students.[73] Tate's comments seem both brave and sad: brave because Tate courageously reexamined his life at a point in his career when most have turned on the automatic pilot, and sad because it shows how much the academy often forces working-class academics to erase crucial parts of who they are. Furthermore, his comments demonstrate how rejecting class origins or ignoring class differences can profoundly affect teaching (and scholarship), as well as the relationship many working-class academics have with their institutions, but especially the relationship they have with their students.

Because the subject of class has been "academe's dirty little secret," according to Patricia Sullivan,[74] working-class academics like Tate often can develop unhealthy attitudes toward their work. Before he returned to his roots, Tate felt "discomfort in the academy" and held "negative feelings" toward it. But his "turn to [his] rediscovered past," combined with his "attempts to cease denying" it, provided "something worthwhile in the academy" for him: It infused and invigorated his "pedagogical work." In the long run, a greater affinity with his students developed, and Tate acquired "newfound confidence" from it. Before his return, he was "inclined to use the textbook, the syllabus, the content of the course as barriers to protect [him] from [his] students," whereas the return allowed him to open up. He writes: "I am attempting to use the strength that a better understanding of my past has given me not as a barrier between myself and my students, but as a means to understand them more compassionately—and thus, hopefully[,] to teach them more effectively, more imaginatively."[75] By reevaluating and reconnecting with his past, Tate reinvented himself as a teacher and as a scholar.

After reading Tate's narrative and others like it, I began to think that my life as a nongifted academic wasn't so bad after all. Being a late bloomer has had its advantages. As a giftless working-class academic, I hadn't uprooted myself, at least not in such dramatic fashion as reported by the bookish prodigies in many working-class academic narratives. Whenever I tried, I was considered more of a weed to be picked than a flower ready to bloom. Also, I didn't need to go back twenty or thirty years to those roots, not when my aunt was telling me I could have been a real doctor or my mother was reminding me to take the Sanitation test a few months before I obtained my doctorate. Then there's the irreversible and un-erasable view of those who knew me in my youth as "the one who got shot." I've always known I can't "escape" my past. To some, my having been shot still overshadows all my accomplishments—my doctorate, articles in prestigious academic journals, the publication of a scholarly book, and the high regard in which I am held by my students. People can change, but the experiences that caused the change don't. For many, it's not the changed person but the unchanged event that stands out.

Not long ago I attended a grand reunion at St. Charles for most of its graduating classes, from its founding in 1964 to 1994. It was held in the school auditorium, the same place where I received my communion and confirmation. It also was where, high on mescaline, I walked onto the stage during our graduation dance party to receive tribute for being voted class clown. I wasn't trying to be a comedian as a student there. I simply started clowning around because it gave me something to do. I wasn't entirely enthralled with my schoolwork, so goofing off filled up the time. You can imagine how upsetting it was when my mother learned of it. It was bad enough I wasn't studious; the dishonor further confirmed my waywardness. Clearly, I was heading more in the direction of getting shot by the time I entered high school rather than reading hundreds of books, as Richard Rodriguez had done by the time he entered his. Long before that, I'm sure plenty of people saw me as a troublemaker, a fucked-up kid with a dim future. Maybe those early impressions are too imprinted on people's minds no matter what I've achieved since then, thereby making it virtually impossible for me to escape my past even if I wanted to. As time went on, it became clearer to me why my father was so mistaken to advise me to pretend as if my past was different from the one I'd lived through. It can't be done.

Five minutes after I arrived at the reunion, a hulking figure walked over to me and placed a beefy arm around my shoulders. "Order any pizzas lately?" he said, chuckling. I didn't recognize him. He'd gained a pile of weight and had aged considerably for someone, as I learned, who'd been two grades below me. As one would expect, we'd had nothing to do with each other in school. I also barely knew him from hanging out at The Station and around the ball fields. He sure as hell remembered me, though. He removed his arm from my shoulders, stepped back, and pretended to fire six-shooters from an imaginary holster, imitating a character in a Hollywood western.

While I was bewildered—what was I supposed to say, "It's nice seeing you again too"?—I was neither flustered nor embarrassed, just as I wasn't when I ran into my former high school classmate at the College of Staten Island. It didn't bother me that he had brought up the shooting, other than its being awkwardly weird, because I think about that night nearly every day, despite the advice my father gave me about doing otherwise. Mind you, it doesn't haunt me, materializing as an unwanted, nightmarish memory. As crazy as it sounds, I summon it. For one thing, it makes me so astonishingly grateful to be alive, to love life, in its entirety, no matter what. Even when the shit hits the fan, it's better to have it splash across your face than to have the gravedigger's dirt thrown on it. It also acts as a reminder of where I'm from and who I am. And who I am is not a Scholarship Boy. I'm more a teacher (man) than a scholar (boy). For me, teacher (man) has a more reassuring ring to it, confirming that when I settled into teaching there was some mastery to it from the start, unlike how other working-class academics admit to their discomfort inside the classroom. If I can speak for my students, it may be better that I wasn't a Scholarship Boy. I never needed to go back to figure out how to connect with them, especially students from the working class or "average" or "below-average" students. I don't zero in on the "gifted" students and ignore the rest. Moreover, the ER scene turned out to be a powerful force in my teaching. The intensity and attention I devote to each classroom moment derives from it (as does every moment). My effectiveness as a teacher therefore has always been grounded in my past. I've never tried to escape it or needed to recapture it. It's always been a welcoming source of inspiration. Not an embarrassing source of desperation.

In "Passing: A Family Dissemblance," Patricia Sullivan concludes that working-class academics are not only physically removed from their homes but inhabit "a metaphysical world light years from home" as well.[76] In many ways, being giftless meant that I had never left, even metaphysically. To my family and friends, I hadn't. Because of these things, I wonder if I settled (instinctively?) upon the value of not erecting a barrier between me and my students or wielding the tools of the trade, like books, to build a pedagogical wall between us. As a giftless student I had seen how books were often used against me and others, sometimes literally, like when Sister Louis Marie clobbered Jay Ruane with one. Obviously, it wasn't that severe for everyone, but I don't recall a time when the nuns and lay teachers presented books as user-friendly. In addition, books were rarely read contextually, or as a way for us to find meaning, or even simply as a pleasant experience. Instead, they were used to regiment our "progress," or in my case my backwardness. Identifying individual illiteracy, rather than promoting general literacy, was the primary focus. Reading enabled teachers to grade, classify, and standardize students. Books were their tool with which to rank us. As a child I failed to see the legitimacy of this approach. I am not making this up in hindsight. Even at that age, like many children, I had a visceral sense of the joyless, perfunctory existence of books in my life at school (and at home). I'm the first to concede that I wasn't bookish in the first place, but what mostly constituted reading in grade school and high school back then (and still, sadly, to this day) seemed pointless.[77] One minute I might be answering questions based on a passage about volcanic activity in ancient Athens and the next minute I'd be answering equally goofy questions based on a passage about the history of haberdashery in London. In high school, when we were asked to read a book—which I likely didn't until I was shot—we were told by our teachers what to think of them and what they meant, with the exception of two, Mr. Larson and Mr. Keck. Interestingly, I can't remember a single name of all those others.

Most teachers ignored me because I wasn't bookish, which is the academic fate of the nongifted. I was therefore unworthy of instruction. I admit that some of my academic indifference and obstinacy may have been born out of resentment or even spite. I'm sure many teachers considered me stubborn and incorrigible, which I probably was. It wouldn't take long before I might be written off entirely, perhaps as early as October, or classified as inept, along with the other poor performers. But just like in Little League Baseball, where all players, no matter how badly they play, must appear in an inning or two, so too did a "bad" reader get to read now and then. For both player and reader alike, though, it could be an embarrassing proposition. Whenever mandatory readings occurred, with students reading aloud in alphabetical order or row by row, weak readers like me were told "that's enough" after a few sentences. Judging the sequence of readers, I would scan ahead trying to calculate the passage I might have to read, practicing it in my head in advance of being called on. It rarely worked. It was impossible to gauge how much the better students would be permitted to read. Unlike the gifted, I considered reading an insidious teaching device to make me look bad and books as impenetrable "things," certainly not "tools" of the trade, that the nuns and lay teachers used to separate the wheat from the chaff. *That* was my experience with books growing up giftless. There was nothing transcendental about them. I never viewed books as assisting me across the great divide of class. I considered them an albatross. Books were instruments of domination, wielded by the dominant to subordinate the lesser or marginal students like me.

As a teacher, I don't use books to distinguish and judge the good apples from the bad. Doing so, Sharon O'Dair points out, ultimately "institutionalizes subordination and thus class."[78] From the moment my students walk into my classroom I want to ground them in the very real, material conditions of their lives and the lives of others. Working with your hands was considered "real work" among family and friends, and that idea resonates in my teaching practices because my pedagogy can best be described as hands-on, and I don't necessarily mean mine. Ethnographic projects and research are the cornerstones of my writing courses. In my literature classes, students design their own tests. In my Romantic Movement course, for instance, I have produced a fifteen-page, single-spaced handout on "The Atlantic Slave Trade," along with one on "The Ways of Women" and "Game of Tomes: The Rise of the Publishing Industry and Reading Public." The last one runs to twenty-five pages. Each student is responsible for coming up with at least three questions based on that unit, that handout. In a classroom of thirty-five students I compile a list of forty to forty-five questions. (There is a fair amount of redundancy.) We go over the list to determine the most important ones for them to answer, typically about twenty-five. Those will be the questions that will appear on the test. This practice operates at two levels, the micro and the macro. For one thing, it makes the students better readers, "close" readers.

For another, it empowers them. Finally, this entire democratic process reinforces the material, really allows—in the case of "The Atlantic Slave Trade"—that ugly, despicable practice of trafficking in human flesh sink into their head. This is evident when they take *their* test, with almost all of them getting a perfect score.

In that same course, they must "discover" their own essay topics, whether it's comparing *Pride and Prejudice* with the movie *Maid in Manhattan* or contrasting enclosed literal and figurative spaces in "Monk" Lewis's *The Monk* with our own postmodern claustrophobic world. Clearly, much of this "discovery" is based on our classroom discussions, grounded in the present, which is of my own doing, I admit. It seems to me that developing critical literacy skills through literary works should involve situating students in an "immediate" social and political context rather than present it exaltedly as "timeless," semi-holy artifacts, often done to separate the good, the bad, and the ugly. Nor should it be put forth as potential boot-strapping apparel that will save some and damn the rest. To me, that means delivering "literature" as close to home as possible. This methodology undoubtedly stems from my earlier giftless experiences, while the writing assignments I assign and the literature I select originates out of it. I saw how teachers sometimes used books to maintain distance or relied on the curriculum to erect boundaries, as Gary Tate acknowledged, or—to put it more bluntly—to establish the condition of *us* (teachers and a handful of bright students) versus *them* (the rest of the mediocre and dull ones).

Since I knew what it was like to be one of *them*, I haven't developed an antagonistic attitude toward my students or sought to erect barriers to be crossed or stopped at. I've been unwilling to wedge a book between me and any of my students, not after what I went through. I want to make books appealing to students rather than employ them as enemies of their mental states. When I became a teacher I swore a silent oath to avoid rote instruction like a disease and not use the curriculum to protect me from my students. I was determined to make learning student-based, a state that can be achieved even in a seemingly dead-end curriculum like my Grammar and Style class, a course designed to be highly interactive around the theme of "Living Languages." I knew that different ways of knowing and experiencing the world were not valued in the academic discourse community. (On the street I was considered witty and a pithy storyteller, yet in school I was "illiterate" and ignorant.) I place a premium on those differences. I don't automatically categorize such differences as deficits, even hoping to encourage nontraditional or giftless students to feel that they belong. I don't value some students over others because they've already pocketed some cultural capital. In my experience, teachers tend to advance such students and hold back the rest—often unconsciously, I suspect. This classification operates as a subtle form of oppression, with profound social consequences. In all probability, it means that the giftless will more likely be hauling trash because that's what they were destined to do. With even greater adverse social consequences, they might be doing it while believing that learning and knowledge are for the privileged and not a right to be enjoyed by all. Only the elite (and thus "The Man") gain from it. Knowledge is rigged against them. In addition, we never hear their stories because they didn't "escape." I'm an odd bird for the unglamorous reason that I was shot almost to death. I guess it takes that kind of extraordinary event for some of us to begin altering our giftless track records and tell our side of the story.

Having been one of those countless giftless working-class kids, I feel obliged to invite all my students into the conversation, generating as many voices as possible. From the time I began teaching writing, I automatically did not "settle for teaching students the discourse of the academy," which remains the prevailing practice, according to Pat Belanoff. She insists that discourse, like books, is frequently used as a device in "dichotomizing" one social class from another.[79] I don't teach academic discourse, pure and simple, even in my literature-based courses, and I'm determinedly inclusive. That I was practicing this method *intuitively*, in my own rudimentary way, before I knew to call it a Dialogic or a Freireian pedagogy, has a lot to do with my giftless background.

As a result, I usually begin assignments by asking students what they already know as a way for them to compare it with what we're about to explore. It may simply begin by my writing a single word on the blackboard—"marriage," "school," "sin," "work," "justice"—and having them free-write about it for five minutes. As they're speaking, I take copious notes, turning our conversation into its own text. I'll often rephrase some of their statements into questions and ask other members of the class to respond to their fellow students. I'll write down those comments as well: The class is constantly being built around student discourse—information and misinformation. Later, we'll compare those statements with the readings and their writing. Now and then I'll circulate a "Newsletter," a series of the most illustrative statements, including some of mine. Sometimes it can get noisy and chaotic, with students firing off answers and talking all at once, and often not to me. At times, I feel as if I've lost control of the class and that therefore little learning is going on—until I remember those deafening-quiet, ultra-structured days back at St. Charles, and the sounds of passive silence I've heard repeatedly in well-managed classrooms elsewhere. As a giftless child, I was left cold by the well-run classroom. I'm the first to admit I was emotionally and intellectually unprepared to gain from such supervision, although a part of me believes I intuitively resisted being treated like a clever robot.

Richard Hoggart argues that the typical Scholarship Boy undergoes a "system of training" that is essentially uncritical and heedless, turning him into a "blinkered pony" because he has become an "expert imbiber and doler-out" of information and knowledge.[80] Richard Rodriguez repeated this claim when he suggested that the Scholarship Boy experiences learning as an "imitative and unimaginative process,"[81] becoming "a great mimic" who rarely has "an opinion of his own."[82] To Hoggart and Rodriguez, the Scholarship Boy tends to absorb learning with little reflection and processes it like a thoughtless machine, largely as a set of doctrines and accomplishments that will prove his worth. He becomes a shining example to his teachers of the value of being a bookish drone. At that exchange rate, cultural capital has enormous value. It can be exchanged for social mobility, placing the dutiful, credulous child inside the prestigious corridors of the Ivory Tower.

Being giftless meant that I was a bucking horse rather than a blinkered pony. I was either too incompetent or too unwilling to become an expert imbiber and doler-outer, and it seemed that much of what passed for vital information was mostly part of a capricious disciplinary system that had little to do with the real world. I couldn't stomach having lessons shoved down my throat so that I could regurgitate them on command. I knew that's what "good" students were supposed to do, so I guess I wasn't "good" enough in that respect. I'm not trying to make myself sound as if I were some wise old pedagogue as I sat in my fifth-grade class, rolling my eyes in conscious mistrust of the limitations of rote instruction as we recited the names of state capitals. It was more visceral than that. I also don't want to overlook something else that likely was going on: Plain and simple, I probably wasn't a "good" student because I lacked a disciplined mind and/or didn't have the right temperament. Who knows if one gave birth to the other, how my undisciplined mind emerged from my temperament. Both may have sprung from my upbringing. All that time sitting by myself in strange rooms for hours on end after being shuttled from one home to another had made me more reflective than methodical. Countless hours alone as a boy had afforded me more time than normal to ponder—errantly—life's larger issues, such as the fragility of human relationships, which overshadowed the minutiae of my schoolwork. I just couldn't wrap my head around what seemed like trivia when the world around me required greater scrutiny.

A great deal of that time in cousin Andrew's room or anywhere else was spent day-dreaming, losing myself in a dappled mental world for the purposes of survival. These are not quite the qualities compatible with official academic approval. If anything, they usually signal an untrained, unproductive mind. It's the "imitative and unimaginative" child who shines in the classroom, for the most part, the future Scholarship Boy or Scholarship Girl. I wish I could say otherwise, but schools aren't exactly in the business of reflection. They're in the business of accounting. Now that I'm on the other side of the divide, I can see that what passes for knowledge in many classrooms doesn't involve calling for student introspection but rather the teacher's conducting student inspections.

Both skeptical and unimpressed with what was supposed to pass for knowledge, I didn't think to mimic it. In all likelihood, my reaction to my own system of training accounts for why as a giftless working-class academic I have insisted that learning be extraordinarily real and engaging. I would sooner work for the Sanitation Department than deliver the dull rote instructions I had received as a student and that still generally passes for learning in many classrooms to this day. (It doesn't help that state and federally mandated tests hamper even the most imaginative teachers at our public schools, constituting as they do officially sanctioning motorized learning.) That I wasn't terribly enamored with my teachers I'm sure had a lot to do with the kind of teacher I became as well, having never turned them into the kind of "over important" figures Hoggart describes.[83] Carol Faulkner maintains in "Truth and the Working Class in the Working Classroom" that as a bookish, "successful student" she "learned" to retain "a too deferential attitude toward authority," which "made [her] too accepting of traditional approaches" when she first started teaching.[84] Linda Brodkey admits that as a "good Catholic girl" she "succumbed so readily" to what she now views "as senseless hours of tedious exercises, distracting at best and debilitating at worst." While slogging through this game, she "learned to trade [her] words for grades and degrees." In doing so, she "trusted teachers" but "distrusted" herself. "[T]o make matters even worse," she adds, she was a child "who lived by rule."[85] Not exactly a good Catholic boy from the working class, I never felt loyal to authority, and I think this pointed me toward democratic pedagogy (unconsciously?) because I've never been "too accepting of traditional approaches." I also trust my students to find their way, even if that means bumbling along in their thinking. If they don't trust themselves, I trust I'm providing them with some guidance to do so, maybe not right then and there but, I hope, at least some time in the future.

Another less obvious way teachers maintain distance is by taking themselves way too seriously, which was part of Tate's story before his "return." As he explained, he stopped being so darn self-imposing, and he became a better teacher because of it. My giftless upbringing taught me that uptight, intimidating teachers didn't get very far with their subjects, unless they were the "good" ones, the students who jumped through hoops. In some ways, I am now the proud class clown in my classroom, a different kind from the one I was as a student. Humor, even the self-deprecating kind that spared an ass-kicking from bullies, can go a long way in the classroom. As that old educational ad used to say, it makes learning "fun-damental." Moreover, humor, as Freud informs us, connects us to one another. Laughter often reveals that *we* get it. We get the joke. It can also reveal that students "get" how delightful learning can be. In my youth, some teachers seemed so distantly alien as to appear inhuman. I was shocked whenever I ran into one of them outside of school. In class, they looked so glum teaching I thought that if the material they considered essential to our educational survival brought them so little joy, then maybe I'd actually be better off dying cheerfully ignorant than depressingly intelligent. Some embodied both masochism and sadism: They were unhappy making us miserable. In addition, humorless teachers were also the worst listeners, rarely interested in what any of us had to say. It was *their* time we were wasting if we didn't learn, and it was our fault if we didn't understand *their* lesson plans. Some were so full of themselves and their agendas that we might as well not even have been there. All in all, I see being a good listener as key to being a good teacher, as long as the listening is done joyfully, perhaps even compassionately. That's why I take dictation. (Maybe, Mom, I should dust off the court reporting machine, finally. I could take down student talk, verbatim.) Listening demonstrates you're present, engaged in the moment, not riveted to the past and not tied to the future. You know, as I wrote those words it sure sounded an awful lot like the epiphany I had in the ER. See: I told you at the beginning of this Not-So-Short-Story it was the worst thing and the best thing that ever happened to me. Now do you finally believe me?

In re-crossing the great divide of class, many working-class academics want to reclaim greater kinship with "those left behind" (even if only in the figurative sense). On the whole, those left behind were not gifted, suggesting that the return involves a symbolic reconnection with those of so-called average, borderline, or even slow intellects. It is, in effect, a form of solidarity through re-identification. Essentially the return brings working-class academics closer, in spirit, to the giftless of their former working-class world. The return also seems to bring academics like Tate and Zandy closer to their students. In seeking to become more comfortable in their own skins as working-class academics by re-identifying with the scores of "others" from their past, many working-class academics open up inside their own classrooms. They become less vigilant about hiding the residual markers of their working-class past, which may have been hidden under the veneer of pretentious academic (im)posturing. They become less gifted, so to speak. For Tate, who shares constructing the curriculum with his students, and for Zandy, who advocates practicing a working-class democratic pedagogy, becoming better teachers meant setting up classrooms wherein there is room for the giftless and average student to participate as fully as the gifted in the development of the curriculum.

Their approaches question the built-in elitism of academic mobility because working-class academics now see the earlier disconnection they felt with their students as potentially related to their identification with their teachers when they were gifted students. Both stemmed from the same principle, that education is dominated by a hierarchical structure, with the teacher institutionally on top and only the best and the brightest with access to such heights. Time and time again, books are the primary measuring devices and the primary vehicle by which to secure such plateaus. Singling out gifted students in a classroom that is composed of mostly average or giftless working-class kids is one way to impose undemocratic class relations through the very ordinary practice of teaching. For Tate, Zandy, and others, the return may animate creating a more egalitarian learning experience for their students and inspire the establishment of a curriculum grounded in social justice. They became more-gifted teachers by reevaluating the meaning of being gifted Scholarship Boys and Girls. It may have taken Zandy and Tate twenty and thirty years, respectively, to get there, but they had to go back before they could go ahead.

In my case, being giftless seems to have been a blessing rather than a curse. I didn't have to reach far back in order to return to my students because I didn't go that far ahead or away. It never occurred to me that school learning was transcendental—socially or spiritually—or that books offered salvation or compensation. I started paying more attention to my schoolwork and became a library rat because I'd nearly had my head shot off by a cop during a botched robbery. Furthermore, in my youth I wasn't gifted enough to impress my teachers with any hint of someday becoming a speaker of elite English, of being identified linguistically as a kid who could read, write, or talk my way around ending up a Sanitation worker or a telephone repairman. My language never matched my teachers', and it rarely met the minimum competency set by those inane standardized tests.

After reading *Strangers in Paradise*, Gary Tate reports in "Halfway Back Home," "I found myself in that book."[86] I can't say that about any of the narratives I've read, especially about the countless descriptions of gifted, bookish children whose families encouraged them and who escaped their working-class conditions. I used to think being different was a bad thing, but perhaps my weakness has been a kind of strength, not unlike how being shot turned out to be the best thing that ever happened to me. You see, even fake doctors can turn out to be real teachers. And something tells me that not being a Scholarship Boy turned me into a better Teacher Man.

11
This Is It

When you open your eyes again you watch him fingering the rosary beads, murmuring in Latin. You know what it means. It's the third time you've gained consciousness. Each one is more ominous than the previous. But this takes the cake. Three strikes and you're out. (Words escape you, so you fall back on clichés.) The first time the black nurse refused to answer a basic question: Am I going to die? The second time you can tell from the look in your mother's eyes you will never see her again. Hearing the last rites seals it: You won't be alive much longer. You're a dead man before you've had time to become a man. Sadness and remorse flood every strand of your being. You're awash with intense emotions and the intensity of the moment. This is it: The End.

And what a foolish way for it to happen, you think. It's a hollow, inconsequential death born out of a selfish, asinine life. If there is an "if," you know you'll do it differently. For a moment books surround your bullet-ridden body. The vision lasts only for a moment. It soon vanishes. Back to reality and the mess you're in, all because of how you lived. Or didn't live. Or didn't live a-live. Or something. No time to mince words. It doesn't matter anyway. It actually makes perfect sense. Such a stupid death should follow such a thoughtless life.

So you accept it. There's really nothing else to do. You're certainly not going anywhere. It is what it is. For some inexplicable reason, you're not afraid. You're not afraid to die; maybe you just don't want fear to be the final feeling, the last emotion or thought you'll ever experience or have. Maybe there's something better to go out with than dreading the unknown. So you stick with the explicit tangibility of the moment, however searing it is. In fact, its strength is something undeniable, something to grasp.

Besides, there's no hiding from the stark truth of this particular moment; its clarity is practically blinding: This is the final moment. *The* Moment, with a capital "M" and a weighty stress on the "the." It's not "a" *moment*. There may never, ever, be another one you'll ever experience, ever again. Strangely, the laundry list of stupid thought and action has brought this most disarming moment together. But your (foolish) life doesn't flash before you. Possibly you don't want it to. If it did, you wouldn't be riveted inside the moment. Instead, the past actually melts away. And there's no horizon. There's no future either. It starts to feel palpable, as if this tiny moment has taken on a life of its own, outside of all the other moments, yet inside all of them at the same time. It begins to feel like an eternity, as if it might last forever. Something extraordinary is taking place. Heightened consciousness seems transformative. It's deliberate. You're not looking to get out of it, to escape this horrible final moment. You've got your head fully wrapped around it. At the same time, there's something inescapable taking place. Free will and inevitability joined together. This exact moment has specially arrived—as all of them do, you'll discover. For the present, it's right now. It's happening, pure and simple, this irresistible moment in time . . . as you're about to die. There's no getting around it. No getting around that fact and its place in the present.

And you don't want to get around it, or over it, or past it, because it could be lost. To lose the last moment you might ever have would be as wasteful as the life you've lived up to this point. You stay with it, grasp it for what it is, possibly your last experience. You might be dead after it—ever after. So you don't wish for some other moment to save you, or crave to be someone else, or desire to be somewhere else. If you did, the present moment would vanish into thin air. Besides, it's useless to think otherwise, to evade *this* moment with thoughts of the past or the future. There's no avoiding who you are at this present time. You can't dance around the fundamental reality that you're a fifteen-year-old kid on the verge of death after having been shot by a cop while trying to rob a pizza delivery driver. There it *is*. You're in a hospital so close to the end that you're receiving the final church sacrament. Nothing else matters. No other *it* exists. Nothing exists. And nothing will matter or exist ever again. You have no past. You have no future. You have only the moment. It's all right here before you. This. Is. It.

And that's when it hits you: The Moment. The absolute present. You exist purely inside existence and living eagerly deep down inside of *the* moment like never before, as if it's your last, which it very well could be. That's why it feels the way it does, as you draw the entire world into it with you, becoming conscious of the forces at work. The mind is infused with total awareness of the purity and beauty of this exact moment. Nothing else. There is nothing else. No before, no after. Only now.

The here-and-now is the burning sun of enlightenment. Accepting it brings a groundswell of enigmatic energy and power. You feel more alive than you've ever felt in your life: here and now on the brink of death. And then you're free. You're free from a conceptual past and an illusory future. If you die now, you know that you've lived more extraordinarily inside this moment than all the others combined. It makes you aware that of all the billions of moments that took place in the past and of all of the billions of moments that will take place in the future, there never has been, nor will there ever be, a moment like this one.

When you wake the next day you realize it's true of all the moments, not just yours, but also only yours and yours alone, and everyone else's, alone, and theirs separately, all because of consciousness, in all its clarity. It's a marvelous paradox: Each of our lived moments is unique, except yours is more unique than theirs and theirs is more unique than yours.

Being shot was the worst thing that happened to you; it was the best thing that happened to you too. It couldn't be any other way. The experience can't be divided into more or less acceptable parts, no more than any moment can be divided into anything other than what is being completely offered. You spend the rest of your life attentively enfolding the fineness of each and every moment to the best of your ability. It's perfect and complete as it is. In doing so, it slowly dawns on you that by being present in the present the past will be marked by the wonder of each brilliantly lived moment and the future will arrive astoundingly as each brilliantly lived moment moves toward it.

At the finest point of death you learned life must be lived expansively at each tiny trace.

What began as a wrong ends up as a rite of passage.

Sometimes the best education begins closest to The End.

Notes

8. "It's not too late to take the Sanitation test"

1. What, exactly, is "the working class" anyway? For that matter, what are classes? According to Paul W. Kingston in *The Classless Society*, classes don't exist in the United States. He contends that groups of people having a common economic experience and who hold similar social positions don't significantly share distinct, life-defining experiences, like family life, marriages, and raising children. Even "morality" is classless because Americans are remarkably divided in their responses to divorce, pornography, or swearing, regardless of their income (145). Meanwhile, Americans from very different income groups might have the same cultural tastes in music or clothes. In *The Working-Class Majority*, Michael Zweig agrees with Kingston about the unimportance of income and lifestyle in assessing whether class exists in America. However, Zweig sharply departs from Kingston's interpretation of these two ideas because he believes that the nation is profoundly class-oriented. "Class is determined not by income and lifestyle," he maintains, "but by the relative standing in power relations at work and in the larger society" (41). Taking a decidedly more Marxist approach to the topic, he states, "Class is first and foremost a product of power asserted in the production process" (12). David Harvey's vigorous analysis of Marx's work in *The Limits to Capital* carries this idea one step further by combining "production and distribution in the context of class relations" (42). These twin forces, he believes, determine the amount of temporal and spatial control one has over one's life, and that power, or the lack thereof, drives class relations. Viewing social relations in this way illustrates the existence of class in the United States. In my varied work experiences, for instance, the amount of power or control I had over time and space established my class. Whether as a grocery clerk, typesetter, apple picker,

landscaper, adjunct professor, warehouse operator, junior staff writer, or handyman, I had virtually no authority over where I had to be and when I had to be there. And in those jobs I always felt like a member of the working class. But now, as an assistant professor of English, other than my office hours and class schedule (which still can be fudged), I have near-total control over where I have to be and when I have to be there. I also feel the most middle class I have ever felt in my life. So, yes, even gangsters can be working class because their bosses maintain control over their whereabouts. The "organization," after all, operates as a highly transparent hierarchy of the division of labor.

2. Jake Ryan and Charles Sackrey, eds., *Strangers in Paradise: Academics from the Working Class.* 1984. Lanham, Md.: University Press of America, 1996, p. 187.

3. Ibid., p. 285.

4. C. L. Barney Dews and Carolyn Leste Law, eds., *This Fine Place So Far from Home: Voices of Academics from the Working Class.* Philadelphia: Temple University Press, 1995, pp. 37–38.

5. Michelle Tokarczyk and Elizabeth Fey, eds., *Working-Class Women in the Academy: Laborers in the Knowledge Factory.* Amherst: University of Massachusetts Press, 1993, p. 72.

6. Richard Rodriguez, *Hunger of Memory: The Education of Richard Rodriguez.* New York: The Dial Press, 2004, p. 137.

10. Re-Gifted

1. In the beginning of the film *Working Girl* the main character, Tess, played by Melanie Griffith, informs her friend she can't attend her own surprise birthday party because she has her speech class to go to that night. In another scene, Tess is listening to a recording of her boss trying to imitate her diction and inflection. Her boss, played by Sigourney Weaver, is a Wellesley graduate who's temporarily occupying her parents' Upper East Side brownstone after relocating from Boston to New York. Tess knows that if she wants to move up in the world she needs to drop her working-class speech markers and adopt the language of the ruling class. I didn't drop mine so consciously. For one thing, when I was at Johnson & Wales I was surrounded by plenty of New Englanders and no one ever said anything about my "New York accent." I certainly didn't think of dropping it then and adopting a very heavy New England accent, which they had, and which was undoubtedly a New England working-class accent. BU was different. There were students from all over the country and everyone sounded the same, including many foreign students from Saudi Arabia and Brazil who spoke impeccable English. The requirements of their (upper) social class had wiped out regionalism—from as far away as the Sahara. I simply noticed that the students there and in class spoke a certain way. If I wanted to participate in class (which I did a lot of) "comfortably," and fit in generally, I needed to sound more like them and less like the people back home.

2. Richard Rodriguez, *Hunger of Memory: The Education of Richard Rodriguez.* New York: Bantam Books, 1983, p. 62.

3. John Edgar Wideman, *Brothers and Keepers: A Memoir.* Boston: Mariner Books, 2005, pp. 26–27.

4. Jake Ryan and Charles Sackrey, eds., *Strangers in Paradise: Academics from the Working Class.* 1984. Lanham, Md.: University Press of America, 1996, p. 115.

5. Ibid., p. 203.

6. Renny Christopher, "A Carpenter's Daughter." In *This Fine Place So Far from Home: Voices of Academics from the Working Class,* ed. C. L. Barney Dews and Carolyn Leste Law. Philadelphia: Temple University Press, 1995, p. 140.

7. Irvin Peckham, "Complicity in Class Codes: The Exclusionary Function of Education." In Dews and Law, *This Fine Place So Far from Home,* p. 274.

8. Linda Brodkey, "Writing on the Bias." *College English* 56.5 (1994), p. 535.

9. Ibid., p. 533.

10. Rodriguez, *Hunger of Memory,* p. 49.

11. Ibid., p. 5.

12. Karen Fitts and Alan W. France, "Production Values and Composition Instruction: Keeping the Hearth, Keeping the Faith." In *Coming to Class: Pedagogy and the Social Class of Teachers,* ed. Alan Shephard, John McMillan, and Gary Tate. Portsmouth, N.H.: Boynton/Cook, 1998, p. 49.

13. Donna Langston, "Who Am I Now? The Politics of Class Identity." In *Working-Class Women in the Academy: Laborers in the Knowledge Factory,* ed. Michelle M. Tokarczyk and Elizabeth A. Fay. Amherst: University of Massachusetts Press, 1993, p. 64.

14. Mike Rose, *Lives on the Boundary: A Moving Account of the Struggles and Achievements of America's Educationally Unprepared.* New York: Penguin, 1990, p. 23.

15. Terry Eagleton, *The Gatekeeper.* New York: St. Martin's Press, 2001, p. 52.

16. Richard Hoggart, *The Uses of Literacy.* 1957. New Brunswick, N.J.: Transaction Publishers, pp. 226–27.

17. Rodriguez, *Hunger of Memory,* pp. 62–63.

18. Victor Villanueva Jr., *Bootstraps: From an American Academic of Color.* Urbana, Ill.: National Council of Teachers of English, 1993, pp. 6–8.

19. Keith Gilyard, *Voices of the Self: A Study of Language Competence.* Detroit: Wayne State University Press, 1991, p. 33.

20. Brodkey, "Writing on the Bias," p. 532.

21. Janet Zandy, "Introduction." In *Calling Home: Working-Class Women's Writing, An Anthology,* ed. Janet Zandy. New Brunswick, N.J.: Rutgers University Press, 1990, p. 13.

22. Robert Brown, "Robert Brown." In Ryan and Sackrey, *Strangers in Paradise,* p. 133.

23. Bob Cole, "Bob Cole." In Ryan and Sackrey, *Strangers in Paradise,* p. 49.

24. Fitts and France, "Production Values and Composition Instruction," p. 48.

25. Patricia A. Sullivan, "Passing: A Family Dissemblance." In Shephard, McMillan, and Tate, *Coming to Class*, p. 237.

26. Suzanne Sowinska, "Yer Own Motha Wouldna Reckanized Ya: Surviving and Apprenticeship in the 'Knowledge Factory." In Tokarczyk and Fay, *Working-Class Women in the Academy*, pp. 150–51.

27. Langston, "Who Am I Now?," pp. 61–62.

28. bell hooks, *Where We Stand: Class Matters*. New York: Routledge, 2000, pp. 25–26.

29. Pat Belanoff, "Language: Closings and Openings." In Tokarczyk and Fay, *Working-Class Women in the Academy*, p. 255.

30. Gilyard, *Voices of the Self*, p. 45.

31. Ibid., pp. 128–29.

32. Perhaps the following warrants more than a sidebar: I've long believed that when "gifted" working-class kids are pulled out of the working-class it benefits the child, *and* the class he or she will soon inhabit, but not the working class. In fact, it may even be detrimental to it. For one thing, it maintains middle- and upper-class hegemony. The "favored" sons and daughters of the working class are now part of the ruling class. The "cream" of one class is absorbed into the others. In addition, yanking these "special" kids out of their environment, especially to become academics, removes them from participating intellectually in working-class life. Potentially powerful voices are relocated to other classes. Sure, many return "home" now and then to work for political and social justice that often affects the working class, but it often happens from the margins, not from the inside. That can be a further class hindrance. Many in the working class consider them outsiders, as no longer "one of their own." Added to that impression is an attempt by the economic elite to call intellectuals, especially humanities professors, the "liberal elite" who are out of touch with the average working man and woman. As we've seen in the narratives, some of those "liberal elite" are from the working class. Such labeling is generally unfair; however, based on the "true confessions" in working-class academic narratives, there's some truth in it. Several narrators acknowledge that they longed to get out of the working class because Joe Sixpack was a boorish ignoramus. As a result, many members of the working class look upon such insufferable smugness as further evidence that being bookish is contemptible and strangely shallow. Intellectualism turns ordinary people into extraordinary snobs. In turn, members of the working class become more entrenched in rejecting the rewards of intellectual activities and the advantages of reading, especially among males. In turn, bookish members of the working class grow up in this hostile environment, sensing and frequently experiencing this animosity, including being treated suspiciously for not being authentic members of their own class. They're considered "weirdos" for the passion they have for those "strange tools." This causes and perpetuates the discomfort of growing up bookish in the working class, making "escape" compelling, if not inevitable. Taking gifted students out

of the working class therefore establishes a pattern: The bookish are unwelcome, feel unwelcome, and want to escape; their need to escape and their actions to do so create inevitable ill-will among other members of the working class. Once gone, their new "elite" status brands them as arrogant traitors, furthering the impression that books are not only strange but hostile tools to the overall integrity of working-class life. The upper classes gain from skimming the cream off the top of the lower class, as does the one being skimmed. The loser in the equation is therefore the working class because the very idea of advanced literacy becomes a wedge rather than a uniting force for greater *class* power. Books provide access to mostly *personal* mobility and power. It's as if books are the weaponry in the class struggle—within the working class!

33. Gloria D. Warren, "Another Day's Journey." In Dews and Law, *This Fine Place So Far from Home*, pp. 108–9.

34. Rosa Maria Pegueros, "Todos Vuelven." In Dews and Law, *This Fine Place So Far from Home*, p. 90.

35. Dwight Lang, "The Social Construction of a Working-Class Academic." In Dews and Law, *This Fine Place So Far from Home*, p. 159.

36. Mary Cappello, "Useful Knowledge." In Dews and Law, *This Fine Place So Far from Home*, pp. 127–29.

37. Ryan and Sackrey, *Strangers in Paradise*, p. 103.

38. Naton Leslie, "You Were Raised Better Than That." In Dews and Law, *This Fine Place So Far from Home*, p. 69.

39. Sowinska, "Yer Own Motha Wouldna Reckanized Ya," pp. 152–56.

40. Nathan Green, "Nathan Green." In Ryan and Sackrey, *Strangers in Paradise*, p. 57.

41. Alice Trent, "Alice Trent. In Ryan and Sackrey, *Strangers in Paradise*, p. 223.

42. Christine Overall, "Nowhere at Home." In Dews and Law, *This Fine Place So Far from Home*, p. 210.

43. Stephen Garger, "Bronx Syndrome." In Dews and Law, *This Fine Place So Far from Home*, p. 44.

44. George T. Martin Jr., "In the Shadow of My Old Kentucky Home." In Dews and Law, *This Fine Place So Far from Home*, p. 82.

45. Sharon O'Dair, "Class Matters." In Dews and Law, *This Fine Place So Far from Home*, p. 201.

46. Rodriguez, *Hunger of Memory*, p. 49.

47. Ibid., pp. 30–31.

48. Ibid., p. 68.

49. Sowinska, "Yer Own Motha Wouldna Reckanized Ya," p. 152.

50. Fitts and France. "Production Values and Composition Instruction," p. 52.

51. O'Dair, "Class Matters," pp. 202–3.

52. Ryan and Sackrey, *Strangers in Paradise*, p. 115.

53. Willy Russell, *Educating Rita*. New York: Bloomsbury, 2001, pp. 39–40.

54. Sowinska, "Yer Own Motha Wouldna Reckanized Ya," p. 150.

55. Cole, p. 49.

56. Warren, "Another Day's Journey, p. 108.

57. Gilyard, *Voices of the Self*, p. 105.

58. Laurel Johnson Black, "Stupid Rich Bastards." In Dews and Law, *This Fine Place So Far from Home*, p. 18.

59. Brodkey, "Writing on the Bias," p. 543.

60. Hoggart, *The Uses of Literacy*, p. 229.

61. Rodriguez, *Hunger of Memory*, p. 49.

62. Gilyard, *Voices of the Self*, p. 44.

63. Charles Finder, "Charles Finder." In Ryan and Sackrey, *Strangers in Paradise*, p. 164.

64. Gary Tate, "Halfway Back Home." In Shephard, McMillan, and Tate, *Coming to Class*, 1998, pp. 253–54.

65. Louis Potter, "Louis Potter." In Ryan and Sackrey, *Strangers in Paradise*, p. 186.

66. Carol Faulkner, "Truth and the Working Class in the Working Classroom." In Shephard, McMillan, and Tate, *Coming to Class*, pp. 37–44.

67. O'Dair, "Class Matters," pp. 206–7.

68. Faulkner, "Truth and the Working Class," p. 44.

69. John Ernest, "One Hundred Friends and Other Class Issues." In Shephard, McMillan, and Tate, *Coming to Class*, pp. 34–35.

70. Olivia Frey, "Stupid Clowns of the Spirit's Motive." In Shephard, McMillan, and Tate, *Coming to Class*, pp. 72–75.

71. Zandy, "Introduction," p. 13.

72. Janet Zandy, "The Job, the Job: The Risk of Work and the Uses of Texts." In Shephard, McMillan, and Tate, *Coming to Class*, pp. 295–99.

73. Tate, "Halfway Back Home," pp. 254–59.

74. Sullivan, "Passing," p. 239.

75. Tate, "Halfway Back Home," pp. 255–59.

76. Sullivan, "Passing," p. 237.

77. This kind of lunacy is carried on by the state in its teacher certification exams. Typically, prospective English teachers must answer a series of identification questions, whereby they must recognize that five lines of poetry is from Tennyson, not Wordsworth or Shakespeare or Yeats, as if that's going to determine their effectiveness as reading and writing teachers. If anything, such tests do more harm than good by setting a bad example, demonstrating that the kind of mindless rote material they must study for to become teachers is the same mindless rote material they should be passing on to their students.

78. O'Dair, "Class Matters," p. 207.

79. Belanoff, "Language: Closings and Openings," p. 270.

80. Hoggart, *The Uses of Literacy*, p. 229.

81. Rodriguez, *Hunger of Memory*, p. 44.

82. Ibid., p. 67.
83. Hoggart, *The Uses of Literacy*, p. 229.
84. Faulkner, "Truth and the Working Class," p. 44.
85. Brodkey, "Writing on the Bias," pp. 529–31.
86. Tate, "Halfway Back Home," p. 255.